Tom Kilmartin
W9-BON-533

Introduction to DITA:

A User Guide to the Darwin Information Typing Architecture

Introduction to DITA:

A User Guide to the Darwin Information Typing Architecture

Kylene Bruski
Jennifer Linton

Comtech Services, Inc.

Publisher: Comtech Services
Editor: Nikki Gjestvang
Text Design & Composition: Comtech Services

©2006 Comtech Services, Inc. All rights reservved.

Published by Comtech Services, Inc., Colorado

No part of this publication may be reproduced, stored in a retrieval system or transmitted in any form or by any means, electronic, mechanical, photocopying, recording, scanning, or otherwise, except as permitted under Sections 107 or 108 of the 1976 United States Copyright Act, without either the prior written permission of the Publisher. Requests to the Publisher for permission should be addressed to Comtech Services, Inc., 710 Kipling Street, Suite 400, Denver, CO 80215, (303) 232-7586, www.comtech-serv.com, E-Mail: info@comtech-serv.com

Printed in the United States of America

Libraray of Congress Cataloging-in-Publication Data:

Comtech Services, Inc.
Introduction to DITA: A User Guide to the Darwin Information Typing Architecture
ISBN 0-9778634-0-9

Colophon

This book was authored using DITA markup and methodology in a variety of XML editors. The XML DITA topics and maps were exchanged between Justsystems XMetaL™, PTC Arbortext Editor, Syntext Serna, <oXygen/> XML Editor, EditPad™ Lite, and UEStudio '05. We used the Justsystems XMetaL™ and Mekon™ Mtools FrameMaker™ plugin in the DITA 1.2 Open Toolkit to produce and format the book. You can download the FrameMaker™ plugin from the SourceForge web site (http://sourceforge.net/projects/dita-ot).

Contents

Introduction ... 1
Acknowledgments ... 5
Part I: The Darwin Information Typing Architecture ... 7
Part II: DITA Topics ... 13
Section A: Understanding the Core DITA Information Types ... 19
Lesson 1: Concept Information Type ... 23
Structure elements ... 29
Concept elements ... 31
Concept review questions ... 33
Lesson 2: Task Information Type ... 34
Task elements ... 42
Task review questions ... 48
Lesson 3: Reference Information Type ... 49
Reference elements ... 56
Reference review questions ... 58
Section B: Understanding DITA Elements ... 59
Lesson 4: Block Elements ... 61
Block element definitions ... 63
Block element review questions ... 71
Lesson 5: Phrase Elements ... 72
Phrase elements definitions ... 78
Domain elements ... 80
Typographic elements ... 86
Phrase element review questions ... 87
Lesson 6: Related links ... 88
Related-link elements ... 93
Related link review questions ... 95
Section C: Understanding Topic Metadata ... 96
Lesson 7: Prolog Metadata ... 97
Prolog metadata elements ... 102
Metadata review questions ... 105
Part III: DITA Maps ... 107
Section D: Understanding DITA Map Basics ... 110
Lesson 8: DITA Map Structure ... 112
Map elements ... 122
Map element review questions ... 125
Section E: Understanding DITA Map Attributes ... 126
Lesson 9: Format Attribute ... 128
Format attribute review questions ... 132
Lesson 10: Scope Attribute ... 133
Scope attribute review questions ... 140
Lesson 11: Type Attribute ... 141

Type attribute review questions 145
Lesson 12: Processing Attributes 146
Processing attribute review questions 151
Section F: Understanding Map Linking 152
Lesson 13: Collection-type Attribute 155
Collection-type review questions 163
Lesson 14: Linking Attribute 164
Linking attribute review questions 169
Section G: Understanding Relationship Tables 170
Lesson 15: Relationship Tables 171
Relationship table elements 181
Relationship table review questions 182
Part IV: Content Reuse 183
Section H: Understanding DITA Content Reuse 185
Lesson 16: Conref Attribute 188
Conref attribute review questions 196
Part V: Specialization 197
Section I: Understanding DITA Specialization 199
Lesson 17: Glossary Specialization 205
Specialization review questions 222
Part VI: Processing 223
Section J: Understanding the DITA Open Toolkit 225
Lesson 18: DITA Open Toolkit 226
DITA Open Toolkit review questions 235
Lesson 19: Build Files 236
Modifying Ant build files 240
Ant review questions 254
Section K: Understanding Conditional Processing 255
Lesson 20: Conditional Processing File 256
Conditional processing review questions 269
Appendix A: Samples 271
Comstar overview code 273
Quick Guide to Basic Telephone Use 275
Quick guide code 276
About hold 278
About hold code 278
Holding a call code 279
About transfer 280
About transfer code 280
Transferring a call code 281
About forward 284
About forward code 284

- About conference calls 286
  - About conference call code 286
  - Placing a call code 288
  - Leaving a conference call temporarily code 289
  - Reentering a conference call code 290
  - Consulting privately on the conference call code 291
  - Reentering a call with all people code 292
- About using the telephone's features 293
  - About using the telephone's features code 293
- Warnings 294
  - Warnings code 295
- Glossary 296
  - Glossary code 297
- Comstar map code 301

Appendix B: DITA element glossary 305

Introduction

Welcome to *Introduction to DITA: A Basic User Guide to the Darwin Information Typing Architecture*. The DITA User Guide is designed to provide you with a task-oriented approach to learning the Darwin Information Typing Architecture. You will find conceptual overviews, background information, tutorials, and the sample XML markup you need to get started using DITA.

Who Should Read This Book

Introduction to DITA is designed as a basic learning tool and a reference manual. This user guide is for you if you play any of these roles in your organization:

- information developer who needs to know how to create DITA topics. As an information developer moving to topic-based authoring, Part 2 guides you through basic concepts and lessons to create DITA core information types: concept, task, and reference.
- information architect who needs to know how to create DITA maps, reuse content, and specialize the DITA DTD. Parts 3 and 5 guide you step-by-step through creating DITA maps and DITA specializations.
- production specialist who needs to know how to create output using DITA processing. Part 6 guides you through installing and running the DITA Open Toolkit and processing final deliverables.

What you should know

We provide you with a basic introduction to the DITA model. You may be trying to decide if the DITA model is right for your organization, or you may already be using DITA to create deliverables. In either case, you will find a helpful resource to answer your questions.

Before you start using DITA, you may find understanding topic-based authoring helpful. Topic-based authoring encourages a new approach to developing information deliverables. For more information about topic-based authoring, refer to JoAnn Hackos's *Standards for Online Communication* (Wiley, 1997).

You may find the lessons and examples easier to understand if you have a basic knowledge of HTML, XML, or other tagging languages. For more information about XML, refer to Kay Ethier's and Alan Houser's *XML Weekend Crash Course* (Hungry Minds, 2001).

How to use this book

The conventions used in this book allow you to easily identify DITA terms used in the lessons.

- <elements> — all elements are surrounded by pointy brackets < and >
- *attributes* — all DITA attributes are in italics
- attribute "values" — all DITA attribute values are in quotes
- **lesson actions** — all tags and content added in the lesson steps are in **bold** in the examples

Layout of this book

Various aspects of the DITA model are discussed in this book, including DITA Topics, DITA Maps, Content Reuse, Specialization, and Processing. Each part consists of sections that explain the concepts and include one or more lessons. The lessons include step-by-step procedures and reference information about the corresponding DITA elements and attributes.

DITA version and Open Toolkit version

We have based the information in this book on the OASIS Darwin Information Typing Architecture (DITA) Architectural Specification version 1.0. At the time of this book's release, the OASIS DITA Technical Committee is planning releases of DITA 1.1 and DITA 1.2.

We also provide processing information based on the SourceForge DITA Open Toolkit 1.2 package. New versions of the Open Toolkit continue to be released.

Additional Resources

Many people have written about the Darwin Information Typing Architecture. Articles about the model and approaches to using the model are available on the web. If you search on DITA, you will find many resources. You will also discover that DITA shares search result space with Dita Von Teese, Burlesque and Fetish Star!

Here are some helpful resources to get you started:

- The official DITA OASIS standards committee web site http://www.oasis-open.org/committees/tc_home.php?wg_abbrev=dita
- *The OASIS Darwin Information Typing Architecture (DITA) Language Specification version 1.0 (OASIS Standard, 09 May 2005)* at http://docs.oasis-open.org/dita/v1.0/dita-v1.0-spec-os-LanguageSpecification.pdf
- The *OASIS Darwin Information Typing Architecture (DITA) Architectural Specification version 1.0 (OASIS Standard, 09 May 2005)*at http://docs.oasis-open.org/dita/v1.0/dita-v1.0-spec-os-ArchitecturalSpecification.pdf
- A web site and wiki, provided by the OASIS Technical Committee, that allow you to contribute and gather more information about the DITA standard at http://dita.xml.org
- A collection of articles gathered by the OASIS technical committee. This resource is, at present, the most extensive collection of articles, presentations, and facts about DITA at http://xml.coverpages.org/dita.html
- The web site managed by IBM, the original DITA developer, with a rich collection of DITA information at http://www-128.ibm.com/developerworks/xml/library/x-dita1/
- The forum for DITA questions at http://groups.yahoo.com/group/dita-users/ and http://groups.yahoo.com/group/framemaker-dita/

A number of local DITA User Groups have are established. The user groups continue to be formed to provide resources for people interested in learning more about the DITA model. You can find information about the local DITA user groups at the http://dita.xml.org web site.

Acknowledgments

Many people contributed to the development and success of the *DITA User Guide*. We would first like to thank JoAnn Hackos and Bill Hackos for their significant contributions. Both have generously provided guidance, best practices, support, and their time to produce this book. We also greatly appreciate the time and effort Mark Poston from Mekon provided to help and guide us through the production of this book. He took time away from his family and provided us with templates for a very powerful DITA processing suite using FrameMaker and the DITA Open Toolkit. Don Day, Michael Priestley, and other OASIS DITA Technical Committee members also provided many explanations and much support. The continuous question and answer sessions with Don, Michael, and other members helped clarify the facts about DITA. We would also like to thank the DITA Open Toolkit development community, especially, Yuan Peng Zhang for answering questions about the DITA Open Toolkit functionality. Thanks to all our colleagues at Comtech for their support and help in reviewing and editing the book, especially Nikki Gjestvang, who helped us immensely with editing. Our book would not be what it is without all of their contributions.

Last but not least, we are grateful for our families and their never-ending patience during our extended hours and crazy ways. We could not have written this book without their support.

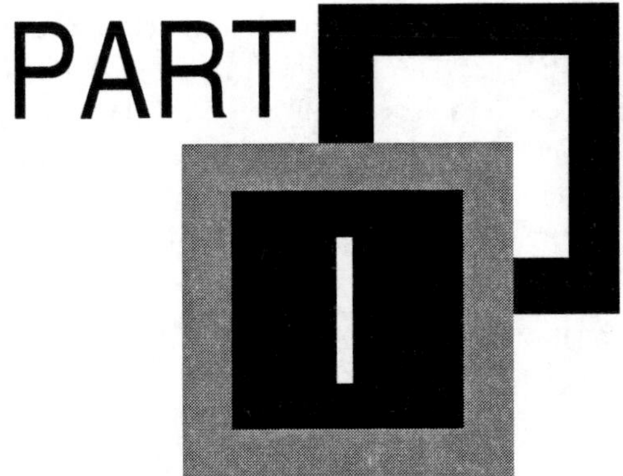

The Darwin Information Typing Architecture

You've heard about XML as a potential new tool for authoring technical content. You're thinking about developing individual topics of content and assembling them into PDFs, help systems, websites, and other deliverables rather than creating monolithic books. You've even heard about the Darwin Information Typing Architecture, a new standard that makes topic-based information development easier and faster to implement. You've come to the right place—an introduction to using the DITA standard to produce your publications.

The Darwin Information Typing Architecture (DITA) is an OASIS Standard that defines an XML architecture for designing, authoring, publishing, and managing content. Content that you develop using the DITA (pronounced dit - uh) model can be easily published to print, PDF, the web, help systems, and other deliverables, depending upon the needs of your users.

The core set of DITA information types provides information architects and information developers with a solid starting point. The core set of information types consists of the concept, the task, and the reference. These three information types represent the vast majority of content produced to support users of our technical information. You will find that each core information type contains a standard set of content units, expressed as XML elements, that encompass the essential content that you need to develop useful and reusable content.

But developing individual topics that match the DITA information types is only the starting point. DITA provides many mechanisms that allow you to build print and online deliverables quickly and easily, as well as create specialized structures to accommodate unique information requirements and use metadata attributes and content-specific element names to make assembly faster and easier and search and retrieval more dynamic:

- DITA maps
- DITA relationship tables
- DITA specialization
- DITA metadata attributes and XML element names

DITA maps provide you with the means of assembling any number of topics into sequences like tables of contents for print and online deliverables. You add DITA topics one by one to a DITA map, using the map construction principles to organize your topics into first-, second-, or third-order headings. The hierarchies you now manage with heading levels are easily managed by the hierarchy of a DITA map.

DITA maps are only one way of handling relationships among topics. By creating DITA relationship tables in your DITA maps, you can easily add and manage related-topic links. The relationships help you to build an information-centered web site or a help system that leads users from one topic they need to the related information that supports successful task performance.

DITA doesn't stop there. If you find that your content does not easily conform to the structure already built into the standard set of information types, DITA provides a mechanism that lets you create special structures. By using DITA specialization techniques, you can start with the standard information types and build new XML elements that best describe your content or even remove or rename standard DITA elements that your information developers don't need. Specialization allows you, for example, to add a list of required tools to a hardware installation task and label the list precisely or to create a special reference information type to accommodate specifications, parameters, or other data your customers require.

Finally, DITA accommodates the requirement of most information developers to handle content variations within a single topic, rather than creating multiple copies of the content with slight variations. The task of maintaining multiple instances of the same or nearly the same content has always been a thorn in the side of most information developers. DITA helps you manage the pain by providing you with conditional processing capabilities to specify elements of content you want to include or exclude from a particular deliverable. For example, if you have instructions that differ in detail among product versions, you can accommodate those differences by labeling them with metadata attributes. The process is very similar to using conditional text in desktop publishing but it is more reliable and precise.

DITA also provides the mainstay of XML authoring by using XML element names to identify content units in a topic. By labeling your task content as steps rather than ordered lists, you can easily find and reuse specific steps rather than all ordered lists in your content. By labeling reference material as a syntax diagram rather than as a paragraph, you can easily develop a dictionary-like deliverable with all the command names and their syntax diagrams. Meaningful labels in DITA are used to replace the standard format labels that we have traditionally used in desktop publishing. A style name like paragraph becomes short description, context, information, or stepresult in DITA.

Once your content conforms to the standards for DITA topics and you have mapped your content into the various deliverables your customers require, you can use the Open Source DITA Toolkit to produce your outputs. Or, you can use the tools available through your content management system. During the production processing steps, you associate one or more style sheets with your format-free XML contact, accommodating various print specifications, PDF, HTML, and any number of help systems and other deliverables. You can also transfer your XML topics, DITA maps, and relationship tables to your localization service provider. Because you are working in format-free XML, you or your service provider can transform your XML topics into the forms required by translation memory systems and other translators' tools. Using the same transforms, your localization service provider can return the translated versions of your topics back to your content repository.

By using all the mechanisms available to you in DITA, you can support the full range of tasks that make up your information-development life cycle.

Reaping the Benefits of DITA

Some people think of DITA as a set of XML-based tools or out-of-the-box Document Type Definitions (DTDs) or schemas that you can immediately use to begin authoring topics with sound XML structure. Certainly, DITA provides you with an open-source, enabling technology that you can download at no cost. It also provides you with the energy, commitment, and investment of DITA developers worldwide who contribute to the OASIS DITA Technical Committee to improve the DITA specification and tools. With DITA, you receive

- a fully tested DTD or schema for XML-based authoring
- a community of developers investing in improvements to the DITA model
- an open source toolkit you can use to produce your own output in multiple media without having to invest in costly tools

- a thoroughly developed approach to information development originating with OASIS and now encompassing many other companies, large and small, that find value in a standards-based approach

But DITA is more than a tool set. DITA represents a standard for the design and development of technical content, the first such broadly based standard in the information-development community.

What business advantages do you gain with DITA?

DITA provides a number of advantages to organizations that are seriously committed to managing information. Both large organizations with content contributors dispersed globally and small organizations with a few individuals working together will benefit from a topic-based, standards-governed approach to content management. DITA adopters find that they can

- reuse information quickly and easily across multiple deliverables
- respond positively to requests for customized information delivery
- respond quickly to changing business and customer needs
- reduce the cost of maintaining and updating information
- enable continuous publishing to keep abreast of content changes
- share information across the global enterprise
- assemble content from multiple resources
- share information with business partners throughout the product support life cycle
- collaborate on content creation with marketing, sales, support, training, and information development
- reduce the cost of localization and the time to market for translated content
- increase the global reach of information, products, and services
- reduce the technical debt caused by inadequate, incorrect, and unusable legacy information

By using DITA to produce topics according to the business rules of each information type, you create content that can easily be shared among a wide variety of deliverables. Because the topics are designed and developed to promote consistency of presentation and content, you can develop a repository of building blocks that can be assembled in multiple ways, including new ways that you have not invented yet. You can assemble the topics based on products, services, audiences, geographies, languages, customer job roles, industries—almost anything that presents you with a business advantage.

The promise organizations and information developers have made for years of providing customized information to meet the specific needs of individual customers is possible without prohibitive expense and time commitments. Many information developers are reluctant to promise support for customization because they cannot support the cost of transforming information for individual customers given their existing desktop publishing tools. With DITA's ability to facilitate new mappings of topics to tables of content and its ability to support conditional processing from master documents that contain a range of information, you are able to respond quickly to requests for customized content without creating a burden on authors and publishers.

As business and customer needs change, you can add new topics to your repository, modify existing topics, add variations to the topics, and publish restructured content. You can respond quickly to changing needs by implementing continuous publishing. Rather than waiting for a new product release to correct errors in content or revise topics so that they answer user questions more successfully, you can update individual topics immediately.

Because topics are authored once and used in multiple DITA maps, you reduce the cost of maintaining and revising topics. You can include task topics in assemblies delivered to different audience groups, add basic concepts for new users and advanced concepts for expert users, and link to detailed reference information that may be extracted directly from source material.

DITA facilitates sharing information across your enterprise because authoring is based on a common XML standard. Some authors will use XML-based authoring tools that provide a full range of functionality. Some authors will continue to use well-known word processing tools with the addition of XML capabilities. Some authors will complete XML-based forms with required information. Others will import XML content into high-end design tools to support creative information design. Some authors, especially software professionals, may even choose to author by inputting tags directly in basic text editors. All of these methods are supported by the DITA standard.

Not only can you share information with colleagues throughout your enterprise and from every part of the development life cycle and the product support chain, but you can also share information with business partners. If you and your suppliers agree to use the DITA standard, you have the means to exchange information resources without laborious and time-consuming restructuring. If you send information to customer organizations, you can provide those resources using the DITA standard. Even if you and your business partners have your own DITA specializations, the hierarchical design principles upon which DITA is built enable you to generalize those individual specializations back to the core information types.

Perhaps one of the most powerful advantages you gain using the DITA standard is to reduce the cost of localization and translation. Once topics are written, reviewed, and approved, they can be transformed to the sources required by translation memory systems. Only new or revised topics even need to be sent for translation, eliminating the need to reapply translation memory to unchanged topics. By building localization and translation early into the information-development life cycle, you give the translators more time to research terminology and develop sound content in your target languages, and you begin to reduce the time needed at the end of the cycle waiting for translations to be completed.

Because DITA maps can be assembled for every language you need, you also eliminate the high costs of desktop publishing at the end of a project. By referencing the translated topics in your DITA maps, you can generate multiple-language output quickly.

Finally, DITA and topic-based authoring, by enabling content reuse, decreasing content assembly time and costs, facilitating localization and translation, and giving authors a standard for content creation, allow you to devote valuable time to minimalizing existing content, promoting usability, correcting errors, filling gaps, and making your content more valuable to your customers and your organization.

PART II DITA Topics

Topic-based authoring has been a mainstay of technical information development since we first began developing help systems. We learned quickly enough that we couldn't split our existing books into help topics by making every heading level a new topic. Information originally designed with a unique narrative flow no longer made sense nor assisted users in finding exactly the content they needed. We had to rethink the types of information that our help systems should include and create a new set of standards for their development. The result is topic-based authoring.

Authoring in topics provides information developers with a way to create distinct modules of information that can stand alone for users. Each topic answers one question: "How do I ...?" "What is ...?" "What went wrong?" Each topic has a title to name its purpose and contains enough content for someone to begin and complete a task, grasp a basic concept, or look up critical reference information. Each topic has a carefully defined set of the basic content units that are required and accommodates other optional content. As information developers learn to author in topics and follow sound authoring guidelines consistently, you gain the flexibility to publish information written by many different writers and subject-matter experts that looks and feels the same to the users.

Not only has topic-based authoring become the norm for well-designed help systems, information architects have learned that designing consistently structured topics facilitates readability and information access in traditional, more linear book structures. Readers are able to identify task-based topics in sections and chapters because the tasks look the same and contain the same essential content units. Readers learn that conceptual and background information is always located in the same position in the table of contents with respect to the tasks. Readers come to depend upon standard reference sections that contain similarly structured details for ease of lookup.

The core information types in DITA, task, concept, and reference, support the structures that underlie most well-designed technical information. Any organization that follows best practices in information architecture will find the core DITA structure to be a good fit. But the core DITA information types also challenge us to become even more disciplined in structuring information according to a set of carefully defined business rules. The benefit of such disciplined information structuring is the consistent presentation of information that helps you build reader confidence and simplify the reader's task of knowing how to navigate and use your information.

Use topic-based authoring to build customer value

Authoring in structured topics provides you with a sophisticated and powerful way to deliver information to your user community. You will experience benefits that decrease your development costs and time to market, as well as provide increased value to your customers:

- Structured topics contain only the information needed to understand one concept, perform one procedure, or look up one set of reference information.
- Structured, topic-based authoring promotes consistency in the presentation of similar information.
- Topics can be reviewed by subject-matter experts as soon as they are ready. They need be reviewed only once, even if they appear in multiple deliverables, reducing the burden on reviewers.
- Topics can be translated before entire volumes are complete, reducing the time to market for global customers. Topics in multiple languages can be combined into language-specific deliverables without extra desktop publishing time and expense.
- Assembling topics into multiple deliverables can be automated, reducing production time and costs.
- Consistently structured topics are easier to reuse in multiple deliverables.
- Structured topics may be combined in new ways to meet changes in product solutions, work structures, geographies, industries, or other customer configurations.
- Topics are easier to update immediately instead of waiting for the next release of an entire library of documents.

- Consistently structured topics help users build a firm mental model of the types of information you are presenting.
- Consistently structured topics help users navigate more quickly to the information they need.

If one of your business goals is to use information topics in multiple deliverables, you need to build a repository of topics that are clearly defined according to a standard set of information types. DITA provides you with such a standard as a starting point. DITA gives you the capability to expand upon its core information types when you need to accommodate the special needs of your customers and your information.

Conducting a content inventory

If your information is like most in the technical information industry, you have a great diversity of structures in your information, especially if topics are embedded in the threaded narrative sections and chapters of books. Your first job is to inventory your content to identify its range and diversity. In most cases, you will find lots of tasks, containing step-by-step instructions for reaching a specific goal. The dominance of the task in technical information is why DITA includes the task as one of the three core information types. Accompanying tasks, you are likely to find background, descriptive, and conceptual information that explains what something is and how it works. DITA labels such supporting information "concepts." You will also find tables, lists, diagrams, process flows, and other information that can be labeled as "reference," the information that no one wants to memorize but must be easy to look up.

Once you have completed your content inventory, you need to carefully analyze the three core information types provided with DITA. The standard structure for task, concept, and reference is presented in detail in the first section of this book. Experiment with accommodating your content to the standard structure. In more than 80 percent of the cases we've researched, the content easily fits into a standard DITA structure.

Where you may encounter difficulties is with the diversity of your own content rather than with the DITA information types. Some of the content in your inventory will not even meet your own guidelines. Often, that content was written by people long gone from your organization or was influenced by subject-matter experts who wanted it their way rather than following your authoring guidelines.

Our recommendation is to focus on the essential underlying structure of your content rather than the idiosyncrasies and accidents of individual writers over the years. If you find an odd structure in a task, for example, ask if that structure is the best way of conveying the information to the user or if the task can be rewritten following the structure of a standard DITA information type. Most of the time, you will find that the standard is a good solution.

One of the more common problems you will find with some of the content you examine is mixed structure. Tasks start out with long discussions of background information. Concepts include step-by-step procedures. Tables of reference material end up with concepts in the footnotes or tasks incorporated into table cells. Although mixed information types are possible in DITA, in most cases, we don't recommend them. Consider that by separating information carefully and rigorously into the neat information-type buckets provided, you will have information that you can present much more dynamically and flexibly to users. If users wants to know the steps of a task, they won't have to skip over background that they don't want to think about yet. You can refer them to that conceptual and background information through a related-topic reference or a hypertext link rather than embed lengthy conceptual information in the task.

Notice the difference between the two task topics in Figure 2.1. The well-structured task follows the DITA model, clearly omitting descriptive information about menus and screens. The well-structured task also ensures that action steps begin with commands and that step results are not incorrectly labeled as steps, as well as separating steps from additional information.

By chunking your information according to well-defined DITA information types rather than combining types randomly, you gain flexibility in distributing your information to people who need it most. You also make the relationships among chunks of information more obvious. If you believe that users will profit from reading background information before performing a task, you can use related-topic links to ensure that they know about the relationship and why reviewing the concept or background is advantageous.

Note: Tabbed interfaces in help topics facilitate the movement back and forth among related topics. Once users find a concept, they can immediately link to one or more tasks simply by clicking on a task tab at the top of the screen. At any point in the online navigation, you can make clear the relationship among a concept, one or more tasks, and a set of reference material.

Adding your own information types to the core DITA set

Although you will find that most technical information fits neatly into the core DITA information types, you may discover that you have special information types that cannot be accommodated by the standard content units or that you want to label those content units with more descriptive XML tag names. At that point, you need to pursue specialization.

Well-Structured, Minimalist DITA Task	Poorly Structured Task
Selecting a Language, Product, Unit, and Lesson (task title) Use the Menu Screen, the first screen you see, to select the Language, Product, Unit, and Lesson you want to work on. (short description) 1. Click on any Language/Product that appears in the left frame of the Menu Screen. (step-command) You may need to scroll to see all the Languages on your CD. (step-information) 2. Click on a Unit tab on the right frame. (step-command) All the Lessons available in that Unit appear. (step-result) 3. Click once on any Lesson to go to the Activities Selection Screen. (step-command) The selected Lesson may take a few minutes to load. (step-information) Every time you return to the Menu Screen, the last Unit and Lesson you worked on is highlighted. (task-result)	Selecting a Language, Product, Unit, and Lesson (task title) The Menu Screen (another title) When you run the RS program, the first screen you will see is the Menu Screen. In this screen, you select a Language, Product, Unit, and Lesson. (menu description) The Menu Screen has two frames: * A frame for selecting a Language and Product (left side). * A frame for selecting a Unit and Lesson (right side). (more menu description) All the Languages on the CD will appear in the Language/Product frame on the left. If you are using the online version of RS, all available Languages should be visible here. You may need to scroll to see all the Languages on your CD. (more menu description) 1. Select any Language/Product in the Language frame by clicking on it. (step-command) 2. The Units will appear. (no step; a result?) 3. All the Lessons available to you in that Unit will appear, after you click on a Unit tab. (misstated step with result first) 5. Click once on any Lesson to continue to the Activities Selection Screen. There may be a delay as the program loads the selected Lesson. (step-command and step-information) Every time you return to the Menu Screen, the last Unit and Lesson you worked on will be highlighted. (task-result)

Figure 2.1 Comparison of DITA and non-DITA task structures

Consider an example in the semiconductor industry. Much detailed information about a chip design is contained in an information type called a register description. Although a register description falls into the class of reference information types, it has some specific and detailed content that should be presented consistently and labeled by its semantic content. By specializing on the core reference information type, you can build a register description specialization that standardizes the register content with appropriate XML element names, assisting the writers and providing additional metadata to facilitate search. Many similar opportunities for specialization may present themselves in your content. But be careful to exhaust the possibilities of the core information types before pursuing the differences.

In the specialization section of this book, you will find step-by-step instructions to help you create a specialized information type. Do so sparingly. The more different information types you present to writers and readers, the more opportunities there are for confusion. With too many choices of information types, an information developer is more likely to chose incorrectly. With too many subtle differences in the presentation of information, your users are more likely to become confused when they are unable to find the standard set of content that they have come to expect.

SECTION A

Understanding the Core DITA Information Types

The DITA standard provides three core information types:

- concept
- task
- reference

Figure 2.2 provides an illustration of the core information types.

CONCEPT	TASK	REFERENCE
Header Information Title Short Description Prolog	Header Information Title Short Description Prolog	Header Information Title Short Description Prolog
conbody Section Paragraph Lists Tables Images Examples Related links	taskbody Context Pre-requisites Steps Step-elements Result Examples Post requirements Related links	refbody Section Paragraph Properties lists Tables Syntax Examples Related links

Figure 2.2 Core information types

The core information types share a common base structure, which consists of a title, short description, prolog, body, and related links. This common base structure is illustrated in Figure 2.3. Each core information type has, in addition, a unique set of specific content units that define the internal structure of that information type. For example, a task contains steps and other content units needed to structure procedural information. Most of the unique content units in the core information types are defined within the topic body.

Note that the common base structure shared by the core information types demonstrate DITA's hierarchical structure. In DITA, the base structure is referred to as a base topic type. Concept, task, and reference are derived from the base structure contained in the base topic.

Topic Element	Contains all other elements (<task>, <concept>, <reference>, <topic>)
Title	Contains the subject of the topic
Short Description	Contains a short description of the topic
Prolog	Contains various kinds of topic metadata, such as change history, audience, product, and so on
Body	Contains the actual topic content: paragraphs, lists, sections - whatever the information type allows
Related links	Contains cross reference links to supporting information

Figure 2.3 Base structure of the core information types

Concept information type

The base structure of the concept information type consists of the root concept element, title, short description, prolog, concept body, and related links. The root concept element is derived from the topic element in the base structure. The concept body is derived from the body element in the base structure. The concept body contains the section and the example content units that are part of the base body element in the base topic structure. Figure 2.4 provides a visual representation of the relationship between the base topic structure and the structure of the concept information type.

Task information type

The base structure of the task information type consists of the root task element, title, short description, prolog, task body, and related links. The root task element is derived from the topic element in the base structure. The task body is derived from the body element in the base structure. The task body contains steps, step, and other content units required to structure the steps in a procedure. Figure 2.5 provides a visual representation of the relationship between the base topic structure and the structure of the task information type.

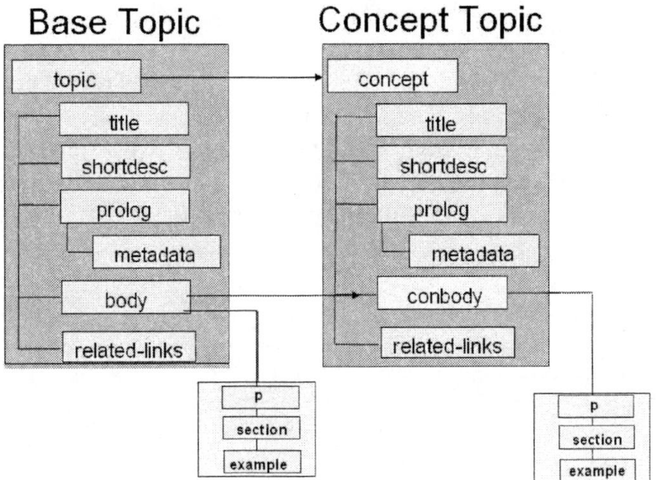

Figure 2.4 Base structure of a concept topic

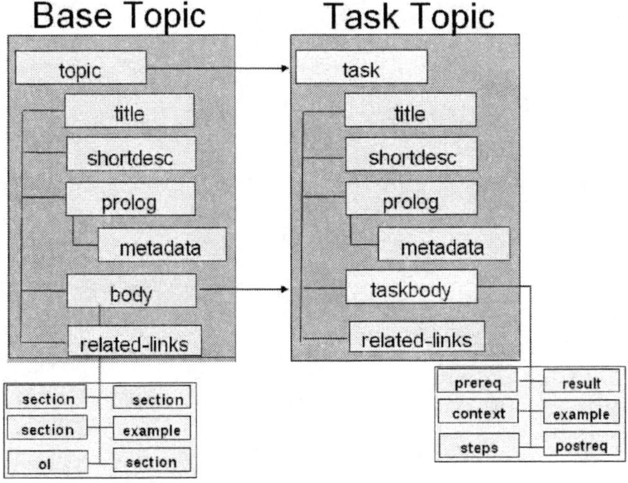

Figure 2.5 Base structure of a task topic

Reference information type

The base structure of the reference information type consists of the root reference element, title, short description, prolog, reference body, and related links. The root reference element is derived from the topic element in the base structure. The reference body is derived from the body element in the base structure. The reference body contains the properties content unit, which uses the same structure as a simple table in the base topic structure. Figure 2.6 provides a visual representation of the relationship between the base topic structure and the structure of the reference information type.

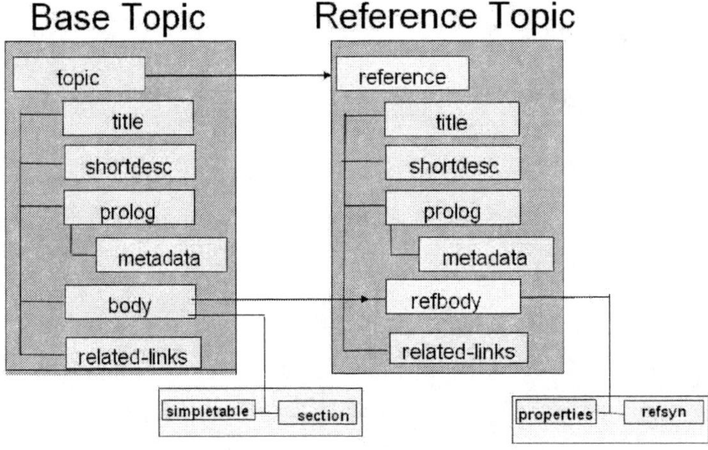

Figure 2.6 Base structure of a reference topic

LESSON 1

Concept Information Type

Concepts provide information that users need to complete tasks successfully. They respond to the user's question, "What is this about?" In implementing a topic-based architecture, you want to begin by developing your tasks. But, for each task, you may need to develop conceptual, descriptive, or background information. Based on your list of tasks, consider if your user needs more knowledge of the product, service, or environment to complete the task.

Unfortunately, much of the conceptual information included in technical documentation is not related to task performance. Others in the organization often ask writers to include snippets of information with little or no relevance to the user's performance. In the DITA model, consider first what concepts are absolutely essential and then ensure that the concepts are stand-alone topics that you can reuse in more than one context.

You may find that identifying and writing a concept is difficult. You may also find it difficult to differentiate between concept information and reference information. Concepts should directly support task performance. If users understand a core concept or knows how a product functions, they should be able to perform tasks and reach their goals more quickly, confidently, and with fewer errors. Some examples of concepts are product overviews, process maps, and introductions to groups of tasks.

In DITA, concepts must include a title and a conbody, the only required elements. A simple concept consists of a title and one or more paragraphs contained in the conbody. Short description, prolog, and related links are all optional. You can include additional structural content units in the conbody, such as paragraphs, sections, examples, and definition lists. A conbody can contain one or more sections or examples with their own titles.

Following the lesson, you will find a list and detailed descriptions of the concept elements, including elements not discussed in this lesson. For a complete list of elements you can use to write a concept, see the *DITA Language Specification.*

Creating a concept topic

This lesson explains the basic DITA elements you use to create a concept topic.

In this lesson, you learn to

- add elements used in each information type, such as <title>, <shortdesc>, <prolog>, and <related-links>
- add a unique *ID* attribute to your topic root element
- add elements specific to the concept information type, such as <concept>, <conbody>, <p>, <dl>, <dlentry>, <dt>, and <dd>

1. Start a new DITA concept topic.

   You can start a new DITA topic in an XML editor or in a text editor. In most XML editors, you can choose **file > new > DITA concept topic**. The XML tool usually includes a DTD declaration and XML declaration automatically. If you choose to use a text editor, start your concept topic by including the example markup shown below. The markup below is an example of what to include for your XML declaration, DTD declaration, and your root element.

   The XML declaration identifies the file as an XML document. The DTD declaration points to the DTD you want to validate your topic structure against. The DTD declaration includes a relative path to your DITA concept DTD. The root element, concept, is the container element for all other elements and identifies the topic as a concept topic.

   ```
   <?xml version="1.0" encoding="utf-8"?>
   <!DOCTYPE concept PUBLIC "-//OASIS//DTD DITA CONCEPT//EN"
     "concept.dtd">
   <concept>
   </concept>
   ```

2. Assign an *ID* attribute and value to the concept element.

   Each *ID* you add to your topic must be unique to that topic. You use the unique *ID* to reference the topic in a DITA map. You can use letters, numbers, and underscores in your *ID*.

   Most content management systems assign a unique *ID* to every topic you create automatically. If you are not using a content management system, consider using your topic title as the unique *ID*. Be careful to omit the spaces between words.

   For this concept, we recommend using the unique *ID*: "AboutConferenceCalls"

```
<?xml version="1.0" encoding="utf-8"?>
<!DOCTYPE concept PUBLIC "-//OASIS//DTD DITA CONCEPT//EN"
   "concept.dtd">
<concept id="AboutConferenceCalls">
</concept>
```

3. Insert <title> element start and end tags between the <concept> start and end tags and include title text.

   The title is the first content unit you include in every topic. Adding the title at the beginning of every topic ensures that the end user can identify the topic. You can include the topic title in your table of contents and site maps, and you can use it as link text for navigation through your topic set. Be certain that your concept title clearly communicates the subject of your topic. You may consider developing a naming convention for your task, concept, and reference topic titles to distinguish the topics for the user.

```
<concept id="AboutConferenceCalls">
   <title>About conference calls</title>
</concept>
```

4. Add <shortdesc> element start and end tags after your title, and include a short description of your topic.

   The short description briefly introduces the content of your concept topic. Although the short description is not required, we recommend you include it in every topic. You can use the short description to provide a brief statement to display in search engine results or as a mouse-over for a help topic.

```
<concept id="AboutConferenceCalls">
   <title>About conference calls</title>
   <shortdesc>Use a conference call to speak with more
         than two people in two different locations at the
         same time.</shortdesc>
</concept>
```

5. Add <prolog> element start and end tags after your short description, and include metadata for your concept topic.

   In this concept topic prolog, include author information. The <author> element is one of the metadata attributes you can use in the <prolog> element. In the <author> element, enter the topic author's name. For more information about prolog metadata elements, see Lesson 7: Prolog Metadata. You can also refer to the *DITA Language Specification* for a complete list of prolog elements.

```
<concept id="AboutConferenceCalls">
   <title>About conference calls</title>
   <shortdesc>Use a conference call to speak with more
      than two people in two different locations at the
      same time.</shortdesc>
   <prolog>
      <author>John Smith
      </author>
   </prolog>
</concept>
```

6. Add the <conbody> element start and end tags after the prolog.

   The concept body contains most of the content in the concept topic. All other information you write about a concept is placed inside the <conbody> element container.

```
<concept id="AboutConferenceCalls">
   <title>About conference calls</title>
   <shortdesc>Use a conference call to speak with more
      than two people in two different locations at the same
      time.
   </shortdesc>
   <prolog>
      <author>John Smith
      </author>
   </prolog>
   <conbody>
   </conbody>
</concept>
```

7. Add <p> element start and end tags between the <conbody> element tags.

   A concept can include any of the basic block elements, such as paragraph, bulleted list, numbered list, and table. Use block elements to structure your concept information in the concept body. For more information about block elements, see Lesson 4: Block Elements.

```
<conbody>
   <p>Use one of the following types of conference calls
      to speak with multiple people.</p>
</conbody>
```

8. Add a definition list to your concept.

   A definition list provides a convenient structure for defining terms, describing components of a system or product, or including information that falls naturally into a two- or three-column table. A definition list uses the <dl>, <dlentry>, <dt>, and <dd> elements. The <dl> element is the container element for your definition list. You can include multiple <dlentry> (definition list entries) element containers in the <dl>. For each <dlentry>, you must include at least one <dt> (definition term) and <dd> (definition description).

The definition list example below describes different types of conference calls.

```
<p>Use one of the following types of conference calls
   to speak with multiple people.</p>
<dl>
   <dlentry>
      <dt>Three-way conference call</dt>
      <dd>Three-way conference calling connects two
         other people to a call.</dd>
   </dlentry>
   <dlentry>
      <dt>Multi-line conference call</dt>
      <dd>Multi-line conference calling connects you
         to more than two but fewer than eight other
         people on a call.</dd>
   </dlentry>
   <dlentry>
      <dt>Dial-in conference call</dt>
      <dd>Dial-in conference calling uses a single
         conference call number to connect multiple
         people.</dd>
   </dlentry>
</dl>
```

9. Add a <related-links> container after your concept body element container and before your <concept> element end tag.

   You can use related links to point your user to other concept, task, or reference topics.

```
   </conbody>
      <related-links>
         <link href="SettingUpConfCall.dita"
            scope="local"/>
      </related-links>
</concept>
```

10. Save your concept topic as AboutConferenceCalls.dita.

    The following example shows the complete concept topic you created.

AboutConferenceCalls.dita

```
<?xml version="1.0" encoding="utf-8"?>
<!DOCTYPE task PUBLIC "-//OASIS//DTD DITA Concept//EN"
   "concept.dtd">
<concept id="AboutConferenceCalls" xml:lang="en-us">
   <title>About conference calls</title>
   <shortdesc>Use a conference call to speak with more
      than two people in two different locations at the same
      time.</shortdesc>
   <prolog>
      <author>John Smith
      </author>
   </prolog>
   <conbody>
      <p>Use one of the following types of conference
         calls to speak with multiple
         people.</p>
      <dl>
         <dlentry>
            <dt>Three-way conference call</dt>
            <dd>Three-way conference calling connects
               two other people to a call.</dd>
         </dlentry>
         <dlentry>
         <dt>Multi-line conference call</dt>
            <dd>Multi-line conference calling connects
               you to more than two but fewer than eight
               other people on a call.</dd>
         </dlentry>
         <dlentry>
            <dt>Dial-in conference call</dt>
            <dd>Dial-in conference calling uses a single
               conference call number to connect multiple
               people.</dd>
         </dlentry>
      </dl>
   </conbody>
      <related-links>
         <link href="SettingUpConfCall.dita"
            scope="local"/>
      </related-links>
</concept>
```

Figure 2.7 shows what a rendered concept topic looks like.

About conference calls

Use a conference call to speak with more than two people in two different locations at the same time.

Use one of the following types of conference calls to speak with multiple people.

Three-way conference call
: Three-way conference calling connects two other people to a call.

Multi-line conference call
: Multi-line conference calling connects you to more than two but less than 8 other people on a call.

Dial-in conference call
: Dial-in conference calling uses a single conference call number to connect multiple people.

Figure 2.7 Concept example rendered

Structure elements

Structure elements are the base elements that you can use with every DITA information type. Use structure elements to create the base topic structure and organize the content. Structure elements are the topic container, title, short description, prolog, and body. The DITA DTD requires that you include a topic container, title, and body in every topic you develop. The other structure elements are optional. You use the elements described in this lesson in the core information types—concept, task, and reference. The structure elements are listed here in the order that you might use them.

<task> <concept> <reference> elements

Use one of the core DITA information types as the top-level container (root element).

<title> title

Use the <title> element at the beginning of a topic to specify the heading for the entire topic. You can also use the <title> element to label sections or examples.

<titlealts> title alternatives

Use the <titlealts> element to specify alternative titles for your topic. The alternative titles may appear in web navigation, a table of contents, related links, or search results. The <titlealts> is a container for the <navtitle> and <search> title elements. The <titlealts> element is optional. If you do not use the <titlealts> element, the text in the <title> element is used for navigation windows, table of contents, related links, and search results.

<navtitle> navigation title

Use the <navtitle> element to specify an alternative title for your topic. The navtitle is usually shorter than the full title in the <title> element. The <navtitle> element is used in navigation windows or other online tables of content. The <navtitle> is located in the <titlealts> element and is optional.

<searchtitle> search title

Use the <searchtitle> element to specify a meaningful search title for your topic. The <searchtitle> element is used in search result summaries. It is located in the <titlealts> element and is optional.

<shortdesc> short description

Use the <shortdesc> element to provide the initial sentence or paragraph that summarizes the purpose or content of the topic. The <shortdesc> adds information to the topic title in search results and link previews. If you do not want to use the short description in your link previews, you can turn off the short description with your style sheet.

<prolog> prolog

Use the <prolog> element as a container for the topic-level metadata. The metadata you can specify in the <prolog> element includes author, audience, copyright information, tracking dates, and permissions. For a complete list of <prolog> elements, see Lesson 7: Prolog Metadata.

<body> body

Use the <body> element as the container for the main content of the <topic> element. The <body> element can contain block elements, phrase elements, and links. In the core task, concept, and reference information types, the <taskbody>, <conbody>, and <refbody> elements take the place of the base <body> element.

<related-links> related links

Use the <related-links> element to specify topics that the reader might want to consult after reading the topic. Although you can add related links to every topic with this element, we strongly recommend that you create your linking structure using a relationship table rather than embedding links in each topic. Changing a relationship table once in a DITA map is much easier than changing links embedded in individual topics. To create a relationship table, see Lesson 15: Relationship Tables.

The following example illustrates how to use the structure elements described above.

```
<concept>
   <title>How PUB$ Estimator simplifies project
      planning</title>
      <titlealts>
         <navtitle>Simplified project
            planning</navtitle>
         <searchtitle>Simplified project planning with
            PUB$ Estimator</searchtitle>
      </titlealts>
   <shortdesc>This section explains how PUB$ can simplify
      project planning. Included are the tasks accomplished
      with PUB$ and the worksheets that correspond to each
      task.</shortdesc>
   <prolog>
      <author>John Smith</author>
   </prolog>
   <conbody>
   </conbody>
</concept>
```

Concept elements

The elements you can use in a concept are primarily block elements. For definitions of block elements, see Lesson 4: Block Elements. Concepts restrict the structure that authors can use but provide considerable flexibility.

For example, the <p> element can only be located at the beginning of a concept. After you add a <section> or <example> element to a concept, you can only use another <section> or <example>. You cannot insert paragraphs between sections and examples. All <p> elements must be inside the <section> or <example> elements.

The following example illustrates how to use the elements in a concept topic.

```
<conbody>
   <p>The two-phase method of planning is so named
      because the planning and estimating process is
      comprised of two phases: the information planning
      phase and the content planning phase.  As you will
      see, the phases of project planning closely resemble
      the phases of product development.</p>
   <section>
      <title>The information planning phase</title>
      <p>During the information planning phase, the
         nature of the project is defined. The information
         plan can be likened to a product requirements
         document for a software development project.</p>
      <p>While studying the information needed by
         potential users and deciding on the best method to
         package the information, you can also create
         preliminary estimates based upon your initial
         research.</p>
   </section>
   <example>
      <image href="informationplanphase.jpg"></image>
   </example>
   <section>
      <title>The content planning phase</title>
      <p>After reviewing and gaining approval for your
         information plan, you reach the content planning
         phase. The content plan is analogous to the product
         specifications for a software or hardware
         project.</p>
      <p>During the content planning phase, you revise
         your preliminary estimates to reflect your detailed
         project specifications. At this point, you have
         enough information to develop a more reliable
         estimate of the time, staffing, and budget
         necessary.</p>
   </section>
   <example>
      <image href="contentplanphase.jpg"></image>
   </example>
</conbody>
```

Concept review questions

1. What question does a concept topic try to answer for the user?
2. What is the base structure of a concept?
3. What is the purpose of a document type definition (DTD)?
4. Where is a short description used during output?
5. Where is the <p> element located in a concept?
6. What is the file extension for a concept topic?

LESSON 2

Task Information Type

Tasks are the essential building blocks of technical content. They respond to the user's question, "How do I …?" When you implement a topic-based architecture, you should always begin by planning and authoring the tasks that the users must perform.

To identify tasks for your information plan, consider performing a user and task analysis. Associate tasks with each user role you identify. Then, follow the basic instructions in this lesson to develop your task topics.

In the lesson, you create a task that begins with a title, followed by a short description, prolog, task body, and related links. The only required elements in a task are the title and the task body. A simple task includes a title and one or more steps in the task body. All the other elements are optional. In the task body, you can include semantic elements, such as prerequisites, steps, examples, and results. The steps container allows you to include individual step elements. Each step begins with a command sentence and continues with additional information, notes, choice tables, step results, and step examples.

Following the lesson, you will find a list and more detailed descriptions of the task elements, including elements not discussed in the lesson. For a complete list of task elements, see the *DITA Language Specification.*

Creating a task topic

This lesson explains the basic DITA elements you use to create a task topic.

Many of the elements added to the beginning of your task topic are general topic structure elements. If you would like more information about the purpose of the <title>, *ID* attribute, <shortdesc>, and <prolog> elements and how to use them, see Lesson 1: Concept Information Type.

In this lesson, you learn to

- add elements specific to the task information type, such as <task>, <taskbody>, <context>, <steps>, <step>, <cmd>, <info>, <note>, and <result>
- create a choice table using elements, such as <choicetable>, <chhead>, <choptionshd>, <chdeschd>, <chrow>, <choption>, <chdesc>

1. Start a new DITA task topic.

   You can start a new DITA topic in a text editor or in an XML editor. In most XML editors, you can choose **File > New > DITA Task Topic** . The XML tool usually includes a DTD declaration and XML declaration automatically. If you choose to use a text editor, start your task topic by including the example markup shown below. The markup below is an example of what to include for your XML declaration, DTD declaration, and your root element.

```
<?xml version="1.0" encoding="utf-8"?>
<!DOCTYPE task PUBLIC "-//OASIS//DTD DITA TASK//EN"
   "task.dtd">
<task>
</task>
```

2. Assign an *ID* attribute and value to the task element.

   Use letters, numbers, and underscores to add your *ID*.

   For this task, we recommend using the unique *ID*: TransferringACall.

```
<?xml version="1.0" encoding="utf-8"?>
<!DOCTYPE task PUBLIC "-//OASIS//DTD DITA TASK//EN"
   "task.dtd">
<task id="TransferringACall">
</task>
```

3. Insert <title> element start and end tags between the task start and end tags and include title text.

   Your task title describes the action the user must take.

```
<task id="TransferringACall">
   <title>Transferring a call</title>
</task>
```

4. Add <shortdesc> element start and end tags after your title, and include a short description of your topic.

   The short description briefly introduces the content of your task topic. Although the short description is not required, you should include it in every topic. The short description for a task provides your readers with an overview of what they will accomplish in the task. You can use the short description to provide a brief statement to display in search engine results or as a mouse-over for a help topic.

```
<task id="TransferringACall">
   <title>Transferring a call</title>
   <shortdesc>When you transfer a call to another
      person in your office, you have two ways of handling
      the transfer.
   </shortdesc>
</task>
```

5. Add <prolog> element start and end tags

   For your task topic, include author metadata.

```
<task id="TransferringACall">
   <title>Transferring a call</title>
   <shortdesc>When you transfer a call to another person
      in your office, you have two ways of handling the
      transfer.
   </shortdesc>
   <prolog>
      <author>John Smith</author>
   </prolog>
</task>
```

6. Add the <taskbody> element start and end tags after your prolog.

   The task body element is a container for most of the content in the task topic. All other information you write about a task is placed inside the <taskbody> element container.

```
<task id="TransferringACall">
   <title>Transferring a call</title>
   <shortdesc>When you transfer a call to another person
      in your office, you have two ways of handling the
      transfer.
   </shortdesc>
   <prolog>
      <author>John Smith</author>
   </prolog>
   <taskbody>
   </taskbody>
</task>
```

7. Add <context> element start and end tags as the first element between your task body start and end tags.

   The <context> element helps the user understand the purpose of the task and provides required background information. The context for a task should not include an entire concept topic. If the user needs more context, consider developing a concept topic.

```
<taskbody>
   <context>
      <p>When you transfer the call without speaking to
         the person, it is an unannounced transfer. When you
         speak to the person receiving the transferred call,
         it is an announced transfer.
      </p>
   </context>
</taskbody>
```

8. Add <steps> after the <context> container.

   The task body uses a <steps> container to add each step. The <steps> container surrounds the individual steps so you can more easily use all the steps in another task. Each step uses the <step> element. For each step, you must include a command. Use the <cmd> element to write a single sentence stating the action for the step.

```
<taskbody>
   <context>
   </context>
   <steps>
      <step>
         <cmd>Press the transfer button.</cmd>
      </step>
      <step>
         <cmd>Dial the number.</cmd>
      </step>
      <step>
         <cmd>Transfer the call.</cmd>
      </step>
   </steps>
</taskbody>
```

9. Add further step information after your command using the <info> element container.

   In the <info> element container, you can add block elements, such as paragraphs, lists, and notes. You can also include a <note> element in the <info> element container and distinguish admonishments, such as note, tip, or caution using the type attribute.

```
<steps>
   <step>
      <cmd>Press the transfer button.</cmd>
   </step>
   <step>
      <cmd>Dial the number.</cmd>
      <info>Dial the number manually, use your pre-defined
```

```
            speed dial keys, or go to your company directory.
         </info>
      </step>
      <step>
         <cmd>Transfer the call.</cmd>
         <info>
            <note>If you announce a call and the person
               refuses the transfer, do not hang up the phone.
               Press the transfer button again to retrieve the
               call on your phone.</note>
         </info>
      </step>
   </steps>
```

10. Add a choice table in the step element container.

A choice table allows you to present your user with different options to complete the step. The <choicetable> element sets up a two-column table to display a choice option in one column and a description in the second column. In DITA XML markup, you must use a series of elements to design a table, including <chhead>, <choptionhd>, <chdeschd>, <chrow>, <choption>, and <chdesc>.

The first element in the <choicetable> is <chhead>. The <chhead> (choice head) allows you to label the columns. The <chhead> uses the <choptionhd> and <chdeschd> to specify each column label. In the example below, use Type of announcement and Steps to complete as the column heads.

After you set up the column headers, you must add the <chrow> element to insert a second row. Each <chrow> container allows <choption> and <chdesc> to create two columns. You enter your choice table content in the choice option and choice description content units.

```
<steps>
   <step>
      <cmd>Transfer the call.</cmd>
      <choicetable>
         <chhead>
            <choptionhd>Type of Announcement
            </choptionhd>
            <chdeschd>Steps to complete
            </chdeschd>
         </chhead>
         <chrow>
            <choption>Announce a call transfer
            </choption>
            <chdesc>
               <ol>
                  <li>Speak to the person.</li>
```

```
                <li>Hang up the phone.</li>
            </ol>
        </chdesc>
    </chrow>
    <chrow>
        <choption>Transfer a call unannounced
        </choption>
        <chdesc>
            <ul>
                <li>Hang up the phone.</li>
            </ul>
        </chdesc>
    </chrow>
</choicetable>
<info>
    <note>If you announce a call and the person
        refuses the transfer, do not hang up the phone.
        Press the transfer button again to retrieve the
        call on your phone.</note>
</info>
</step>
</steps>
```

11. Finally, add task <result> start and end tags before your end <taskbody> element container.

    Task topics don't require that you include a result, but a result statement helps the users verify that they performed the task correctly. In the result container, provide the users with information about what they accomplished in the task. You may also add a task example and a post requirement. For more information about the task <example> element and <postreq> element, see the Task Elements at the end of this lesson.

```
<taskbody>
    <context>
    </context>
    <steps>
    </steps>
    <result>The call is transferred.
    </result>
</taskbody>
```

12. Add <related-links> element start and end tags after the <taskbody> element container and before your <task> element end tag.

    In the related links, you can provide multiple links to other topics associated with this task. For example, you might use a related link to lead the reader to the next task in a sequence of tasks or to a concept that helps the reader perform the tasks correctly.

```
<task>
   <taskbody>
   </taskbody>
      <related-links>
         <link href="AboutTransfer.dita" scope="local"/>
      </related-links>
</task>
```

13. Save the task topic as TransferringACall.dita.

    The following example shows the complete task topic you created.

TransferringACall.dita

```
<?xml version="1.0" encoding="utf-8"?>
<!DOCTYPE task PUBLIC "-//OASIS//DTD DITA Task//EN"
   "task.dtd">
<task id="TransferringACall" xml:lang="en-us">
   <title>Transferring a call</title>
   <shortdesc>When you transfer a call to another person
      in your office, you have two ways of handling the
      transfer.
   </shortdesc>
   <prolog>
      <author>John Smith</author>
   </prolog>
   <taskbody>
      <context>
         <p>When you transfer the call without speaking
            to the person, it is an unannounced transfer.
            When you speak to the person receiving the
            transferred call, it is an announced transfer.
         </p>
      </context>
      <steps>
         <step>
            <cmd>Press the transfer button.</cmd>
         </step>
         <step>
            <cmd>Dial the number. </cmd>
            <info>Dial the number manually, use your
               pre-defined speed dial keys, or go to your
               company directory. </info>
         </step>
         <step>
            <cmd>Transfer the call.</cmd>
```

```
            <choicetable>
               <chhead>
                  <choptionhd>Type of Announcement
                  </choptionhd>
                  <chdeschd>Steps to complete
                  </chdeschd>
               </chhead>
               <chrow>
                  <choption>Announce a call transfer
                  </choption>
                  <chdesc>
                     <ol>
                        <li>Speak to the person.
                        </li>
                        <li>Hang up the phone.</li>
                     </ol>
                  </chdesc>
               </chrow>
               <chrow>
                  <choption>Transfer a call
                     unannounced</choption>
                  <chdesc>
                     <ul>
                        <li>Hang up the phone.</li>
                     </ul>
                  </chdesc>
               </chrow>
            </choicetable>
            <info>
               <note>If you announce a call and the
                  person refuses the transfer, do not hang
                  up the phone. Press the transfer button
                  again to retrieve the call on your phone
                  station.</note>
            </info>
         </step>
      </steps>
      <result>The call is transferred.</result>
   </taskbody>
      <related-links>
          <link href="AboutTransfer.dita" scope="local"/>
      </related-links>
</task>
```

Figure 2.8 shows what a rendered task topic looks like.

Transferring a call

When you transfer a call to another person in your office, you have two ways of handling the transfer.

When you transfer the call without speaking to the person, it is an unannounced transfer. When you speak to the person receiving the transferred call, it is an announced transfer.

1. Press the transfer button.
2. Dial the number. Dial the number manually, use your pre-defined speed dial keys or go to your company directory.
3. Transfer the call.

Type of Announcement	Steps to complete
Announce a call transfer	a. Speak to the person. b. Hang up the phone.
Transfer a call unannounced	• Hang up the phone.

Note: If you announce a call and the person refuses the transfer, do not hang up the phone. Press the transfer button again to retrieve the call on your phone station.

The call is transferred.

Figure 2.8 Task example rendered

Task elements

You can use the elements described below in the task information type. The task elements are listed here in the order that you might use them when writing a task.

<prereq> prerequisite

Use the <prereq> element to specify anything that the user needs to know or do before starting the task. This information may include actions that must be completed first or a list of equipment that the user needs to complete the task.

If you are referring the user to another section, put the reference links needed for the prerequisite in the related-links section rather than into the prerequisite paragraph.

The following example illustrates how to use the <prereq> element.

```
<taskbody>
   <prereq> Before you generate a new dependencies
      worksheet, research your organization's average hours
      per page for similar documents. You can base this
      average on past project histories, industry averages,
      or an educated guess.</prereq>
</taskbody>
```

<context>context

Use the <context> element to identify the purpose or goal of the task, as well as to indicate to the users what they gain by completing the task. While the context information may contain some basic conceptual information, it should not replace or recreate a related concept topic.

The following example illustrates how to use the <context> element.

```
<taskbody>
   <context>
      <p>PUB$ sets up your dependencies worksheet with
         an average ranking of 3 for each dependency. After
         PUB$ returns control to you, you may want to change
         the rankings to reflect your specific
         circumstances.</p>
   </context>
</taskbody>
```

<steps> steps and <steps-unordered> steps unordered

Use the <steps> element to create a numbered list of all the steps that the user must follow to complete the task. The <steps> element is the container for all of the individual <step> elements that your task contains. If your task only has one step or if the steps do not need to be performed in order, use a <steps-unordered> element instead.

<step> step

Use the <step> element to develop each step that the user must follow to complete the task. Each <step> element must be in the <steps> container and must begin with a <cmd> element. Each <step> in a <steps> list may be rendered as a numbered step. Each <step> in a <steps-unordered> list may be rendered as an unnumbered step. You may use one or more <step> elements within each <steps> or <steps-unordered> element.

<cmd> command

Use the <cmd> element to describe the action the user needs to take in a <step> element. The description should be written in the imperative (Press the button), and it should be no more than one sentence. The <cmd> element must be the first element in the <step> element.

<info> information

Use the <info> element to add information needed to complete a step beyond the instruction in the <cmd> element. The description should be brief and should contain minimal conceptual information.

<note> note

Use the <note> element to call attention to a particular point in the <info> element. The <note> can be designated as caution, warning, or note, depending on the attribute you select for the element.

<stepxmp> step example

Use the <stepxmp> element to show the user how to perform the step. The example may include a few words, a paragraph, a figure, a table, or other information to illustrate the task. Step examples often provide specific data-entry characters.

<stepresult> step result

Use the <stepresult> element to explain the expected outcome of a step, such as a dialog box opening or a progress indicator appearing. Step results assure users that they are on track. They are not required for every step.

<substeps> sub-steps

Use the <substeps> element to break a step down into a series of actions. This element is a container for the individual <substep> elements. If you need to use <substeps>, consider creating a new task instead so that the steps are not embedded in another task. Use <substeps> only when necessary.

<substep> sub-step

Use the <substep> element to develop each sub-step that a user must follow to complete the step. The <substep> element has the same structure as the <step> element, but it cannot contain another level of <substeps> or <choice> or <choice-table> elements.

The following example illustrates how to use the <step> elements.

```
<taskbody>
   <steps>
      <step>
         <cmd>Select a cell in the dependency row you
            want to change.</cmd>
         <info>After setting up the dependencies
            worksheet, PUB$ selects a cell in the first
            dependency row. If you don't want to change this
            dependency ranking, select a cell in another
            dependency row.</info>
      </step>

      <step>
         <cmd>Enter the new ranking.</cmd>
         <substeps>
            <substep>
               <cmd>While holding down the Control key,
                  type the appropriate ranking (1 to 5).
               </cmd>
```

```
                <info> The cell that corresponds to your
                   entry is shaded.
                   <note type="caution"> The Control key
                      works only with the number keys at the
                      top of your keyboard. Use those numbers
                      to change dependency rankings. If you
                      use the keypad on the right side of
                      your keyboard, you delete information
                      in the selected cell.</note>
                </info>
             </substep>
          </substeps>
          <stepresult>After you change the dependency
             ranking, PUB$ multiples your average hours per
             page by each multiple to calculate a new hours
             per page projection. PUB$ then selects a cell in
             the next dependency row and returns control to
             you.</stepresult>
       </step>
    </steps>
</taskbody>
```

<choices> choices

Use the <choices> element to create a list of options that the user may select to complete the task. The <choices> element is a container for the individual <choice> elements.

<choice> choice

Use the <choice> element to develop each option that the user can select. The <choice> element must be in a <choices> container. The <choice> items are bullets when rendered.

The following example illustrates how to use the <choices> elements.

```
<taskbody>
   <steps>
      <step>
         <cmd>Start the PUB$ program.</cmd>
         <choices>
            <choice>Click Yes if you want to include
               the new skill in the factor formula.
            </choice>
            <choice>Click No if you don't want to include
               the new skill in the factor formula.
            </choice>
         </choices>
      </step>
   </steps>
</taskbody>
```

<choicetable> choice table

Use the <choicetable> element to create a table of options that the user may select to complete the task. The <choicetable> element is a container for the individual <choice> elements.

<chhead> choice head

Use the <chhead> element to override the default heads in a choice table. The <chhead> element is used in the <choicetable> container. It contains the <choptionhd> and <chdeschd> elements.

<choptionhd> choice option head

Use the <choptionhd> element to change the default head on the first column of a choice table. The <choptionhd> element is used in the <chhead> container. The default value of <choptionhd> is Options.

<chdeschd> choice description head

Use the <chdeschd> element to change the default head on the second column of a choice table. The <chdeschd> element is used in the <chhead> container. The default value of <chdeschd> is Description.

<chrow> choice row

Use the <chrow> element to create a row in a choice table. The <chrow> element is used in the <choicetable> container. The <chrow> element contains the <choption> and <chdesc> elements.

<choption> choice option

Use the <choption> element to describe an option that the user can choose to accomplish the step. One <choption> element is used in each <chrow> element.

<chdesc> choice description

Use the <chdesc> element to provide a description for the option in the corresponding <choption> element. The description explains why the user would choose that option or the result of making that choice. One <chdesc> element is used in each <chrow> element.

The following example illustrates how to use the <choicetable> elements.

```
<taskbody>
   <steps>
      <step>
         <cmd>Enter the file names of any labor costs
            summary reports.</cmd>
         <choicetable>
            <chhead>
               <choptionhd>If</choptionhd>
               <chdeschd>Then</chdeschd>
            </chhead>
```

```
            <chrow>
               <choption>You have previously generated
                  labor costs summary reports</choption>
               <chdesc>The links must be updated and
                  maintained. Type the file names in the
                  spaces provided, indicate whether each
                  file is currently open, and click Enter.
                  If a file is closed, PUB$ opens it before
                  updating the information.</chdesc>
            </chrow>
            <chrow>
               <choption>You have not generated one or
                  both of these reports.</choption>
               <chdesc>Check the box that corresponds
                  to the missing report, and click Enter.
               </chdesc>
            </chrow>
         </choicetable>
      </step>
   </steps>
</taskbody>
```

<result> result

Use the <result> element to describe the expected outcome of the entire task. The <result> element could include a final description using figures, tables, or audiovisual cues that show the users that they have successfully completed the task. The <result> element is used after the <steps> container.

The following example illustrates how to use the <result> element.

```
<taskbody>
   <steps>...</steps>
   <result>The weekly hours tracking workshop has been
      saved by PUB$. Control of the worksheet has been
      restored to you. </result>
</taskbody>
```

<example> example

Use the <example> element in a task to display the expected outcome of the entire task. The <example> element could include code samples, figures, screen shots, and other samples that show the users how they should have completed the task. The <example> element is used after the <result> container.

The following example illustrates how to use the <example> element.

```
<taskbody>
   <steps>...</steps>
   <example>Let's take a look at the weekly total costs
      tracking worksheet that Renee generated for the month
      of March (Figure 5.21)
      <fig>
         <title>Serendipity's weekly total costs tracking
            worksheet</title>
         <image href="WeeklyTotalCostsExample.jpg">
         </image>
      </fig>
   </example>
</taskbody>
```

<postreq> post requirement

Use the <postreq> element to specify anything that the user needs to know or do after completing the task. This information may include actions that need to be completed before the user can see the expected results, such as rebooting the computer, or information that the user needs to read or cross-reference to verify the completion of the task. The <postreq> element is often supported by links to the next task or tasks in the related-links section.

The following example illustrates how to use the <postreq> element.

```
<taskbody>
   <steps>...</steps>
   <postreq>After you have entered your initial
      dependency rankings, you can change any of them by
      repeating steps 1 and 2. Notice how the hours per page
      projection is affected by each change.</postreq>
</taskbody>
```

Task review questions

1. What question does a task topic try to answer for the user?
2. What is the base structure of a task?
3. What is the difference between a concept and a task document type definition (DTD)?
4. What is the first element in a step and what function does it serve?
5. What is the difference between the context and short description elements?
6. What is the difference between choices and a choice table?
7. What does a choice table accomplish?

LESSON 3

Reference Information Type

Reference topics are essential for the successful performance of technical tasks. In fact, many competent and expert users depend more heavily on reference information than they do on step-by-step tasks. By building stand-alone reference topics, you have the flexibility of building unique deliverables that emphasize reference content, including command reference lists, error codes, specifications, parameters, and glossary terms.

Because reference information is often in lists or tables, the reference information type provides elements that facilitate list and table development.

A reference topic begins with a title, followed by a short description, prolog, reference body, and related links. The only required elements of a reference topic are the title and the reference body. A simple reference topic consists of a title and a list or a table contained in the reference body. You can structure your information further within the reference body using a property table, ordered and unordered lists, simple tables, and complex tables.

Following the lesson, you will find a list and more detailed descriptions of the reference elements, including elements not discussed in this lesson.

Creating a reference topic

This lesson explains the basic DITA elements you use to create a reference topic.

Many of the elements added to the beginning of your reference topic are general topic structure elements. If you would like more information about how to use the <title>, *ID* attribute, <shortdesc>, and <prolog> elements and their purpose, see Lesson 1: Concept Information Type.

In this lesson you learn to

- add standard elements used in the reference information type such as <reference> and <refbody>
- create a properties table using elements, such as <properties>, <prophead>, <proptypehd>, <propvaluehd>, <propdeschd>, <property>, <proptype>, <propvalue>, and <propdesc>

1. Start a new DITA reference topic.

   You can start a new DITA topic in a text editor or in an XML editor. In most XML editors, you can choose **File > New > DITA Reference Topic** . The XML tool usually includes a DTD declaration and XML declaration automatically. If you choose to use a text editor, start your task topic by including the example markup shown below. The markup below is an example of what to include for your XML declaration, DTD declaration, and your root element.

```
<?xml version="1.0" encoding="utf-8"?>
<!DOCTYPE reference PUBLIC "-//OASIS//DTD DITA
   REFERENCE//EN" "reference.dtd">
<reference>
</reference>
```

2. Assign a unique *ID* to the topic.

   Use letters, numbers, and underscores to add your *ID*.

   For this reference, we recommend using the unique *ID*: "QuickGuide"

```
<?xml version="1.0" encoding="utf-8"?>
<!DOCTYPE reference PUBLIC "-//OASIS//DTD DITA
   REFERENCE//EN" "reference.dtd">
<reference id="QuickGuide">
</reference>
```

3. Begin the reference with the <title> element start and end tags in the reference container.

   Reference topic titles need to facilitate quick lookup.

```
<reference id="QuickGuide">
   <title>Quick Guide to Basic Telephone Use
   </title>
</reference>
```

4. Add <shortdesc> element start and end tags after the <title> container.

   The short description for a reference topic provides your users with an overview of the lists, tables, and other reference information in the topic.

```
<reference id="QuickGuide">
   <title>Quick Guide to Basic Telephone Use</title>
   <shortdesc>The Quick Guide provides a brief
      description of the buttons on your phone.
   </shortdesc>
</reference>
```

5. Add <prolog> element start and end tags after your short description, and include metadata specific to your task topic.

   For your reference topic, include author metadata.

```
<reference id="QuickGuide">
   <title>Quick Guide to Basic Telephone Use</title>
   <shortdesc>The Quick Guide provides a brief
      description of each button on your phone.
   </shortdesc>
   <prolog>
      <author>John Smith</author>
   </prolog>
</reference>
```

6. Add <refbody> element start and end tags after your prolog container.

   The <refbody> element contains most of the content in the reference topic. All other information you write about a reference is placed inside the <refbody> element container.

```
<reference id="QuickGuide">
   <title>Quick Guide to Basic Telephone Use</title>
   <shortdesc>The Quick Guide provides a brief
      description of the buttons on your phone.
   </shortdesc>
   <prolog>
      <author>John Smith</author>
   </prolog>
   <refbody>
   </refbody>
</reference>
```

7. Add <properties> element start and end tags between your <refbody> element tags.

   The properties container allows you to create a table for your reference information. A properties table informs users about a term, value, and description in your product. Using the <properties> element to contain your table, you can more easily reuse an entire properties table in another context.

```
<refbody>
   <properties></properties>
</refbody>
```

8. Add <prophead> element start and end tags as the first container between your <properties> element start and end tag.

   You define the column heads in the <prophead> element container using the <proptypehd>, <propvaluehd>, and <propdeschd> elements. The

<proptypehd> element container allows you to insert a column head for your property types. The <propvaluehd> element container allows you to insert a column head for your property values. The <propdeschd> element container allows you to insert a column head for your property descriptions.

```
<refbody>
   <properties>
      <prophead>
         <proptypehd>Action</proptypehd>
         <propvaluehd>Indicator</propvaluehd>
         <propdeschd>Description</propdeschd>
      </prophead>
   </properties>
</refbody>
```

9. Add <property> element start and end tags after your property head container.

   You can insert content for each row using the <proptype>, <propvalue>, and <propdesc> elements in your <property> container. In the columns, you can name the <proptype> you are referencing, such as the name of a particular parameter. Use <propvalue> to describe the values associated with each parameter. Use <propdeschd> to include a detailed description of the parameter.

   The property element provides a container for each row of content. The three element containers, property type, property value, and property description, allow you to create a three-column table. If you decide you don't want to include data in one of the table cells defined by the <proptype>, <propvalue>, and <propdesc> elements, add the element tags without adding text.

```
<refbody>
   <properties>
      <prophead>
         <proptypehd>Action</proptypehd>
         <propvaluehd>Indicator</propvaluehd>
         <propdeschd>Description</propdeschd>
      </prophead>
      <property>
         <proptype>Talk</proptype>
         <propvalue>
            <image href="talk.jpg"/>
         </propvalue>
         <propdesc>Press the talk key to receive a dial
            tone.</propdesc>
      </property>
      <property>
```

```
            <proptype>Speaker phone</proptype>
            <propvalue>
               <image href="speakerphone.jpg"/>
            </propvalue>
            <propdesc>Press the speaker phone button to
               place a call on speaker phone.</propdesc>
         </property>
         <property>
            <proptype>Forward</proptype>
            <propvalue>
               <image href="forward.jpg"/>
            </propvalue>
            <propdesc>Press the forward button to forward
               all incoming calls to another phone number or
               voice mail.</propdesc>
         </property>
         <property>
            <proptype>Transfer</proptype>
            <propvalue>
               <image href="transfer.jpg"/>
            </propvalue>
            <propdesc>Press the transfer button to transfer
               a call to another person.</propdesc>
         </property>
         <property>
            <proptype>Hold</proptype>
            <propvalue>
               <image href="hold.jpg"/>
            </propvalue>
            <propdesc>Press the hold button to place a call
               on hold.</propdesc>
         </property>
         <property>
            <proptype>Mute</proptype>
            <propvalue>
               <image href="mute.jpg"/>
            </propvalue>
            <propdesc>Press the mute button to mute your
               end of the call.</propdesc>
         </property>
      </properties>
   </refbody>
```

10. Add <related-links> element start and end tags after your <refbody> element container and before your <concept> element end tag.

    In reference topics, you rarely use related links because reference topics relate to so many other task, concept, and reference topics. If you include links to all task, concept, and reference topics in your reference topic, it might overwhelm the user.

```
   </refbody>
   <related-links>
      <link href="TransferringACall.dita"
         scope="local"/>
   </related-links>
</reference>
```

11. Save the reference topic as QuickGuide.dita.

    The following example illustrates the complete reference topic you created.

QuickGuide.dita

```
<?xml version="1.0" encoding="utf-8"?>
<!DOCTYPE reference PUBLIC "-//OASIS//DTD DITA
   Reference//EN" "reference.dtd">
<reference id="QuickGuide" xml:lang="en-us">
   <title>Quick Guide to Basic Telephone Use</title>
   <shortdesc>The Quick Guide provides a brief
      description of the buttons on your phone.
   </shortdesc>
   <prolog>
      <author>John Smith</author>
   </prolog>
   <refbody>
      <properties>
         <prophead>
            <proptypehd>Action</proptypehd>
            <propvaluehd>Indicator</propvaluehd>
            <propdeschd>Description</propdeschd>
         </prophead>
         <property>
            <proptype>Talk</proptype>
            <propvalue>
               <image href="talk.jpg"/>
            </propvalue>
            <propdesc>Press the talk key to receive a
               dial tone.</propdesc>
         </property>
         <property>
            <proptype>Speaker phone</proptype>
            <propvalue>
               <image href="speakerphone.jpg"/>
            </propvalue>
            <propdesc>Press the speaker phone button to
               place a call on speaker phone.</propdesc>
         </property>
         <property>
            <proptype>Forward</proptype>
            <propvalue>
               <image href="forward.jpg"/>
            </propvalue>
```

```
            <propdesc>Press the forward button to
               forward all incoming calls to another phone
               number or voice mail.</propdesc>
         </property>
         <property>
            <proptype>Transfer</proptype>
            <propvalue>
               <image href="transfer.jpg"/>
            </propvalue>
            <propdesc>Press the transfer button to
               transfer a call to another person.
            </propdesc>
         </property>
         <property>
            <proptype>Hold</proptype>
            <propvalue>
               <image href="hold.jpg"/>
            </propvalue>
            <propdesc>Press the hold button to place a
               call on hold.</propdesc>
         </property>
         <property>
            <proptype>Mute</proptype>
            <propvalue>
               <image href="mute.jpg"/>
            </propvalue>
            <propdesc>Press the mute button to mute
               your end of the call.
            </propdesc>
         </property>
      </properties>
   </refbody>
      <related-links>
          <link href="TransferringACall.dita"
             scope="local"/>
      </related-links>
</reference>
```

Figure 2.9 shows what a rendered reference topic looks like.

Quick Guide

The quick guide provides a brief description of the buttons on your phone.

Action	Indicator	Description
Talk	TALK	Press the talk key to receive a dial tone.
Speaker phone	SPEAKERPHONE	Press the speaker phone button to place a call on speaker phone
Forward	FORWARD	Press the forward button to forward all incoming calls to another phone number or voice mail.
Transfer	TRANSFER	Press the transfer button to transfer a call to another person.
Hold	HOLD	Press the hold button to place a call on hold.
Mute	MUTE	Press the mute button to mute your end of the call.

Related tasks
Transferring a call

Figure 2.9 Reference example rendered

Reference elements

You can use the reference elements described below in the reference information type. The reference elements are listed here in the order that you might use them when authoring a properties table.

<properties> properties

Use the <properties> element to create a properties table to list all the details the user must know for the corresponding task topic. The <properties> element is the container for all the individual <property> elements your reference contains.

<prophead> property head

Use the <prophead> element to specify the property type, property value, and property description column heads for the properties table. The <prophead> element is the container for the three <proptypehd>, <propvaluehd>, and <propdeschd> elements. Each of these elements can only occur once within the <properties> element.

<proptypehd> property type head

Use the <proptypehd> element to specify the type heading for the properties table. The <proptypehd> is the first element in the <prophead> element.

<propvaluehd> property value head

Use the <propvaluehd> element to specify the value head for the properties table. The <propvaluehd> is the second element in the <prophead> element.

<propdeschd> property description head

Use the <propdeschd> element to specify the description head for the properties table. The <propdeschd> is the last element in the <prophead> element.

<property> property

Use the <property> element to create a row in a property table. The <property> element contains the <proptype>, <propvalue>, and <propdesc> elements.

<proptype> property type

Use the <proptype> element to define the property type for the row in the properties table. One <proptype> element can be used in each <property> element.

<propvalue> property value

Use the <propvalue> element to define the value of the specified property type. One <propvalue> element can be used in each <property> element.

<propdesc> property description

Use the <propdesc> element to describe the property type in one row of the properties table. One <propdesc> element can be used in each <property> element.

The following example illustrates how to use the <properties> elements.

```
<properties>
   <prophead>
      <proptypehd>Character Graphic</proptypehd>
      <propvaluehd>Code Point</propvaluehd>
      <propdeschd>Description</propdeschd>
   </prophead>
   <property>
      <proptype>A</proptype>
      <propvalue>41</propvalue>
      <propdesc>A Capital</propdesc>
   </property>
   <property>
      <proptype>a</proptype>
      <propvalue>61</propvalue>
      <propdesc>a Small</propdesc>
   </property>
  <property>
      <proptype>B</proptype>
      <propvalue>42</propvalue>
      <propdesc>B Capital</propdesc>
   </property>
   <property>
      <proptype>b</proptype>
      <propvalue>62</propvalue>
      <propdesc>b Small</propdesc>
```

```
        </property>
        <property>
            <proptype>C</proptype>
            <propvalue>43</propvalue>
            <propdesc>C Capital</propdesc>
        </property>
        <property>
            <proptype>c</proptype>
            <propvalue>63</propvalue>
            <propdesc>c Small</propdesc>
        </property>
    </properties>
```

Figure 2.10 illustrates a rendered properties table. The table format will vary depending on your stylesheet.

Character Graphic	Code Point	Description
A	41	A Capital
a	61	a Small
B	42	B Capital
b	62	b Small
C	43	C Capital
c	63	c Small

Figure 2.10 Properties table rendered

Reference review questions

1. What is the base structure of a reference?
2. What is the container element for the body of the reference?
3. What tags do you use to create column heads in a properties table?
4. Is there any limit to the number of columns that you can have in a properties table?
5. Is there any limit to the number of rows that you can have in a properties table?

SECTION B

Understanding DITA Elements

In the first three lessons, you learned to apply the required elements and some of the optional structure elements to a DITA concept, task, and reference topic. DITA has 171 elements that you can use to create your DITA topics. The DITA elements may also contain attributes which enhance their functionality. In this guide, we do not discuss all elements or all the attributes. For a complete list of the DITA elements and their attributes, see the *DITA Language Specification*.

DITA topic elements may be grouped into five categories: structure, block, phrase, related-link, and metadata elements. Structure elements, as described in the concept lesson, provide the overall structure for each information type. Block elements provide structure for basic content, such as paragraphs and lists, and also provide containers for other elements. Phrase elements are used inline in your content to label information semantically.

Related links allow you to link topics together. Metadata elements allow you to categorize your information to facilitate search and retrieval and conditional processing.

Figure 2.11 illustrates how the elements are ordered in a DITA topic.

Document Type Declaration

Structure elements

Metadata elements

Structure element

Block Elements

Phrase element

Domain element

Related-link elements

```
<?xml version="1.0" encoding="utf-8"?>
<!DOCTYPE concept PUBLIC "-//OASIS//DTD DITA Concept//EN" "concept.dtd">
<concept id="AboutConferenceCalls" xml:lang="en-us">
<title>About conference calls</title>
<shortdesc>Use a conference call to speak with more than two people in two
different locations at the same time. </shortdesc>
<prolog>
 <metadata>
  <prodinfo>
    <prodname>ComStar Phones</prodname>
    <brand>ComStar</brand>
  <prodinfo>
 </metadata>
</prolog>
<conbody>
  <p>About conference calls</p>
  <section><p>There are several basic types of conference calls
   you can  make using your telephone. </p>
  <dl>
    <dlentry>
      <dt><keyword>Three-way</keyword> conference call</dt>
      <dd>Three-way conference calling allows you to connect two
        other people to the call.This feature can be accessed on your
        phone through the <uicontrol>Conf-3</uicontrol> key
        located on your phone.</dd>
    </dlentry>
    <dlentry>
      <dt><keyword>Multi-line</keyword> conference call</dt>
      <dd>Multi-line conference calling allows you to connect more than two but
       less than 8 other people to the call.This feature can be accessed on your
       phone through the <uicontrol>Conference</uicontrol>
       key located on your phone</dd>
    </dlentry>
    <dlentry>
      <dt><keyword>Dial-in</keyword> conference call</dt>
      <dd>Dial-in conference calling allows you to set up a conference call number
         that multiple people can call to speak with each other.</dd>
    </dlentry>
  </dl>
  </section>
  <example>
  <title>Using an image in your example</title>
  <image href="Topics\InformationTypes.jpg"></image>
  </example>
</conbody>
<related-links>
  <link href="AboutTransferringACall.dita" scope="local"/>
  <link href="../../Glossary.dita" scope="peer"/>
  <link href="http://www.comtech-serv.com/Comstar"  scope="external"/>
</related-links>
</concept>
```

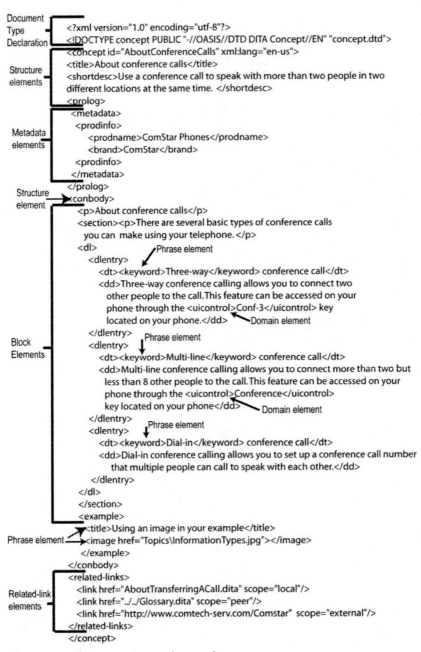

Figure 2.11 Element structure in a topic

LESSON 4

Block Elements

Block elements are the standard content units used by authors to define the structure of blocks of text. Some block elements may look familiar because they share the same names as HTML elements. Block elements include paragraph, list, table, and example. Section is also a block element that serves as a container element for other block elements. You can use most block elements in every information type. However, the rules in the Document Type Definition (DTD) for each information type restrict the use of some block elements. For example, you can use a section in a concept but not in a task.

Adding block elements

This lesson explains the basic block elements used to add to a DITA topic.

In this lesson, you learn to add elements you can use in each information type, such as <p>, <ul>, and <li>.

1. Start a new concept topic.

   Refer to Lesson 1: Creating a Concept Information Type to create the basic structure.

2. Add <p> element start and end tags between the <conbody> element start and end tags.

   You can include any of the basic block elements, such as paragraph, bulleted list, numbered list, and tables in your topics. In this concept, you can add as many paragraphs as needed at the beginning of your concept body container. However, each information type allows or disallows block elements in different places. See the *DITA Language Specification* to determine where you can add block elements in your information types.

   You can find more information about block elements in Lesson 4: Block Elements.

```
<conbody>
   <p>In this chapter, you will learn how to use the
      features of your phone. If you have any questions
      about these features, contact your system
      administrator.</p>
   <p>The features discussed in this chapter are</p>
</conbody>
```

3. Add <ul> start and end tags to your concept after the second paragraph container.

   An unordered list presents information to the user when the order of the item is not relevant, such as a list of tools needed to complete a task. The unordered list container uses <li> elements to separate each list item. Using a list item container allows you to reuse the set of items in other contexts.

   The following example illustrates the <ul> and <li> elements.

```
<conbody>
   <p>In this chapter, you will learn how to use the
      features of your phone. If you have any questions
      about these features, contact your system
      administrator.</p>
  <p>The features discussed in this chapter are</p>
  <ul>
     <li>automatic callback</li>
     <li>automatic preselect</li>
     <li>automatic speakerphone answer</li>
  </ul>
</conbody>
```

4. Save the topic as AboutPhoneFeatures.dita.

   The following example illustrates a concept topic using block elements.

AboutPhoneFeatures.dita

```
<?xml version="1.0" encoding="utf-8"?>
<!DOCTYPE concept PUBLIC "-//OASIS//DTD DITA CONCEPT//EN"
"concept.dtd">
<concept id="AboutTelephoneFeatures">
   <title>About using the telephone's features</title>
   <shortdesc>Your Comstar telephone has many features
      that allow you to handle calls in a variety of
      powerful ways.</shortdesc>
   <conbody>
      <p>In this chapter, you will learn how to use the
         features of your phone. If you have any questions
         about these features, contact your system
         administrator.</p>
      <p>The features discussed in this chapter
         are</p>
```

```
        <ul>
            <li>automatic callback</li>
            <li>automatic preselect</li>
            <li>automatic speakerphone answer</li>
            <li>background music</li>
            <li>call forwarding</li>
            <li>call waiting</li>
        </ul>
    </conbody>
</concept>
```

Figure 2.12 shows a sample of how this topic is rendered using our stylesheet.

About using the telephone's features

Your Comstar telephone has many features that allow you to handle calls in a variety of powerful ways.

In this chapter, you will learn how to use the features of your phone. If you have any questions about these features, contact your system administrator.

The features discussed in this chapter are

- automatic callback
- automatic preselect
- automatic speakerphone answer
- background music
- call forwarding
- call waiting

Figure 2.12 Block elements example rendered

Block element definitions

The following block elements are used in the DITA model.

<p> paragraph

Use the <p> element to group text . The <p> element is the most common element used in a topic. You can use the <p> element in the body of your topic, in a <section>, or in an <example> . The number of <p> elements used in a topic is unlimited.

<section> section

Use the <section> element to organize subtopics in the body of a larger topic. All information types except task allow the <section> element in the body element. You cannot include a section in an example, but you can follow an example with a section and vice versa. You can include a title in a section. One of the ways you can build hierarchy within your topic is to add a title to your section.

<example> example

Use the <example> element to illustrate the content of a topic. Illustrations used in the <example> element may include images, code, output, and discussions. You cannot include an example in a section; you can follow a section with an example and vice versa. In an example, you can include a title. One of the ways you can build hierarchy within your topic is to add a title to your example.

<fig> figure

Use the <fig> element as a container to include a figure caption and an image in your content. Adding a figure caption to your figure is optional but recommended.

The following example below illustrates how to use the elements described above.

```
<conbody>
   <p>The two-phase method of planning is so named
      because the planning and estimating process comprises
      two phases: the information planning phase and the
      content planning phase. As you will see, the phases of
      project planning closely resemble the phases of
      product development.</p>
   <section>
      <title>The information planning phase</title>
      <p>During the information planning phase, the
         nature of the project is defined. The information
         plan can be likened to a product requirements
         document for a software development project.
         You conduct preparatory research to learn the
         nature of the product and its potential market.
         You learn who will use the product and what tasks
         they will accomplish with the product.</p>
   </section>
   <example>
      <fig><title>Product Information Plan</title>
      <image href="ProductInfoPlan.jpg"/></fig>
   </example>
</conbody>
```

<sl> simple list

Use the <sl> element as the container for all simple list items. The output of a simple list does not use bullets or numbering to distinguish each list item. Therefore, the simple list should only be used for short lists that do not need additional formatting to distinguish each item. If your list is more complex, we recommend using the <ul> or <ol> items.

<sli> simple list item

Use the <sli> element to separate each item in the list.

The following example illustrates how to use the <sl> and <sli> elements.

```
<conbody>
   <p>The dominant characteristics of Monotype Old
      English Text are</p>
   <sl>
      <sli>Serif: rounded</sli>
      <sli>Thick and thin: marked contrast</sli>
      <sli>Stress: diagonal</sli>
   </sl>
</conbody>
```

<ul> unordered list

Use the <ul> element to list items where the sequence of each item is not relevant. The items within the <ul> element are typically formatted with bullets, circles, or other symbols. To create sub-unordered lists, nest <ul> elements in other <ul> elements. However, nesting more than one level of <ul> elements makes the list more difficult for the reader to understand. The <ul> element is the container for all unordered list items.

<li> list item

Use the <li> element to separate each item in the list. More than one <li> element can be added to each <ul> element.

The following example illustrates how to use the <ul> element.

```
<conbody>
   <p>Before adding or deleting a row or column in your
      projected hours worksheet, gather the following
      information:</p>
   <ul>
      <li>File names of the linked projected labor and
         total costs worksheets</li>
      <li>File names of the linked monthly hours, labor,
         and total costs tracking worksheets</li>
   </ul>
</conbody>
```

<ol> ordered list

Use the <ol> element to list items where the sequence of the each item is important. The items in an ordered list are typically numbered. To create sub-ordered lists, nest <ol> elements in other <ol> elements. However, nesting more than one level of <ol> elements can make the list more difficult for the reader to understand. The <ol> element is the container for all ordered list items.

<li> list item

Use the <li> element to separate each item in the list. More than one <li> element can be added to each <ol> element.

The following example illustrates how to use the elements listed above.

```
<conbody>
   <p>The code page provides a map to the characters.
      As you enter your document into a file at a terminal,
      the code page ties together your keyboard entry and
      the characters in the character set.</p>
   <ol>
      <li>Each keyboard character is translated into a
         hexadecimal code point.</li>
      <li>The code page matches the code point to a
         character identifier ID.</li>
      <li>The character set matches the character
         ID to the image of the character—the image
         that will be printed in your document.</li>
   </ol>
</conbody>
```

<dl> definition list

Use the <dl> element to list terms and their corresponding definitions. The <dl> element is the container for all elements in a definition list.

<dlhead> definition list head

Use <dlhead> as the container element for column heads for the terms and descriptions within the definition list. This element is optional and may be used only once in a definition list.

<dthd> term head

Use <dthd> to specify a term column head for the definition list. One <dthd> element can be added to the <dlhead> element but is not required. The <dthd> element is the first element added to the definition list head.

<ddhd> definition head

Use <ddhd> to specify a definition column head for the definition list. One <ddhd> element can be added to the <dlhead> element but is not required.

<dlentry> definition list entry

Use the <dlentry> element in the <dl> element as a container for each term and definition. A separate <dlentry> element is used each time a new term and definition are introduced. Multiple <dlentry> elements can be used for each <dl>.

<dt> definition term

Use<dt> to identify the word or phrase to be defined. If multiple terms share the same definition, multiple <dt> elements can be added to the <dlentry> element.

<dd> definition description

Use the <dd> element to provide the definition for the corresponding term. If a term has multiple definitions, multiple <dd> elements can be added to the <dlentry> element.

The following example illustrates how to use the elements described above.

```
<conbody>
   <dl>
      <dlhead>
         <dthd>term</dthd>
         <ddhd>definition</ddhd>
      </dlhead>
      <dlentry>
         <dt>dome</dt>
         <dd>A hemispherical vault or roof.</dd>
         </dlentry>
      <dlentry>
         <dt>doctor</dt>
         <dt>PhD</dt>
         <dd>A person trained and licensed to practice
            the healing arts, as medicine or surgery.
         </dd>
         <dd>A person holding the highest degree given by
            a university.</dd>
      </dlentry>
   </dl>
</conbody>
```

<table> table

Use the <table> element to create a complex table. Complex tables provide you with control over the display properties and layout of the table. The <table> element is the container for all of the complex table elements. For a list of all table element attributes, see the *DITA Language Specification.*

<tgroup> table group

Use the <tgroup> element to specify the display properties for the columns, rows, spanning, header, footer, and body of the complex table. The <tgroup> element with column specifications is required when using a complex table.

<colspec> column specification

Use the <colspec> element to specify the column information, such as column name, number, cell content alignment, and column width. The column name, number, cell content alignment and column width are all specified using attributes in the <colspec> element. Use the *colname* attribute to specify the column name. Use the *cols* attribute to specify the number of columns. Use the *align* attribute to align the cell content. Use the *colwidth* attribute to specify the width of each column.

<thead> table head

Use the <thead> element to define the heads for the table columns. The <thead> element is used in the <table> container. It contains multiple <row> and <entry> elements.

<tbody> table body

Use the <tbody> element to define the body of the table. The <tbody> element is the container for multiple <row> and <entry> elements.

<row> row

Use the <row> element to define a single row in the table. Each <row> element contains multiple <entry> elements, each indicating a different column. The number of <entry> elements in the body of the table should match the number of <entry> elements in the <thead> element.

<entry> entry

Use the <entry> element to define a single cell in the table. The number of <entry> elements defined in the <tbody> element must match the number of <entry> elements defined in the <thead> element.

The following example illustrates how to use the table elements described above.

```
<conbody>
   <table>
      <tgroup cols="4">
         <colspec colname="COLSPC0" colwidth="76*"/>
         <colspec colname="COLSPC1" colwidth="76*"/>
         <colspec colname="COLSPC2" colwidth="25*"/>
         <colspec colname="COLSPC3" colwidth="25*"/>
      <thead>
         <row>
            <entry colname="COLSPC0" align="left">
       Worksheet</entry>
    <entry colname="COLSPC1" align="left">
       Orientation</entry>
            <entry colname="COLSPC2" valign="top">
          US Letter</entry>
            <entry colname="COLSPC3" valign="top">
       US Legal</entry>
         </row>
      </thead>
      <tbody>
         <row>
            <entry>Dependencies worksheet</entry>
            <entry>Vertical</entry>
    <entry>100%</entry>
    <entry>100%</entry>
         </row>
         <row>
            <entry></entry>
            <entry>Horizontal</entry>
    <entry>100%</entry>
    <entry>100%</entry>
         </row>
         <row>
            <entry>Weekly tracking worksheets
            </entry>
            <entry>Vertical</entry>
    <entry>no</entry>
    <entry>no</entry>
         </row>
         <row>
            <entry></entry>
            <entry>Horizontal</entry>
    <entry>45%</entry>
    <entry>60%</entry>
         </row>
      </tbody>
      </tgroup>
   </table>
</conbody>
```

Figure 2.13 shows what a rendered table looks like.

Worksheet	Orientation	US Letter	US Legal
Dependencies worksheet	Vertical	100%	100%
	Horizontal	100%	100%
Weekly tracking worksheets	Vertical	no	no
	Horizontal	45%	60%

Figure 2.13 Complex table example rendered

<simpletable> simple table

Use the <simpletable> element to describe tabular information that has a simple layout. The simple table is less sophisticated than the complex table. You cannot control the format of the table. The <simpletable> element is the container for <sthead>, <strow>, and <stentry> elements.

<sthead> simple table head

Use the <sthead> element to define the heads for the table columns. The <sthead> element contains one or more <stentry> elements. It is optional and can be used only once within the <simpletable> element.

<strow> simple table row

Use the <strow> element to create a row in the simple table. The <strow> element is used in the <simpletable> container. It contains the <stentry> element.

<stentry> simple table cell (entry)

Use the <stentry> element to define a single cell in the table. Use this element to define both the content for each cell and the column heads for the entire table. To define the column heads, use one or more <stentry> elements within the <sthead> element. To define the content for each cell in the table, use the <stentry> element in the <strow> element. The number of <stentry> elements within each <strow> element must match the number of <stentry> elements used within the <sthead> element.

The following example illustrates how to create the simple table described above.

```
<conbody>
   <simpletable>
      <sthead>
         <stentry>Worksheet</stentry>
         <stentry>Prerequisites</stentry>
      </sthead>
```

```
        <strow>
            <stentry>Monthly hours tracking worksheet
            </stentry>
            <stentry>Projected hours worksheet</stentry>
        </strow>
        <strow>
            <stentry>Monthly labor costs tracking worksheet
            </stentry>
            <stentry>Projected hours worksheet</stentry>
        </strow>
    </simpletable>
</conbody>
```

Block element review questions

1. Where would you place block elements within your topic?
2. List five of the most commonly used block elements.
3. What is the difference between an ordered list and an unordered list?
4. What is the difference between a table and a simple table?
5. When would you use a section?
6. Which of these elements contains a title: section, paragraph, and/or example?

LESSON 5

Phrase Elements

Phrase elements describe the words or phrases that occur inside a structure or block element. Phrase elements include elements used inline in sentences to mark items, such as index terms, keywords, and cross references. Phrase elements also include domain and typographic elements. Domain elements occur inline to describe specific subject matter, such as a syntax diagram or an interface control. Typographic elements affect the output format of a word or phrase. Typographic elements include italic, bold, and underscore.

Domain elements

Domain elements describe text associated with a specific subject area. Use domain elements to add structure and semantic tags to your information. The information contained in your domain tags is used to optimize search and retrieval. The domains included in DITA are associated with software products, programming information, and user interfaces. Other domains may include elements for training material and Application Programming Interfaces (APIs). Depending on the subject matter you are writing about, you may want to add new domain-specific elements by specializing DITA. For more information about specialization, see Part IV: Introduction to Specialization.

Typographic elements

Use typographic elements when your information cannot be formatted properly using the semantic DITA tags. In DITA, the typographic tags include italic, bold, teletype, superscript, subscript, and underscore. DITA best practices discourage the use of most typographic elements. We recommend that you find or define an appropriate semantic tag that identifies text by its content rather than its formatting. For example, if you identify a word as a <uicontrol>, you can easily format it on output as bold, italic, or underscore. If you tag the same word as bold, your format cannot be easily changed on output. Remember that the word you emphasize in your source language may not be the same word that a translator must emphasize in a target language. Many languages do not include any of the common typographic elements found in English, so use typographic elements sparingly if your information is translated into other languages.

Adding phrase elements

This lesson explains the basic phrase elements to add to a DITA topic.

In this lesson, you learn how to add phrase elements, such as <keyword>, <uicontrol>, and <xref>, that you can use in each information type.

1. Open the TransferringACall.dita task topic you created in Lesson 2: Task Information Type.

```
<?xml version="1.0" encoding="utf-8"?>
<!DOCTYPE task PUBLIC "-//OASIS//DTD DITA Task//EN"
   "task.dtd">
<task id="TransferringACall" xml:lang="en-us">
   <title>Transferring a call</title>
   <shortdesc>When you transfer a call to another person
      in your office, you have two ways of handling the
      transfer.</shortdesc>
   <prolog>
      <author>John Smith</author>
   </prolog>
   <taskbody>
      <context>
         <p> When you transfer the call without speaking
            to the person, it is an unannounced transfer.
            When you speak to the person receiving the
            transferred call, it is an announced transfer.
         </p>
      </context>
      <steps>
         <step>
            <cmd>Press the transfer button.</cmd>
         </step>
         <step>
            <cmd>Dial the number.</cmd>
            <info>Dial the number manually, use your
               pre-defined speed dial keys or go to your
               company directory. </info>
         </step>
          <step>
              <cmd>Transfer the call.</cmd>
              <choicetable>
                 <chhead>
                    <choptionhd>Type of Announcement
             </choptionhd>
             <chdeschd>Steps to complete
             </chdeschd>
                 </chhead>
                 <chrow>
                    <choption>Announce a call transfer
                    </choption>
```

```
                    <chdesc>
                       <ol>
                          <li>Speak to the person.</li>
                          <li>Hang up the phone.</li>
                       </ol>
                    </chdesc>
                 </chrow>
                 <chrow>
                    <choption>Transfer a call unannounced
                    </choption>
                    <chdesc>
                       <ul>
                          <li>Hang up the phone.</li>
                       </ul>
                    </chdesc>
                 </chrow>
             </choicetable>
              <info>
                 <note>If you announce a call and the
                    person refuses the transfer, do not hang
                    up the phone. Press the transfer button
                    again to retrieve the call on your phone
                    station.</note>
              </info>
           </step>
      </steps>
      <result>The call is transferred.</result>
   </taskbody>
      <related-links>
         <link href="AboutTransfer.dita" scope="local"/>
      </related-links>
</task>
```

2. Add <keyword> element start and end tags around the word "transferring" in your <title> element container.

   The <keyword> element highlights words or phrases in an abstract, title, subject heading, content notes, or general text to identify words you may want to use in a special context, such as a glossary or a search engine. In the example below, transferring might be a term a user looks up in a glossary or types into a search engine. See the *DITA Language Specification* to learn where you can add keywords.

```
<task id="TransferringACall" xml:lang="en-us">
   <title><keyword>Transferring</keyword>
      a call</title>
   <taskbody>
   </taskbody>
</task>
```

3. Add <uicontrol> element start and end tags around the word "transfer" in the first step command.

   You can use the user interface control element to identify button names, entry fields, menu items, or other user interface controls. Using semantic elements, such as <uicontrol>, helps users find information more easily. You can create a unique format for a semantically tagged phrase element without using a typographic element like bold or italic.

```
<taskbody>
   <steps>
      <step>
         <cmd>Press the <uicontrol>transfer
            </uicontrol> button.
         </cmd>
      </step>
   </steps>
</taskbody>
```

4. Add <xref> element start and end tags around the phrase "company directory" in the second step info container.

   The <xref> container identifies a term or phrase you want to cross reference to another piece of information. To use the <xref> element correctly, you must include a path location and target file to the content you want to cross reference.

   To add a cross reference path location and target file, add an *href* attribute in the <xref> element. In the example below, the *href* attribute points to another DITA task, AccessingDirectory.dita. The cross-reference element creates a hyperlink to the information you reference in the *href* attribute. You can link to information in the same topic using the topic filename, topic *ID*, and element *ID* in your *href* attribute value. Or you can link to an external topic or document using the topic file name and *ID* in your *href* attribute value. You can also use the *type* attribute to specify the type of link. In this case, set the *type* attribute to "task" to link to another DITA task. You can also link to figures, tables, concepts, references, and other types of information.

```
<taskbody>
   <steps>
      <step>
         <cmd>Dial the number.</cmd>
```

```
            <info>Dial the number manually, use your
               pre-defined speed dial keys or go to your
               <xref href="AccessingCompanyDirectory.dita"
               type="task">company directory</xref>.
            </info>
         </step>
      </steps>
   </taskbody>
```

5. Save the document as TransferringACall.dita.

TransferringACall.dita

The following example illustrates the Transferring a call topic using phrase elements.

```
<?xml version="1.0" encoding="utf-8"?>
<!DOCTYPE task PUBLIC "-//OASIS//DTD DITA Task//EN"
   "task.dtd">
<task id="TransferringACall" xml:lang="en-us">
   <title><keyword>Transferring</keyword>
      a call</title>
   <shortdesc>When you transfer a call to another person
      in your office, you have two ways of handling the
      transfer.</shortdesc>
   <prolog>
      <author>John Smith</author>
   </prolog>
   <taskbody>
      <context>
         <p> When you transfer the call without speaking
            to the person, it is an unannounced transfer.
            When you speak to the person receiving the
            transferred call, it is an announced transfer.
         </p>
      </context>
      <steps>
         <step>
            <cmd>Press the <uicontrol>transfer
               </uicontrol> button.
            </cmd>
         </step>
         <step>
            <cmd>Dial the number.</cmd>
            <info>Dial the number manually, use your
               pre-defined speed dial keys or go to your
```

```
            <xref
            href="AccessingCompanyDirectory.dita"
            type="task">company directory</xref>.
         </info>
      </step>
      <step>
         <cmd>Transfer the call.</cmd>
         <choicetable>
            <chhead>
               <choptionhd>Type of Announcement
               </choptionhd>
               <chdeschd>Steps to complete
               </chdeschd>
            </chhead>
            <chrow>
               <choption>Announce a call transfer
               </choption>
               <chdesc>
                  <ol>
                     <li>Speak to the person.</li>
                     <li>Hang up the phone.</li>
                  </ol>
               </chdesc>
            </chrow>
            <chrow>
               <choption>Transfer a call unannounced
               </choption>
               <chdesc>
                  <ul>
                     <li>Hang up the phone.</li>
                  </ul>
               </chdesc>
            </chrow>
         </choicetable>
         <info>
            <note>If you announce a call and the
               person refuses the transfer, do not hang
               up the phone. Press the transfer button
               again to retrieve the call on your phone
               station.</note>
         </info>
      </step>
   </steps>
   <result>The call is transferred.</result>
</taskbody>
<related-links>
   <link href="AboutTransfer.dita" scope="local"/>
</related-links>
</task>
```

Figure 2.14 shows what a rendered topic with phrase elements looks like.

Transferring a call

When you transfer a call to another person in your office, you have two ways of handling the transfer.

When you transfer the call without speaking to the person, it is an unannounced transfer. When you speak to the person receiving the transferred call, it is an announced transfer.

1. Press the transfer button.
2. Dial the number. Dial the number manually, use your pre-defined speed dial keys or go to your company directory.
3. Transfer the call.

Type of Announcement	Steps to complete
Announce a call transfer	a. Speak to the person. b. Hang up the phone.
Transfer a call unannounced	• Hang up the phone.

Note: If you announce a call and the person refuses the transfer, do not hang up the phone. Press the transfer button again to retrieve the call on your phone station.

The call is transferred.

Figure 2.14 Phrase and domain element example rendered

Phrase elements definitions

The following phrase elements are used in the DITA model.

<keyword> keyword

Use the <keyword> element to highlight important words or phrases in an abstract, title, subject heading, content notes, or general text to increase your information's ability to be searched. The <keyword> element does not usually affect the format of the text during processing. The <keyword> element cannot contain additional markup (elements or attributes).

<ph> phrase

Use the <ph> element to assign metadata to your information to locate it for future reuse, flagging, or filtering. The <ph> element usually does not change the format of the text during processing. However, you can use the element to apply specific formatting and processing to the marked up phrases with your style sheet.

The following example illustrates how to use the <keyword> and <ph> elements.

```
<conbody>
   <p>This section explains how
      <ph><keyword>PUB$</keyword> simplifies
         project planning</ph>.  Included are the tasks
         accomplished with <ph><keyword>PUB$
         </keyword></ph> and the worksheets that
         correspond to each task.</p>
</conbody>
```

<term> term

Use the <term> element to identify words requiring an extended definition or explanation. The <term> element also links the identified word to matching glossary entries. The <term> element does not affect the format of the text during output.

The following example illustrates how to use the <term> element.

```
<conbody>
   <p>The first three major type concepts defined in
      this chapter are <term>type family</term>,
      <term>typeface</term>, and <term>type
      font</term>.  Illustrations help you compare type
      styles and select those most suitable for your
      applications.</p>
</conbody>
```

<xref> cross reference link

Use the <xref> element to create a link in the content of your document. The <xref> element is used inline in the text of your topic, preferably at the end of a sentence. It is not used at the end of the topic like the <related-links> element. The target for this link can be a specific element in the same topic, another topic, or an external source.

Use the *type* attribute in the <xref> element to specify the target for your link. Possible values for the type attribute are "fig," "table," "li," "section," "concept," "task," and "reference." To link to an external source, use the *scope* attribute. The <xref> should be used sparingly, if at all, because a link in the middle of a sentence may distract the reader and increase the cost of maintaining and translating the topic. Instead of <xref>, consider using either a relationship table in your map or the <related-links> element at the end of each topic.

The following example illustrates how to use the <xref> element.

```
<taskbody>
   <steps>
      <step>
         <cmd>Type <codeph>ant all</codeph> and
            press Enter to begin testing.</cmd>
         <stepresult>The testing process completes in
            3-10 minutes, depending on the speed of your
            machine. When testing completes, the
            confirmation message "BUILD SUCCESSFUL"
            displays.
            <note type="note">To read more about the DITA
               Open Toolkit options and functions, see
               <xref href="C:\DITAOT\doc\DITA-readme.html"
               scope="external">DITA-readme</xref> on
               your local hard drive.
            </note>
         </stepresult>
      </step>
   </steps>
</taskbody>
```

Domain elements

The following domain elements are used in the DITA model. The element descriptions refer to specific content used in programming, software, and user interfaces.

Programming elements

Use the programming elements to define programming syntax or give examples of programming-specific information. Some descriptions for the common programming elements are included here. For the complete list of programming elements, see the *DITA Language Specification.*

<codeblock> code block

Use the <codeblock> element to represent multiple lines of programming code. The information in the <codeblock> element is formatted as a monospaced font and preserves carriage returns and spaces in the element.

The following example illustrating how to use the <codeblock> element was created using the <codeblock> elements.

XML Recipe

```
<conbody>
   <section>
      <codeblock>
         <?xml version="1.0"?>
         <recipe>
            <title>Scrambled eggs</title>
               <ingredient>Ingredient</ingredient>
               <ingredient_list>
                  <list_item>5 eggs</list_item>
                  <list_item>1/2 cup milk</list_item>
                  <list_item>1 tbsp butter</list_item>
               </ingredient_list>
               <instructions>Melt butter......
               </instructions>
         </recipe>
      </codeblock>
   </section>
</conbody>
```

<parml> parameter list

Use the <parml> element to describe the terms and definitions associated with parameters in an application programming interface. The <parml> is similar to the <dl> element but is designed for documenting programming parameters.

<plentry> parameter list entry

Use the <plentry> element in the <parml> element as a container for each parameter term <pt> and definition <pd>. A separate <plentry> element is used each time a new parameter term and definition are introduced. Multiple <plentry> elements exist for each <parml>.

<pt> parameter term

Use <pt> to identify the parameter term to be defined. If multiple terms share the same definition, multiple <pt> elements can be added to the <plentry> element. If multiple <pt> elements are added, the definition must match both terms.

<pd> parameter description

Use the <pd> element to provide the definition for the corresponding term. If a term has multiple definitions, multiple <pd> elements can be added to the <plentry> element. If you add multiple <pd> elements to the <plentry> element, both definitions must describe the term.

The following example illustrates how to use the parameter list.

```
<conbody>
   <section>
      <p>Listed below are the available properties for a
         checkbox object located in an HTML form.</p>
      <parml>
         <plentry>
            <pt>Checked</pt>
            <pd>Sets the checkbox value to true if the
               checkbox is checked and false if the checkbox
               is not checked.</pd>
         </plentry>
         <plentry>
            <pt>Name</pt>
            <pd>Sets the name attribute for the checkbox
               object on the form.</pd>
         </plentry>
         <plentry>
            <pt>Form</pt>
            <pd>Is used to associate the checkbox object
               to the form in which the checkbox object is
               located.</pd>
         </plentry>
      </parml>
   </section>
</conbody>
```

<apiname> API name

Use the <apiname> element to describe the name of an application programming interface (API), such as a Java class or method name.

The following example illustrates how to use the <apiname> element.

```
<conbody>
   <section>
      <p>Use <apiname>JavaScript</apiname> to
         increase the functionality of your website.
      </p>
   </section>
</conbody>
```

Software elements

Use the software elements to describe the operations of a software program. Some of the most common software elements are listed below. For the complete list of software elements, see the *DITA Language Specification.*

<msgph> message phrase

Use the <msgph> element to list the contents of a message produced by an application or program. Other elements, such as the <varname> element, can be used in the <msgph> element to make the semantic markup of your information more specific.

The following example illustrates how to use the <msgph> element.

```
<taskbody>
   <steps>
      <step>
         <cmd>Delete the dependency for the weekly
            tracking worksheet.</cmd>
         <info>If you recieve the following error, see
            the appendix on error messages:
            <msgph>Can't remove the dependency for the
               worksheet as it is currently in use.
            </msgph></info>
      </step>
   </steps>
</taskbody>
```

<cmdname> command name

Use the <cmdname> element to specify software commands. You can add the <cmdname> element to several of the topic elements, including <title>, <shortdesc>, <body>, <section>, <filepath>, and <msgph>.

The following example illustrates how to use the <cmdname> element.

```
<taskbody>
   <steps>
      <step>
         <cmd>Open a command prompt.</cmd>
         <substeps>
            <substep>
               <cmd>Go to
                  <menucascade>
                     <uicontrol>Start</uicontrol>
                     <uicontrol>Run</uicontrol>
                  </menucascade>
               </cmd>
            </substep>
         </substeps>
      </step>
      <step>
         <cmd>Type <cmdname>cmd</cmdname> in the
            Run window.</cmd></step>
   </steps>
</taskbody>
```

<varname> variable name

Use the <varname> element to define software application variables. The <varname> element is similar to the <var> element except that the <varname> element exists outside of a syntax diagram.

The following example illustrates how to use the <varname> element.

```
<conbody>
   <p>Create a Visual Basic program where you create the
      output "Hello World" by adding two variables:
      <varname>x</varname> and
      <varname>y</varname></p>
</conbody>
```

<filepath> file path

Use the <filepath> element to define the name and location of a reference file. When adding a file path, be sure to include the directories preceding the file to document the full system hierarchy.

The following example illustrates how to use the <filepath> element.

```
<conbody>
   <p>Open the PUB$ weekly timesheet example from
      <filepath>D:\Samples\WeeklyTimesheet.xls
      </filepath>.
   </p>
</conbody>
```

<userinput> user input

Use the <userinput> element to specify information the user must enter. Software programs usually prompt users for this type of information.

The following example illustrates how to use the <userinput> element.

```
<taskbody>
   <steps>
      <step>
         <cmd>Run the PUB$ manual build file.</cmd>
      </step>
      <step>
         <cmd>Type <userinput>ant -f ant\PUB$_PDF.xml
            </userinput></cmd></step>
   </steps>
</taskbody>
```

<systemoutput> system output

Use the <systemoutput> element to represent the output or responses from a software program. The <systemoutput> is a very general element that can represent multiple output types.

The following example illustrates how to use the <systemoutput> element.

```
<taskbody>
   <steps>
      <step>
         <cmd>Run the PUB$ manual build file.</cmd>
      </step>
```

```
        <step>
           <cmd>Type <userinput>ant -f ant\PUB$_PDF.xml
              </userinput></cmd></step>
        <step>
           <cmd>Click Enter.</cmd>
           <stepresult>When the build file has completed
              the processing, you will receive the
              <systemoutput>Build Successful
              </systemoutput> message if the process was
              successful. If the build failed during
              processing, you will receive the
              <systemoutput>Build Failed</systemoutput>
              message.</stepresult>
        </step>
     </steps>
  </taskbody>
```

User interface elements

Use the user interface elements to describe the user interface of a web or software application. Some of the most common user interface elements are listed below. For the complete list of user interface elements, see the *DITA Language Specification*.

<menucascade> menu cascade

Use the <menucascade> element to indicate a series of menu choices in an application. The <menucascade> element is a container for one or more <uicontrol> elements. A simple menu cascade may be formatted as

Start >**Programs** > **Accessories** .

<uicontrol> user interface control

Use the <uicontrol> element to specify button names, entry fields, menu items, or other user interface controls. You can use multiple <uicontrol> elements in a <menucascade> element to identify a sequence of menu choices in a nested menu.

The following example illustrates how to use the elements described above.

```
<taskbody>
   <context>To end your work session, follow these steps:
   </context>
   <steps>
      <step>
         <cmd>Save your worksheet.</cmd>
      </step>
```

```
        <step>
           <cmd>Select<menucascade>
                 <uicontrol>Track</uicontrol>
                 <uicontrol>Return to PUB$ Menu
                 </uicontrol></menucascade>
           </cmd>
        </step>
     </steps>
  </taskbody>
```

Typographic elements

The following typographic elements are used in the DITA model.

<b> bold

Use the <b> element to provide bold emphasis to information.

The following example illustrates how to use the <b> element.

```
<p>In the DITA User Guide examples, each
   <b>change</b> is bolded.</p>
```

<i> italic

Use the <i> element to provide italic emphasis to information.

The following example illustrates how to use the <i> element.

```
<p>In the DITA User Guide examples, each
   <i>attribute</i> is italicized.</p>
```

<sub> subscript

Use the <sub> element to subscript a symbol or text.

The following example illustrates how to use the <sub> element.

```
<p>... H<sub>2</sub>CO<sub>3</sub></p>
```

<sup> superscript

Use the <sup> element to superscript a symbol or text.

The following example illustrates how to use the <sup> element.

```
<p>...  x<sup>2</sup></p>
```

<tt> teletype

Use the <tt> element to output words in a monospace font.

The following example illustrates how to use the <tt> element.

```
<p><tt>In the DITA User Guide examples, each codeblock is created i
n a monospace font.</tt></p>
```

Figure 2.15 illustrates what rendered typographic elements look like.

In our examples, each *attribute* is italicized.
In our examples, each **attribute value** is bolded.
`In our examples, each codeblock contains monospace font.`

Figure 2.15 Typographic elements rendered

Phrase element review questions

1. What is the difference between phrase elements and block elements?
2. When would you use typographic elements?
3. Why should you avoid using typographic elements?
4. What is the purpose of domain elements?
5. Where should you place the <xref> element?
6. What is the benefit of adding phrase elements to your information?

LESSON 6

Related links

You can add related links to a topic to refer the reader to other topics, external references, or web pages.

Related-link elements specify the tags that you use to add related links at the end of a topic. Because related-links are output as hyperlinks, they are most appropriate for electronic delivery. If your output is to print or PDF, the links may not appear in the print or PDF unless you specify a format for the link in your stylesheet.

Although the related-links section at the end of each topic is useful, we recommend that you create links using a relationship table as described in Lesson 15: Relationship Tables. If you create related links at the end of each topic, you cannot as easily reuse the topic because you must guarantee that all the linked topics are output in your DITA map. If a topic is missing, you will get a broken link. If you create a relationship table, all the links are in one place, making them easier to maintain.

Your related links can point to any topic, including

- topics in your information set
- topics outside of your information set but available in a repository in your organization
- documents outside your organization

If you include a link to a non-DITA topic, you must include both a link title and short description in the link metadata. These items ensure that your users understand something about the topic in the link. If you link to a DITA topic in your information set, your processing pipeline extracts both the title and short description to create the link text in the topic. If you choose not to display a short description, you can change this feature when you create your stylesheets.

Adding related-links

This lesson explains how to add related links to your topics.

In this lesson, you learn to add standard elements to create related links in any information type, such as <related-links>, <link>, <linktext>, and <desc>.

1. Open the TransferringACall.dita task topic you created in Lesson 2: Task Information Topic.

   In the TransferringACall.dita task topic, you added a <related-links> container and a <link> element to point to another DITA topic.

```
<?xml version="1.0" encoding="utf-8"?>
<!DOCTYPE task PUBLIC "-//OASIS//DTD DITA Task//EN"
   "task.dtd">
<task id="TransferringACall" xml:lang="en-us">
   <title>Transferring a call</title>
   <shortdesc>When you transfer a call to another person
      in your office, you have two ways of handling the
      transfer.</shortdesc>
   <prolog>
      <copyright>
         <copyryear year="2006"></copyryear>
         <copyrholder>Comtech Services, Inc.
         </copyrholder>
      </copyright>
   </prolog>
   <taskbody>
      <context>
         <p>When you transfer the call without speaking
            to the person, it is an unannounced transfer.
            When you speak to the person receiving the
            transferred call, it is an announced transfer.
         </p>
      </context>
      <steps>
         <step>
            <cmd>Press the transfer button.</cmd>
         </step>
         <step>
            <cmd>Dial the number.</cmd>
            <info>Dial the number manually, use your
               pre-defined speed dial keys or go to your
               company directory. </info>
         </step>
         <step>
            <cmd>Transfer the call.</cmd>
            <choicetable>
               <chhead>
                  <choptionhd>Type of Announcement
                  </choptionhd>
                  <chdeschd>Steps to complete
                  </chdeschd>
               </chhead>
               <chrow>
                  <choption>Announce a call transfer
                  </choption>
```

```
                <chdesc>
                    <ol>
                        <li>Speak to the person.</li>
                        <li>Hang up the phone.</li>
                    </ol>
                </chdesc>
            </chrow>
            <chrow>
                <choption>Transfer a call unannounced
                </choption>
                <chdesc>
                    <ul>
                        <li>Hang up the phone.</li>
                    </ul>
                </chdesc>
            </chrow>
        </choicetable>
        <info>
            <note>If you announce a call and the
                person refuses the transfer, do not hang
                up the phone. Press the transfer button
                again to retrieve the call on your phone
                station.</note>
        </info>
    </step>
  </steps>
  <result>The call is transferred.</result>
</taskbody>
  <related-links>
     <link href="AboutTransfer.dita" scope="local"/>
  </related-links>
</task>
```

2. Add <link> element start and end tags in the <related-links> container after the AboutTransfer.dita link.

   For every related link you want to add, you must use a separate <link> element. Within each link element, specify a value for the *href* attribute. In your *href* attribute, you must point to the target information you want to include using absolute or relative path and file names. The file path must be relative to the topic you are authoring. You also need to include a value for the *format* attribute. If you are outputting to HTML or a help system, indicate that the format is "html" so the processor formats your link according to HTML rules.

   The following example illustrates how using the AboutTransfer.dita and the ../GeneralTopic/Glossary.dita links as empty elements is the same as using start and end <link> element tags.

```
<related-links>
   <link href="AboutTransfer.dita" format="html" />
   <link href="../GeneralTopic/Glossary.dita"
      format="html" />
   <link href="http://www.comtech-serv.com/Comstar"
      format="html">
   </link>
</related-links>
```

3. Add the *scope* attribute to each <link> element.

   You can set the value to "local," "peer," or "external," depending on the location of the target topic. The *scope* attribute tells the processor how to process a link. For more information about the *scope* attribute, see Lesson 10: Scope Attribute.

```
<related-links>
   <link href="AboutTransfer.dita" scope="local"/>
   <link href="../GeneralTopic/Glossary.dita"
      scope="peer"/>
   <link href="http://www.comtech-serv.com/Comstar"
      scope="external">
   </link>
</related-links>
```

4. Add the <linktext> element between the start and end tags of the <link> element for the http://www.comtech-serv.com/Comstar link.

   Not all related links need link text because your processor will automatically use the title from your target topic. For example, when you create your output, your AboutTransfer.dita link uses the title "About Transfer" as the link text in your related-links section.

   For topics that don't have a DITA title element, use the <linktext> element container to specify text for your link. For example, because the http://www.comtech-serv.com/Comstar isn't a DITA topic, you will need to add link text because your processor can't pull text from the web page. If you do not use link text, your processor will use the value you provided in the *href* attribute (i.e., http://www.comtech-serv.com/Comstar).

   For this example, use Comstar Phones as the link text for the http://www.comtech-serv.com/Comstar link.

```
<related-links>
   <link href="AboutTransfer.dita" scope="local"/>
   <link href="../GeneralTopic/Glossary.dita"
      scope="peer"/>
```

```
   <link href="http://www.comtech-serv.com/Comstar"
      scope="external">
      <linktext>Comstar Phones</linktext>
   </link>
</related-links>
```

5. Add <desc> element start and end tags after your <linktext> container.

   The description provides the user with a brief description of the linked topic or resource. We recommend adding a description for external links to provide your user with additional information about the target topic. If you don't provide a description, the processor creates a hyperlink of the text or *href* value for your user to navigate and doesn't include any description.

```
<related-links>
   <link href="AboutTransfer.dita" scope="local"/>
   <link href="../GeneralTopic/Glossary.dita"
      scope="peer"/>
   <link href="http://www.comtech-serv.com/Comstar"
      scope="external">
      <linktext>Comstar Phones</linktext>
         <desc>Order your Comstar phone today.</desc>
   </link>
</related-links>
```

TransferringACall.dita example

The following example shows the complete related-links section in your task topic.

```
<task>
   <taskbody>
   </taskbody>
      <related-links>
         <link href="AboutTransfer.dita" format="html"
            scope="local"/>
         <link href="../GeneralTopic/Glossary.dita"
            format="html" scope="peer"></link>
         <link href="http://www.comtech-serv.com/Comstar"
            format="html" scope="external">
         <linktext>Comstar Phones</linktext>
            <desc>Order your Comstar phone today.
            </desc>
         </link>
      </related-links>
</task>
```

Figure 2.16 shows how related links are rendered.

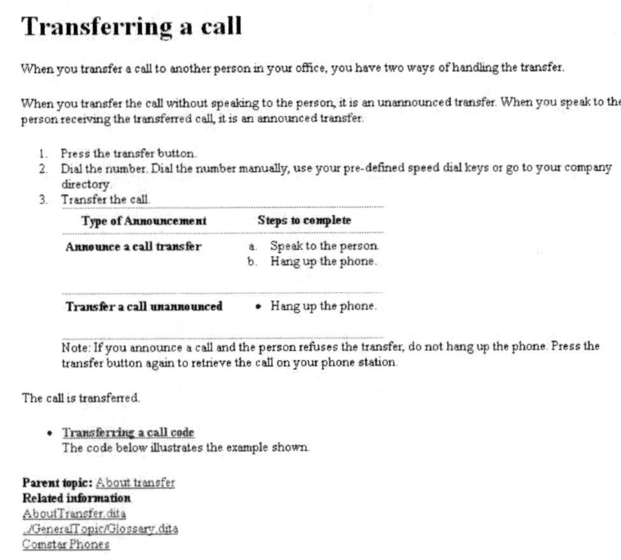

Transferring a call

When you transfer a call to another person in your office, you have two ways of handling the transfer.

When you transfer the call without speaking to the person, it is an unannounced transfer. When you speak to the person receiving the transferred call, it is an announced transfer.

1. Press the transfer button.
2. Dial the number. Dial the number manually, use your pre-defined speed dial keys or go to your company directory.
3. Transfer the call.

Type of Announcement	Steps to complete
Announce a call transfer	a. Speak to the person. b. Hang up the phone.
Transfer a call unannounced	• Hang up the phone.

Note: If you announce a call and the person refuses the transfer, do not hang up the phone. Press the transfer button again to retrieve the call on your phone station.

The call is transferred.

- Transferring a call code
  The code below illustrates the example shown.

Parent topic: About transfer
Related information
AboutTransfer.dita
../GeneralTopic/Glossary.dita
Comstar Phones

Figure 2.16 Related links example rendered

Related-link elements

The following related-link elements are used in the DITA model.

<link> link

Use the <link> element to define the relationships between topics. Use the <linklist> and <linkpool> elements to define groups of links and categorize them using a common attribute. The links will be sorted during output based on these additional attributes.

<linklist> link list

Use the <linklist> element to define a group of related links by giving the group a title. The collection-type attribute defines the group of links and can be set to unordered, sequence, choice, or family. For more information on the collection-type attribute, see Lesson 13: Collection-type Attribute. The list of links will output in the same order you added them to your topic. If you add a <linkpool> element, the order of the links is determined during output.

<linkinfo> link information

Use the <linkinfo> element to add a descriptive paragraph to a list of links.

<linktext> link text

Use the <linktext> element to specify the label or line of text for a link. Use the <linktext> element when the target reference cannot be reached or when the target is a non-DITA topic. During output, the <linktext> information will be output inline within the reference topic.

The following example illustrates how to use the elements described above.

```
<concept>
   <conbody>
   </conbody>
   <related-links>
      <linklist collection-type="sequence">
         <title>Hold</title>
         <link href="AboutHold.dita" type="concept"/>
         <link href="HoldingACall.dita" type="task">
            <linktext>Holding a call</linktext>
         </link>
            <linkinfo>Use these topics for background
               information about the process of holding a
               call.</linkinfo>
      </linklist>
   </related-links>
</concept>
```

<linkpool> link pool

Use the <linkpool> element to group a set of related links that have a common characteristic. These characteristics may be type, audience, source, etc. Use the <linkpool> element in place of the <linklist> element. The order your links are listed in the <linkpool> element does not affect the output. Instead, the processor sorts through the links and determines the order for output. All links within a linkpool inherit any attribute associated with the <linkpool> element. Usually, the type attribute defines the group of links attribute and can be set to concept, task, reference, other, and more. For more information on the type attribute, see Lesson 11: Type Attribute.

The following example illustrates how to use the <linkpool> element.

```
<concept>
   <conbody>
   </conbody>
   <related-links>
      <linkpool type="concept">
         <link href="AboutHold.dita"/>
         <link href="AboutTransfer.dita"/>
         <link href="AboutForward.dita"/>
```

```
        <link href="AboutConfCalls.dita"/>
      </linkpool>
    </related-links>
  </concept>
```

Related link review questions

1. Why should you use related links?
2. What is the difference between the <xref> element and the related-links section?
3. How does the *scope* attribute affect a link in the related-links section?
4. What is the purpose of link text?
5. What is the difference between link list and link pool?

SECTION C

Understanding Topic Metadata

Metadata means data or information about information. For example, the metadata you use to retrieve topics might include the names of the authors and contributors, dates of revisions, version numbers, or security rights. In DITA, you can add metadata to the prolog using elements, such as <author>, <revise>, <rev>, and <audience>.

In a DITA source document, you use descriptive element tags not only to control the content structure and reuse topics and elements, but you use additional markup to describe information in each topic. Because semantic element names are not always sufficient for search and retrieval, DITA provides general metadata markup for each topic. You use the metadata to find topics in your file system and your CMS. You can also build your search engine index using your topic metadata.

We strongly recommend that you plan your metadata at the beginning of your project. Once you add metadata to your topics, it is difficult to change. By planning your metadata, you ensure that your authors correctly apply metadata attributes and values as they create topics.

Be careful to limit the number of metadata attributes you ask authors to include. Too many attributes are harder to maintain and take time to add. Once you have defined your metadata, map the metadata categories to the metadata elements available in the DITA prolog. You will insert most of your topic metadata in the <prolog> element. You can also add metadata to any block of information by applying attributes to individual elements. If you find that the standard DITA metadata elements in the prolog do not meet your metadata needs, you may want to create a metadata specialization.

LESSON 7

Prolog Metadata

Use metadata elements in the <prolog> container to categorize, summarize, and label a topic. The base DITA prolog metadata elements specify the audience for which a topic is intended, the product with which the topic is associated, the hardware or software platform, the topic author, the copyright holder, and date-related information, such as copyright year, date created, and date revised. Prolog metadata elements are optional.

In addition to the general prolog metadata, you can also add the <metadata> element, <keywords> element, and <permissions> element as prolog metadata. In HTML, the keywords metatag helps search engines retrieve a specific list of words to identify content in a full-text search. The search engine uses the keywords you provide to retrieve and rank your topic. You can transport the keywords you identify in your DITA topics to the HTML metatag using your stylesheet.

The <permissions> element allows you to enter security filters for each topic you author.

Adding prolog metadata

This lesson explains how to add product information and keyword metadata to your topic <prolog> container.

In this lesson, you learn to add prolog metadata elements such as <permissions>, <metadata>, and <keywords> that you can use in each information type.

1. Open the TransferringACall.dita task topic that you created in Lesson 2: Task Information Type.

   In the TransferringACall.dita task topic you added a <prolog> container and an <author> element to identify topic author metadata.

```
<?xml version="1.0" encoding="utf-8"?>
<!DOCTYPE task PUBLIC "-//OASIS//DTD DITA Task//EN"
   "task.dtd">
<task id="TransferringACall" xml:lang="en-us">
   <title>Transferring a call</title>
   <shortdesc>When you transfer a call to another person
      in your office, you have two ways of handling the
      transfer.</shortdesc>
```

```
<prolog>
   <author>John Smith</author>
</prolog>
<taskbody>
   <context>
      <p>When you transfer the call without speaking
         to the person, it is an unannounced transfer.
         When you speak to the person receiving the
         transferred call, it is an announced transfer.
      </p>
   </context>
   <steps>
      <step>
         <cmd>Press the transfer button.</cmd>
      </step>
      <step>
         <cmd>Dial the number.</cmd>
         <info>Dial the number manually, use your
            pre-defined speed dial keys or go to your
            company directory. </info>
      </step>
      <step>
         <cmd>Transfer the call.</cmd>
         <choicetable>
            <chhead>
               <choptionhd>Type of Announcement
               </choptionhd>
               <chdeschd>Steps to complete
            </chdeschd>
            </chhead>
            <chrow>
               <choption>Announce a call transfer
               </choption>
               <chdesc>
                  <ol>
                     <li>Speak to the person.</li>
                     <li>Hang up the phone.</li>
                  </ol>
               </chdesc>
            </chrow>
            <chrow>
               <choption>Transfer a call unannounced
               </choption>
               <chdesc>
                  <ul>
                     <li>Hang up the phone.</li>
                  </ul>
               </chdesc>
            </chrow>
         </choicetable>
```

```
            <info>
               <note>If you announce a call and the
                  person refuses the transfer, do not hang
                  up the phone. Press the transfer button
                  again to retrieve the call on your phone
                  station.</note>
            </info>
         </step>
      </steps>
      <result>The call is transferred.</result>
   </taskbody>
      <related-links>
         <link href="AboutTransfer.dita" scope="local"/>
      </related-links>
</task>
```

2. Add a <permissions> element start tag in your prolog container after the <copyright> element end tag.

   In your <permissions> element, add a *view* attribute. The *view* attribute provides a mechanism to add security roles to your topic. The *view* attribute allows you to assign the values all, classified, entitled, or internal.

```
<prolog>
   <copyright>
      <copyryear year="2006"></copyryear>
      <copyrholder>Comtech Services, Inc.</copyrholder>
   </copyright>
   <permissions view="all"/>
</prolog>
```

3. Add <metadata> element start and end tags in your prolog container after the <permissions> element tag.

```
<prolog>
   <copyright>
      <copyryear year="2006"></copyryear>
      <copyrholder>Comtech Services, Inc.</copyrholder>
   </copyright>
   <permissions view="all"/>
   <metadata>
   </metadata>
</prolog>
```

4. Add <keywords> element start and end tags in your metadata.

   In your <keywords> container, you can add multiple <keyword> elements for each term you want to include. You use the words to create metatags in your HTML output.

```
<prolog>
   <copyright>
      <copyryear year="2006"></copyryear>
      <copyrholder>Comtech Services, Inc.
      </copyrholder>
   </copyright>
   <permissions view="all"/>
   <metadata>
      <keywords>
         <keyword>phone</keyword>
         <keyword>transfer</keyword>
         <keyword>transferring a call</keyword>
      </keywords>
   </metadata>
</prolog>
```

TransferringACall.dita

The following example shows how to use the <prolog> element in a task topic.

```
<?xml version="1.0" encoding="utf-8"?>
<!DOCTYPE task PUBLIC "-//OASIS//DTD DITA Task//EN"
   "task.dtd">
<task id="TransferringACall" xml:lang="en-us">
   <title><keyword>Transferring</keyword> a call
   </title>
   <shortdesc>When you transfer a call to another person
      in your office, you have two ways of handling the
      transfer.</shortdesc>
   <prolog>
      <copyright>
         <copyryear year="2006"></copyryear>
         <copyrholder>Comtech Services</copyrholder>
      </copyright>
      <permissions view="all"/>
      <metadata>
         <keywords>
            <keyword>phone</keyword>
            <keyword>transfer</keyword>
            <keyword>transferring a call</keyword>
         </keywords>
      </metadata>
   </prolog>
   <taskbody>
      <context>
         <p> When you transfer the call without speaking
            to the person, it is an unannounced transfer.
            When you speak to the person receiving the
            transferred call, it is an announced transfer.
         </p>
      </context>
```

```
<steps>
   <step>
      <cmd>Press the <uicontrol>transfer
         </uicontrol> button.</cmd>
   </step>
   <step>
      <cmd>Dial the number.</cmd>
      <info>Dial the number manually, use your
         pre-defined speed dial keys or go to your
         company directory.</info>
   </step>
   <step>
      <cmd>Transfer the call.</cmd>
      <choicetable>
         <chhead>
            <choptionhd>Type of Announcement
            </choptionhd>
            <chdeschd>Steps to complete
            </chdeschd>
         </chhead>
         <chrow>
            <choption>Announce a call transfer
            </choption>
            <chdesc>
               <ol>
                  <li>Speak to the person.</li>
                  <li>Hang up the phone.</li>
               </ol>
            </chdesc>
         </chrow>
         <chrow>
            <choption>Transfer a call unannounced
            </choption>
            <chdesc>
               <ul>
                  <li>Hang up the phone.</li>
               </ul>
            </chdesc>
         </chrow>
      </choicetable>
      <info>
         <note>If you announce a call and the
            person refuses the transfer, do not hang
            up the phone. Press the <uicontrol>
            transfer</uicontrol> button again to
            retrieve the call on your phone.</note>
      </info>
   </step>
</steps>
```

```
        <result>The call is transferred.</result>
    </taskbody>
</task>
```

Prolog metadata elements

The following prolog metadata elements are listed in alphabetical order.

<audience> audience

Use the <audience> metadata element to specify the intended audience, job, and experience level for a topic. Use the *type* attribute in the <audience> element to specify the intended audience. Use the *job* attribute to specify the high-level task they are trying to accomplish. Use the *experiencelevel* attribute to specify the end users expected experience level. You may add more than one <audience> metadata element to the <prolog> element to indicate multiple audiences, jobs, or experience levels for the topic.

<author> author

Use the <author> element to specify the name of the topic author. Use the optional *type* attribute with the value of "creator" or "contributor" to indicate the primary author of the topic. You may add multiple <author> elements to the <author> metadata element.

<brand> brand

Use the <brand> element to indicate the manufacturer or brand associated with the product info.

<copyrholder> copyright holder

Use the <copyrholder> element to indicate the entitiy that holds the legal rights to the topic.

<copyright> copyright

Use the <copyright> element to specify the copyright information for a topic. The <copyright> element is the container for the <copyryear> and <copyrholder> elements.

<copyryear> copyright year

Use the <copyryear> element to indicate the copyright year.

<created> created date

Use the <created> element to track the topic creation date. Use the *date* attribute to document the creation date.

<critdates> critical dates

Use the <critdates> element to track the important dates of your topic including the creation and multiple revision dates. The <critdates> element is the container for the <created> and <revised> elements.

<keywords> keywords

Use the <keywords> metadata element to specify index and keyword terms. These terms are used in search indexes and are added to the metadata for HTML output. The <keywords> element is a container for one or more <keyword> elements.

<keyword> keyword

Use the <keyword> element to specify a single index or keyword term for your topic. Multiple <keyword> elements can be added to the <keywords> element.

<metadata> metadata

Use the <metadata> element to add information regarding a particular audience, category, product, keyword, or other metadata. The <metadata> element allows you to include elements, such as <audience>, <keywords>, and <prodinfo>.

<permissions> permissions

Use the <permissions> element to add security filters to your topics. The <permissions> element requires you to include a *view* attribute. The possible values you can use for the *view* attribute are "all", "classified", "entitled", or "internal".

<platform> platform

Use the <platform> metadata element to describe the software or hardware associated with the product.

<prodinfo> product information

Use the <prodinfo> metadata element to provide information regarding the product or products described in your topic. The <prodinfo> metadata element is a container for the <prodname>, <vrmlist>, and <platform> metadata elements.

<prodname> product name

Use the <prodname> metadata element to specify the name of the product described in the topic.

<revised> revised date

Use the <revised> element to track the dates the topic was modified or changed. Use the *modification* attribute to track the last date the topic was modified. Use the *golive* attribute to track the date the product was released. Use the *expiry* date to record when the information should be reviewed or retired.

The following example illustrates how to use the prolog metadata elements described above.

```
<concept id="EstimateProjHours">
   <title>Estimating project hours</title>
   <prolog>
      <author type="creator">Jennifer Linton</author>
      <author type="creator">Kylene Bruski</author>
      <author type="contributor">JoAnn Hackos</author>
      <author type="contributor">Bill Hackos</author>
      <author type="contributor">Nikki Gjestvang
      </author>
      <copyright>
         <copyryear year="2006"></copyryear>
         <copyrholder>Comtech Services, Inc.
         </copyrholder>
      </copyright>
      <critdates>
         <created date="1999-01-01"></created>
         <revised modified="2000-03-01"></revised>
      </critdates>
      <metadata>
         <audience type="administrator" job="planning"
            experiencelevel="novice"/>
         <keywords>
            <keyword>Costs</keyword>
            <keyword>Estimating</keyword>
            <keyword>Tracking</keyword>
            <keyword>Monitoring</keyword>
            <keyword>PUB$</keyword>
         </keywords>
         <prodinfo>
            <prodname>PUB$ Estimator</prodname>
            <vrmlist>
               <vrm version="1.1" release="2"
                  modification="1"/>
            </vrmlist>
            <brand>Comtech Services</brand>
            <platform>Windows 98, 2000, XP</platform>
         </prodinfo>
      </metadata>
   </prolog>
   <conbody>
   </conbody>
</concept>
```

Metadata review questions

1. What is the purpose of metadata?
2. When should you plan your metadata?
3. What kind of metadata can you add to the <prolog> element?
4. What values might you apply to the <prodinfo> element?

PART III DITA Maps

Using DITA maps to create collections of topics for print, web, help, or other deliverables helps you create a collaborative work environment and improve the quality of the information you deliver to your customers. You may want to establish a team of information developers to develop collaboratively the topics for a deliverable. You may want to deliver solution-oriented information to your users rather than sets of manuals specific to individual products. You may want to improve the time to market by synchronizing processes between information and product development. Using DITA maps to create collections of topics improves your ability to deliver information to specific audiences, assemble pre-translated topics for specific locales, and create deliverables for specific products and product solutions.

Mapping your topics into deliverables helps to

- improve writer collaboration
- create solutions-oriented deliverables
- create customized deliverables
- synchronize information development with product-development schedules

Creating a collaborative work environment

Information-development organizations often move to topic-oriented writing to avoid duplication of effort. They find that their colleagues write the same topics in slightly different ways for individual deliverables. Managers hope to reduce redundancy by developing a repository of unique topics that can be reused in multiple deliverables. DITA maps facilitate single sourcing and content reuse. By designing

DITA maps for final deliverables early in the information-development life cycle, information developers avoid duplication of effort at the same time that they understand the context in which a topic will appear.

Creating solutions-oriented deliverables

Users of technical information are often at a disadvantage when they try to use a variety of products, even when these products are developed by the same company. They find that each product has an independently developed set of manuals that may adequately describe how to use each product but fail to explain how the products work together. Solutions documentation is designed to bridge product elements by documenting how they work together and how they can be used together efficiently and effectively.

Topic-based authoring facilitates the development of solutions-oriented deliverables. When you use topics to create your information deliverables, you can create DITA maps that apply to a specific product or to a group of products. You can reference DITA maps for one deliverable into a master map to produce a solutions-oriented collection of your product information.

Creating customized deliverables

Users of technical information often would prefer to collect individual topics from larger documentation sets and create their own personal manuals. Experienced technicians administering and maintaining complex products may need only select reference information to support their tasks. Occasional users may profit from simple task-oriented information because they're unwilling to devote time to learning concepts and studying background. By giving your users access to individual topics or enabling them to search for topics with a controlled vocabulary of metadata attributes and values, you can help them create personalized maps of the information they need.

By allowing users to select the information they need from a collection of topics, you can help them build personalized collections. Using a DITA map, they build personalized deliverables by arranging selected topics into a recommended hierarchy. The map can even group concepts, tasks, and reference information about a particular subject matter into a single deliverable.

Synchronizing information development with product development

By moving from authoring books to authoring topics, information developers can more easily synchronize their schedules with the development of product features and functions. Beginning with user scenarios or use cases that describe how actual users will benefit from new and updated product features and functions, information developers first create a list of task topics. The task topics explain how users will accomplish their goals with the product.

After the task topics are outlined, the information developers begin to string the tasks together into DITA maps, using a hierarchy that best represents how the user might approach the activities. That hierarchy might be chronological, supporting a start-to-finish installation process. The hierarchy might reflect common and less common uses of the product. The DITA map prepares the hierarchy and renders it as a table of contents or the navigation in a help system or web site.

Concept and reference topics can then be developed and organized in the DITA map in relationship to the task topics. With all the topics accounted for and the contexts developed in the maps, the information developers can author topics in whatever order is convenient and corresponds to the availability of source information from requirements, use cases, product specifications, and interviews with product developers, designers, and managers.

By synchronizing the information-development process with product development, you can create topics about more stable product features early, moving to less stable or completed features and functions when they are ready. If product management decides to remove a feature from a deliverable, you need only remove the topic from the DITA map, making last minute changes easier to accommodate. Adding, modifying, or deleting standalone topics in a map is more efficient than extracting topics embedded in chapters and sections of books.

SECTION D

Understanding DITA Map Basics

DITA maps are the backbone of DITA. Maps provide a mechanism for ordering topics and creating a topic hierarchy. For example, you can produce two different API reference manuals, one organizing functions and methods alphabetically and the other organizing them by family. By creating two different maps that reference the same source topics, you can create two deliverables to meet user needs. Because maps consist of lists of topic references, you can reorganize the content in a map simply by changing the order of the topic references. You can distinguish among your maps by applying map and topic metadata. Figure 3.1 illustrates two maps created from the same source topics.

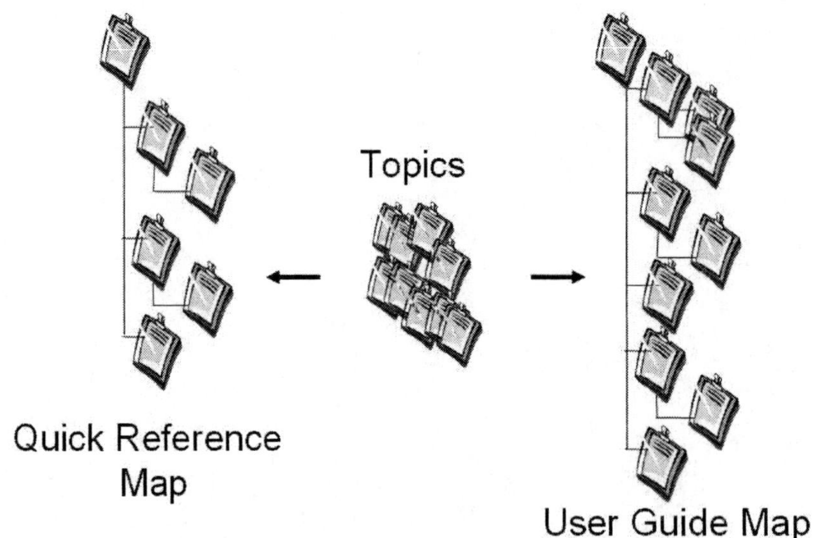

Figure 3.1 Creating multiple maps from a single source

When topics are authored in the chapters and sections of desktop publishing applications, restructuring them is difficult. In DITA, your deliverable isn't tied to the structure in which you author the topics . You can

- place topics in more than one position in a DITA map. For example, a task can occur in more than one place in a task flow.
- create solutions-oriented maps that answer the question "how do these products work together?" You can also create task-oriented maps to answer the question "how do I accomplish my goals?" And, you can create feature-oriented maps to answer the question "what does this product do?"
- create maps to deliver information to specific audiences
- create hierarchies of topics depending on the way you format your output
- include topics in your navigation from different information sets, such as external web sites and other content your staff or another department may have created

The relationships among topics defined in a map can be used to create tables of contents (TOC), site maps, and navigation. DITA maps provide functionality to customize how the output will be rendered using specific map metadata, such as the *href*, *format*, *scope*, *type*, *linking*, and *collection-type* attributes. Additionally, DITA map relationship tables provide linking between topics that do not have direct relationships in the hierarchy. You use the DITA map as the cornerstone for processing the output you need.

Map location

When you create a new map, it is best to place the map file in the same directory that contains the topics. DITA maps have a .ditamap extension so that they can be distinguished from other DITA source files. You might also consider creating smaller maps and storing them in subdirectories (for example, a folder for each major category of your deliverable, such as installation, troubleshooting, and operations) to help you manage topics better. Then you can create a master map that references the smaller maps. Because you can nest the topic folders to any level, you should position the map in a higher level folder that contains all the topics. This folder organization ensures that processing runs without errors.

LESSON 8

DITA Map Structure

DITA maps use a small set of elements to help you create a topic collection and arrange topics into a useful hierarchy.

The map elements allow you to reference topics, create groups of topics, create navigational headings, add map metadata, and more. Map elements dictate the structure of the topics in your final deliverables. Although the number of elements needed to create a map is significantly less than the number used to create topics, the map elements play a special role. The topic reference element builds the structure of the DITA map and is the most widely used map element. The topic reference points to a single topic and includes it in the deliverable.

Topic reference elements create the hierarchical relationships needed to format the deliverable with more than one heading level. By embedding topic references in one another, you can create a hierarchy as many levels deep as you believe necessary.

Metadata in the map allows you to further customize deliverables. You can include the same metadata in your map that you include in your topic. When you include metadata in a map, it is applied to a specific topic reference. However, when you include the metadata in a map, you can change the metadata based on the deliverable and manage the topic metadata in the map rather than in the topic. If you manage the metadata in the topic, it makes the topic less flexible. For example, if you want to include information about an audience, you might assign different audiences to a topic reference depending on the deliverable you are building. But, if you include one specific audience in your topic-level metadata, you may find it difficult to use that topic in more than one map. Some metadata you might include in a DITA map are author, publisher, audience, category, copyright, critical dates, keywords, permissions, and product information.

Lesson 8 contains four exercises:

- Starting a DITA map
- Adding topic references
- Adding topic metadata
- Creating a basic hierarchy

Starting a DITA map

This exercise explains the standard XML markup included in a DITA map.

In this exercise, you learn to add the XML declaration, DTD declaration, and the root <map> element in your DITA map.

1. Start a new DITA map.

   You can start a new DITA map in a text editor or in an XML editor. In most XML editors, you can choose **file > new > DITA map.** The XML tool usually includes a DTD declaration and XML declaration automatically. If you choose to use a text editor, type the markup shown here. Enter the XML declaration as the first line of your file. The DITA map, like other XML files, must have an XML declaration, doctype declaration, and a root element to contain the rest of your structured information.

   ```
   <?xml version="1.0" encoding="utf-8"?>
   ```

2. Enter the document type declaration.

   The document type declaration identifies the DTD you will validate against. For this example, add the path to the folder in which you stored the DITA map DTD.

   ```
   <!DOCTYPE map PUBLIC "-//OASIS//DTD DITA Map//EN"
      "map.dtd">
   ```

3. Add the <map> start and end element tags.

   The map element container is the root element that you use to start your DITA map.

   ```
   <?xml version="1.0" encoding="utf-8"?>
   <!DOCTYPE map PUBLIC "-//OASIS//DTD DITA Map//EN"
      "map.dtd">
   <map>
   </map>
   ```

4. Add a *title* attribute and value to your map element.

   The processor uses the map element title to create a cover page for your print output or add a window name to your online output.

   ```
   <map title="Comstar Phone Guide">
   </map>
   ```

5. Add an *id* attribute to your map element.

   The ID must be unique. A unique ID allows you to easily identify the map you want to process. The ID can contain numbers, letters, and underscores, but it must start with a letter or a number.

```
<map title="Comstar Phone Guide"
   id="Comstaruserguide">
</map>
```

6. Save this file with a .ditamap extension.

Comstaruserguide.ditamap

The following example shows how every DITA map must start.

```
<?xml version="1.0" encoding="utf-8"?>
<!DOCTYPE map PUBLIC "-//OASIS//DTD DITA Map//EN"
   "map.dtd">
<map title="Comstar Phone Guide" id="Comstaruserguide">
</map>
```

Adding topic references

This exercise explains how to add topic references to your DITA map.

In this exercise, you learn to

- add the <topicref> element
- apply an *href* attribute and value to your topic references
- add the *navtitle* and *locktitle* attributes

1. Open the DITA map you started creating in the previous exercise in this lesson.

```
<?xml version="1.0" encoding="utf-8"?>
<!DOCTYPE map PUBLIC "-//OASIS//DTD DITA Map//EN"
   "map.dtd">
<map title="Comstar Phone Guide" id="Comstaruserguide">
</map>
```

2. Insert <topicref> element start and end tags between the <map> start and end tags.
3. Assign the *href* attribute the value **ComstarOverview.dita** in the <topicref> element's start tag.

   The *href* attribute is the most important attribute in a DITA map, pointing to the location of the DITA topic file you want to reference. The *href* attribute value accepts absolute or relative path names to the location of your topic. Your topics may be named with a .dita or a .xml extension. Remember to include this file extension when referencing your file.

   The following example shows what a topic reference looks like. The value of the *href* attribute points to a DITA topic file located in the same folder as the DITA map.

```
<map>

   <topicref href="ComstarOverview.dita"></topicref>
</map>
```

You can also create empty <topicref> elements if you are not going to nest any topic references as child topics between the start and end <topicref> tags. Using empty topic references helps you create a more maintainable map to work with. If you use multiple open and close tags, you are more likely to create an error nesting your topic references. You can find out more about nesting topic references in the exercise covering Creating a Basic Hierarchy later in this lesson.

```
<map>
   <topicref href="ComstarOverview.dita" />
</map>
```

4. Under the ComstarOverview.dita (reference) topicref, add two more <topicref> element containers.

   Assign the *href* attributes the values QuickGuide.dita (concept) and AboutHold.dita (task) respectively. Your map now points to three topics and puts them in the order in which you want them to appear in the table of contents. At this point, all the topic references are at the same level in the hierarchy.

```
<map title="Comstar User Guide" id="Comstaruserguide">
   <topicref href="ComstarOverview.dita" />
   <topicref href="QuickGuide.dita" />
   <topicref href="AboutHold.dita"></topicref>
</map>
```

5. Add a *navtitle* attribute to your AboutHold.dita topic reference container.

   A *navtitle* provides an optional alternative title for different output types. Normally, the default output uses the referenced topic titles for the navigation or table of contents.

   In the example below, the AboutHold.dita topic title is "About Hold," but using the *navtitle* attribute, you shorten the navigation title to "Hold".

```
<map>
   <topicref href="AboutHold.dita"
      navtitle="Hold" />
</map>
```

6. Add a *locktitle* attribute to the <topicref> element.

   In some situations, you may want to use the title you assigned the *navtitle* attribute value instead of the title you originally included in your topic. By default, the processor uses the title from your topic, but you can override this processing functionality when you set the *locktitle* attribute value to "yes". You don't need to repeat the title you used in the topic. You may want to use the *locktitle* attribute if your topic has a long title and you want a shorter title in a navigation pane.

```
<map>
   <topicref href="AboutHold.dita" navtitle="Hold"
      locktitle="yes"/>
</map>
```

Comstaruserguide.ditamap

At this point, your Comstaruserguide.ditamap looks like the example below.

```
<?xml version="1.0" encoding="utf-8"?>
<!DOCTYPE map PUBLIC "-//OASIS//DTD DITA Map//EN"
   "map.dtd">
<map title="Comstar Phone Guide" id="Comstaruserguide">
   <topicref href="ComstarOverview.dita" />
   <topicref href="QuickGuide.dita" />
   <topicref href="AboutHold.dita" navtitle="Hold"
      locktitle="yes"></topicref>
</map>
```

Adding topic metadata

This exercise explains how to apply topic metadata to each topic reference in your DITA map.

Because you apply topic metadata to each topic reference in your map, it helps to understand how to add topic references to DITA maps. You can learn about adding topic references in the exercise, Adding Topic References, earlier in this lesson.

In this exercise, you learn to

- add the <topicmeta> element needed to apply topic metadata in a map
- add four pieces of metadata to a topic including <author>, <publisher>, <copyright>, and <audience>

1. Open your DITA map from the Adding Topic References exercise.

```
<?xml version="1.0" encoding="utf-8"?>
<!DOCTYPE map PUBLIC "-//OASIS//DTD DITA Map//EN"
   "map.dtd">
<map title="Comstar Phone Guide" id="Comstaruserguide">
   <topicref href="ComstarOverview.dita" />
   <topicref href="QuickGuide.dita" />
   <topicref href="AboutHold.dita" navtitle="Hold"
      locktitle="yes"></topicref>
</map>
```

2. Change the QuickGuide.dita topic reference to a container element rather than an empty element.

   If you remove the end slash and insert a <topicref> end tag, you create a container.

```
<topicref href="QuickGuide.dita"></topicref>
```

3. Insert <topicmeta> start and end tags between the QuickGuide.dita <topicref> element start and end tags.

   The topic metadata container allows you to include metadata about a topic you reference in your map. The <topicmeta> element contains similar items to those you include in the internal topic metadata, such as audience, copyright, product, and others.

```
<map title="Comstar User Guide">
   <topicref href="QuickGuide.dita">
      <topicmeta></topicmeta>
   </topicref>
</map>
```

4. Add <author> start and end element tags between the <topicmeta> element start and end tags.

   Inside the author tag, insert the name of the individual, company, or organization that authored the topic you are referencing.

   Note: You can add multiple author elements if needed.

```
<map title="Comstar User Guide">
   <topicref href="QuickGuide.dita">
      <topicmeta>
         <author>Jennifer Linton</author>
         <author>Kylene Bruski</author>
      </topicmeta>
   </topicref>
</map>
```

5. Add <publisher> element start and end tags after the <author> element end tag.

   You can include only one publisher for each topic reference.

```
<map title="Comstar User Guide">
   <topicref href="QuickGuide.dita">
      <topicmeta>
         <author>Jennifer Linton</author>
         <author>Kylene Bruski</author>
```

```
         <publisher>Comtech Services, Inc.</publisher>
      </topicmeta>
   </topicref>
</map>
```

6. Add <copyright> element start and end tags after the <publisher> element end tag.

   In the <copyright> tag, you must insert an empty <copyryear> element. This element is empty because it does not require you to enter information between the start and end tags. However, it does require you to add a *year* attribute to define the copyright year. You can also include an optional <copyrholder> element to identify the copyright owner.

```
<map title="Comstar User Guide">
   <topicref href="QuickGuide.dita">
      <topicmeta>
         <author>Jennifer Linton</author>
         <author>Kylene Bruski</author>
         <publisher>Comtech Services, Inc.</publisher>
         <copyright>
            <copyryear year="2006" />
            <copyrholder>Comtech Services, Inc.
            </copyrholder>
         </copyright>
      </topicmeta>
   </topicref>
</map>
```

7. Add an empty <audience> element tag after the <copyright> element.

   In the <audience> element, you must add a value to the *audience* attribute. You can add as many <audience> elements as needed, assigning a topic reference to multiple audiences, such as an end user or administrator. However, you can also add multiple values in a single audience metadata attribute using space delimiters (i.e., audience="beginner intermediate").

```
<map title="Comstar User Guide">
   <topicref href="QuickGuide.dita" navtitle="Quick start guide">
      <topicmeta>
         <author>Jennifer Linton</author>
         <author>Kylene Bruski</author>
         <publisher>Comtech Services, Inc.</publisher>
         <copyright>
            <copyryear year="2006" />
            <copyrholder>Comtech Services, Inc.
            </copyrholder>
         </copyright>
```

```
            <audience audience="user" />
            <audience audience="administrator" />
        </topicmeta>
    </topicref>
</map>
```

8. Add topic metadata to any topic references in your map.

   Because you can also define metadata in the topics, it may not be necessary to define the metadata in the map. You define the metadata in relation to topic references in the map so that you can apply different metadata to various deliverables. If you apply the metadata in the topic, every deliverable uses the metadata from the topic, making it more difficult to reuse the topic.

Comstaruserguide.ditamap

```
<map title="Comstar User Guide" id="Comstaruserguide">
    <topicref href="ComstarOverview.dita" />
    <topicref href="QuickGuide.dita"
        navtitle="Quick start guide">
        <topicmeta>
            <author>Jennifer Linton</author>
            <author>Kylene Bruski</author>
            <publisher>Raven Printing</publisher>
            <copyright>
                <copyryear year="2006" />
                <copyrholder>Comtech Services, Inc.
                </copyrholder>
            </copyright>
            <audience audience="beginner" />
            <audience audience="intermediate" />
        </topicmeta>
    </topicref>
    <topicref href="AboutHold.dita" navtitle="Hold"
        locktitle="yes">
        <topicmeta>
            <author>John Parsens</author>
            <publisher>Comtech Services, Inc.</publisher>
            <copyright>
                <copyryear year="2006" />
                <copyrholder>Comstar Phones</copyrholder>
            </copyright>
            <audience audience="adminsitrator" />
        </topicmeta>
    </topicref>
</map>
```

Creating a basic hierarchy

Up to this point, you have created a flat, one-level structure for your map. This exercise explains how to create a hierarchy and nest <topicref> elements.

By nesting topic references, you create multiple heading levels in your deliverable. Nesting <topicref> elements sets up the sequence and hierarchy of topics in PDF tables of contents and creates a navigation tree or site index for online output.

In this exercise, you learn to nest <topicref> elements to create hierarchical relationships among your topics.

1. Open your DITA map.

   So far, you have three topic references in a flat, one-level structure.

   ```
   <?xml version="1.0" encoding="utf-8"?>
   <!DOCTYPE map PUBLIC "-//OASIS//DTD DITA Map//EN"
      "map.dtd">
   <map title="Comstar Phone Guide" id="Comstaruserguide">
      <topicref href="ComstarOverview.dita" />
      <topicref href="QuickGuide.dita" />
      <topicref href="AboutHold.dita" navtitle="Hold"
         locktitle="yes"></topicref>
   </map>
   ```

2. Insert <topicref> start and end element tags between the AboutHold.dita <topicref> element start and end tags.

   Point the *href* attribute value to the topic called "HoldingACall.dita".

   Inserting the HoldingACall.dita topic reference between the AboutHold.dita <topicref> start and end tags makes the AboutHold.dita topic the parent of HoldingACall.dita. When you output the map, the AboutHold.dita topic is a first-level heading and the HoldingACall.dita is a second-level heading. Notice in the example that the two </topicref> element end tags are next to each other. Two topic reference end tags next to each other close both the child topic reference container and its parent topic reference container. When you add the next topic in the map, the topic reference starts at the first level of hierarchy again.

   ```
   <map title="Comstar User Guide" id="Comstaruserguide">
      <topicref href="ComstarOverview.dita" />
      <topicref href="QuickGuide.dita"
         navtitle="Quick start guide" />
      <topicref href="AboutHold.dita" navtitle="Hold"
         locktitle="yes" >
         <topicref href="HoldingACall.dita"
            navtitle="Putting a call on hold"></topicref>
      </topicref>
   </map>
   ```

3. Insert additional topic references to create more parent and child relationships.

   Remember to close child topic reference element containers with end tags before closing the parent topic reference elements. Nesting the topic references in one another creates your hierarchy. You can continue to insert topic references in a parent topic reference to any level. However, it is better not to include more than four levels of topic references or the hierarchy will become confusing to the user.

Comstaruserguide.ditamap

The following example is a full map. The conference call section shows how to create multiple child topics.

```
<map title="Comstar User Guide" id="Comstaruserguide">
   <topicref href="ComstarOverview.dita" />
   <topicref href="QuickGuide.dita"
      navtitle="Quick guide">
      <topicmeta>
         <author>Jennifer Linton</author>
         <author>Kylene Bruski</author>
         <publisher>Raven Printing</publisher>
         <copyright>
            <copyryear year="2006" />
            <copyrholder>Comtech Services, Inc.
            </copyrholder>
         </copyright>
         <audience audience="beginner" />
         <audience audience="intermediate" />
      </topicmeta>
   </topicref>
   <topicref href="AboutHold.dita" navtitle="Hold">
      <topicmeta>
         <author>John Parsens</author>
         <publisher>Comtech Services, Inc.</publisher>
         <copyright>
            <copyryear year="2006" />
            <copyrholder>Comstar Phones</copyrholder>
         </copyright>
         <audience audience="adminsitrator" />
      </topicmeta>
      <topicref href="HoldingACall.dita"
         navtitle="Putting a call on hold" />
   </topicref>
   <topicref href="AboutTransfer.dita"
      navtitle="Transfer">
      <topicref href="TransferringACall.dita"
         navtitle="Transferring a call" />
   </topicref>
```

```
    <topicref href="AboutForward.dita"
       navtitle="About forward">
       <topicref href="ForwardingACall.dita"
          navtitle="Forwarding a call"/>
    </topicref>
    <topicref href="AboutConferenceCalls.dita"
       navtitle="About conference calls">
       <topicref href="PlacingACall.dita"
          navtitle="Placing a conference call" />
       <topicref href="
          LeavingAConferenceCallTemporarily.dita"
          navtitle="Leaving a conference call temporarily" />
       <topicref href="ReEnteringAConferenceCall.dita"
          navtitle="Reentering a conference call" />
       <topicref href="
          ConsultingPrivatelyOnTheConferenceCall.dita" />
       <topicref href="ReEnteringACallWithAllPeople.dita"
          navtitle="ReEntering a call with all people" />
    </topicref>
    <topicref href="Warnings.dita"/>
    <topicref href="http://www.comtech-serv.com/Comstar/">
       <topicmeta>
          <linktext>Order Comstar Phones</linktext>
          <shortdesc>Online ordering for your choice
             of any Comstar phones.</shortdesc>
       </topicmeta>
    </topicref>
    <topicref href="../../ComstarPricing.pdf">
       <topicmeta>
          <linktext>Comstar Pricing List</linktext>
          <shortdesc>Comstar phones provide a variety of
             different plans you can purchase to use with
             your phone.</shortdesc>
       </topicmeta>
    </topicref>
    <topicref href="../GeneralTopic/Glossary.dita"/>
</map>
```

Map elements

You can only use map elements in a DITA map. You cannot use the elements in topics or other DITA files. The map elements that you regularly use when creating a map are listed here. For more information on map elements, see the *DITA Language Specification*.

<topicref> topic reference

Use the <topicref> element to create a pointer to a single DITA topic. Use multiple <topicref> tags to point to multiple topics to build your deliverable. Nesting the <topicref> elements in one another creates a hierarchical structure for your readers. You can also use this hierarchy to represent your table of contents, site map, and online navigation. The topic reference *href* attribute is the most important part of the <topicref> element. It points to the path and filename for the DITA topic or external information you reference.

<topichead> topic heading

Use the <topichead> element to add a title to your DITA map that is not used in any topic titles. Use the *navtitle* attribute to enter the title text. Use the <topichead> element, for example, if you want to provide a title, such as Section 3: Project Management, for a section or part that contains multiple topic references. Keep in mind you will need to translate the contents in the *navtitle* attribute if you produce deliverables for different languages. Currently DITA does not provide adequate mechanisms for translating content in an attribute value. You may need to create a transform to put attribute values into translatable element containers. Future versions of DITA plan to fix this problem.

The following example illustrates what a topic head looks like in your DITA map.

```
<map>
   <topicref href="ComstarOverview.dita" />
   <topicref href="QuickGuide.dita" />
   <topichead navtitle="Installation" locktitle="yes">
      <topicref href="SettingUpPhone.dita" />
      <topicref href="ConfiguringPhoneOptions.dita" />
   </topichead>
   <topichead navtitle="Troubleshooting" locktitle="yes">
      <topicref href="PhoneErrors.dita" />
   </topichead>
</map>
```

<topicgroup> topic group

Use the <topicgroup> element to create collections of topic references without affecting the hierarchy. You can apply inheritable attributes to <topicgroup> elements. If you apply an attribute to a group of topic references between topic group start and end tags, all of the topic references also gain this attribute value. You can learn about inheritable attributes in the Understanding Map Attributes section.

This following example illustrates what a topic group looks like in your DITA map. If you want to learn about the *linking* attribute used in this example, see Lesson 14: Linking Attributes.

```
<map title="Comstar User Guide">
   <topicref href="ComstarOverview.dita" />
   <topicref href="QuickGuide.dita"
      navtitle="Quick guide" />
```

```
    <topicgroup collection-type="family">
       <topicref href="AboutHold.dita" navtitle="Hold">
          <topicref href="HoldingACall.dita"
             navtitle="Holding a call" />
       </topicref>
       <topicref href="AboutConferencCalls.dita"
          navtitle="About conference calls">
          <topicref href="PlacingACall.dita"
             navtitle="Placing a conference a call" />
          <topicref href="
             LeavingAConferenceCallTemporarily.dita"
             navtitle="Leaving a conference call temporarily"
             linking="normal"/>
          <topicref href="ReEnteringAConferenceCall.dita"
             navtitle="Reentering a conference call" />
          <topicref href="
             ConsultingPrivatelyOnTheConferenceCall.dita"
             navtitle="Consulting with one party on the
             conference call privately" />
          <topicref href="
             ReEnteringACallWithAllPeople.dita"
             navtitle="ReEntering a call with all people" />
       </topicref>
    </topicgroup>
 </map>
```

<topicmeta> topic metadata

Use the <topicmeta> element to apply topic metadata at the map level. The <topicmeta> element allows you to include alternative text for links, short descriptions that you want to use specifically for an output, author information, keywords, and more. If you apply topic metadata at the map level, it overrides any metadata that authors set in the topics. One important metadata category is keyword. The <keyword> element you would include in the <topicmeta> stores the words you want to associate with this topic reference. You can use these keywords after translating your topics to maintain separate keywords across the same content. If you create different maps for your end users, you can indicate special keywords for a particular deliverable type or audience using the topic metadata. Keep in mind, if you do provide keywords in your map, you may need to translate the text in your maps. If you add text in your map other than references to your topic files and processing attributes, you must translate the text to provide accessible and consistent deliverables for all users.

This following example illustrates what topic metadata keywords look like in your DITA map. You can use these words to add to your search metadata.

```
<topicref href="DITAGettingStarted.dita"
   navtitle="Getting Started with DITA" >
   <topicmeta>
      <keywords>
         <keyword>concept</keyword>
         <keyword>beginner</keyword>
         <keyword>information type</keyword>
    <keyword>DITA</keyword>
         <keyword>Darwin Information Typing Architecture
         </keyword>
         <keyword>topics</keyword>
      </keywords>
   </topicmeta>
</topicref>
```

Map element review questions

1. When should you create a map?
2. What is the structure of a map?
3. How do you determine the parent child hierarchy in a map?
4. Can a topic be used multiple times in the same map?
5. What is the purpose of topic metadata?
6. When would you use a *locktitle* and when would you use a *navtitle*?

SECTION E

Understanding DITA Map Attributes

Although maps provide the structure for your deliverables, map attributes add production functionality to the maps.

The most important attribute in a DITA map is the required *href* attribute. The *href* attribute values add a file path and a file name to the topic you are referencing. If you are working in a file system, the typical format for the *href* attribute value is `systempathandfilename.dita#topicid`. If you omit the # and topic id, the *href* points to the first element (i.e., <concept>, <task>, or <reference>) in the target file. If you use a content management system, the system assigns a unique ID to your topic file. If you are using a CMS, use the unique ID provided by the CMS as the value for the *href* attribute.

Other DITA map attributes facilitate dynamically linking topics and setting processing options and formatting rules. Consider including the *format*, *type*, and *scope* attributes with each of your topic references for identification purposes. Attributes you can apply to groups of topics or to individual topics to help control linking include *collection-type* and *linking*. The processing attributes DITA provides include *toc* and *print*.

Because maps create a hierarchical structure, they establish parent and child relationships among the topics. If you add an attribute to a parent topic reference, all child topics have the same attribute and value, a relationship referred to as inheritance. You can override the inheritance by applying a different value on a child topic reference.

For example, if you assign a topic reference the *toc* attribute value "no", the table of contents will not include that topic reference and all of its child topic references. However, if you set one of the child topic references to the *toc* attribute value "yes", the table of contents will include the child topic.

You can use inheritance to create different print and HTML output using the same DITA map. You can exclude topics from the PDF output by setting the *print* attribute value to "no".

The inheritable attributes you can use in a DITA map include linking, print, toc, audience, product, platform, importance, otherprops, rev, type, locktitle, scope, and format.

LESSON 9

Format Attribute

Use the *format* attribute to indicate the file type you are referencing in your map. You may want to reference other than DITA topics in your map, such as PDFs, doc files, XML files, or web pages. Because a map allows you to reference content other than DITA topics, you must indicate that the topic you are referencing is something other than a DITA file. If you assign the format attribute the value DITA, it instructs your processor to use DITA processing rules. If the topic reference points to a different file format, then the processing engine will not try to process the file referenced.

The default value for the *format* attribute is "dita". Other formats may include "html", "pdf", "txt", "zip", and any other resource you may reference in your deliverable. Setting *format* to "pdf", for example, should cause the PDF simply to be copied into the output directory with a link to it. Your processor will not attempt to process the PDF using DITA processing rules. Any non-DITA topic reference will open in a separate window or application, such as Adobe Reader.

In this lesson, you learn to apply the *format* attribute to your topic references. You should consider using this attribute for each topic reference to provide consistency in your output.

Adding the *format* attribute

This lesson explains the *format* attribute and values you can use in your DITA map.

In this lesson, you learn to

- add the *format* attribute to <topicref> elements
- apply *format* attribute values, such as "dita" and "html"

1. Open the DITA map you created at the end of Lesson 8: DITA Map Structures.

   Your DITA map at this point looks like the following example.

```
<map title="Comstar User Guide" id="Comstaruserguide">
   <topicref href="ComstarOverview.dita" />
   <topicref href="QuickGuide.dita"
      navtitle="Quick guide">
      <topicmeta>
         <author>Jennifer Linton</author>
         <author>Kylene Bruski</author>
         <publisher>Raven Printing</publisher>
```

```
            <copyright>
                <copyryear year="2006" />
                <copyrholder>Comtech Services, Inc.
                </copyrholder>
            </copyright>
            <audience audience="beginner" />
            <audience audience="intermediate" />
        </topicmeta>
    </topicref>
    <topicref href="AboutHold.dita" navtitle="Hold">
        <topicmeta>
            <author>John Parsens</author>
            <publisher>Comtech Services, Inc.</publisher>
            <copyright>
                <copyryear year="2006" />
                <copyrholder>Comstar Phones</copyrholder>
            </copyright>
            <audience audience="adminsitrator" />
        </topicmeta>
        <topicref href="HoldingACall.dita"
            navtitle="Putting a call on hold" />
    </topicref>
    <topicref href="AboutTransfer.dita"
        navtitle="Transfer">
        <topicref href="TransferringACall.dita"
            navtitle="Transferring a call" />
    </topicref>
    <topicref href="AboutForward.dita"
        navtitle="About forward">
        <topicref href="ForwardingACall.dita"
        navtitle="Forwarding a call"/>
    </topicref>
    <topicref href="AboutConferenceCalls.dita"
        navtitle="About conference calls">
        <topicref href="PlacingACall.dita"
            navtitle="Placing a conference call" />
        <topicref href="
            LeavingAConferenceCallTemporarily.dita"
            navtitle="Leaving a conference call temporarily" />
        <topicref href="ReEnteringAConferenceCall.dita"
            navtitle="Reentering a conference call" />
        <topicref href="
            ConsultingPrivatelyOnTheConferenceCall.dita" />
        <topicref href="ReEnteringACallWithAllPeople.dita"
            navtitle="ReEntering a call with all people" />
    </topicref>
```

```
    <topicref href="Warnings.dita"/>
    <topicref href="http://www.comtech-serv.com/Comstar/">
    </topicref>
    <topicref href="../../ComstarPricing.pdf">
    </topicref>
    <topicref href="../GeneralTopic/Glossary.dita"/>
</map>
```

2. Add the *format* attribute to your QuickGuide.dita topic reference and set the value to "dita".

   Because the QuickGuide.dita topic reference is a DITA topic, it is unnecessary to explicitly assign the topic reference the format attribute. However, for consistency, include the format attribute for each topic reference whether it is DITA or not.

   ```
   <topicref href="QuickGuide.dita" format="DITA"></topicref>
   ```

3. Add the *format* attribute for the http://www.comtech-serv.com/Comstar/ topic reference and set the value to "html".

   Because the topic reference is an HTML web page, processing the topic through the DITA processing pipeline causes errors. Indicating that the topic reference *format* is "html" prevents processing errors because the processor doesn't try to process the target file as a DITA topic.

   ```
   <topicref href="http://www.comtech-serv.com/Comstar/"
      format="html" />
   ```

Comstaruserguide.ditamap

The following example shows what a map would look like with the *format* attribute. Most of the format values are "dita", but the example also illustrates other topic references where you must use the *format* attribute.

```
<map title="Comstar User Guide" id="Comstaruserguide">
   <topicref href="ComstarOverview.dita"
      format="dita" />
   <topicref href="QuickGuide.dita" navtitle="Quick guide"
      format="dita">
      <topicmeta>
         <author>Jennifer Linton</author>
         <author>Kylene Bruski</author>
         <publisher>Raven Printing</publisher>
         <copyright>
            <copyryear year="2006" />
            <copyrholder>Comtech Services, Inc.
            </copyrholder>
         </copyright>
         <audience audience="beginner" />
         <audience audience="intermediate" />
      </topicmeta>
```

```
</topicref>
<topicref href="AboutHold.dita"
   navtitle="Hold" format="dita" >
   <topicmeta>
      <author>John Parsens</author>
      <publisher>Comtech Services, Inc.</publisher>
      <copyright>
         <copyryear year="2006" />
         <copyrholder>Comstar Phones</copyrholder>
      </copyright>
      <audience audience="adminsitrator" />
   </topicmeta>
   <topicref href="HoldingACall.dita"
      navtitle="Putting a call on hold"
      format="dita" />
</topicref>
<topicref href="AboutTransfer.dita"
   navtitle="Transfer" format="dita" >
   <topicref href="TransferringACall.dita"
   navtitle="Transferring a call" format="dita" />
</topicref>
<topicref href="AboutForward.dita"
   navtitle="About forward" format="DITA" >
   <topicref href="ForwardingACall.dita"
   navtitle="Forwarding a call" format="dita" />
</topicref>
<topicref href="AboutConferenceCalls.dita"
   navtitle="About conference calls" format="dita">
   <topicref href="PlacingACall.dita"
      navtitle="Placing a conference call"
      format="dita" />
   <topicref href="
      LeavingAConferenceCallTemporarily.dita"
      navtitle="Leaving a conference call temporarily"
      format="dita" />
   <topicref href="ReEnteringAConferenceCall.dita"
      navtitle="Reentering a conference call"
      format="dita" />
   <topicref href="
      ConsultingPrivatelyOnTheConferenceCall.dita"
      format="dita" />
   <topicref href="ReEnteringACallWithAllPeople.dita"
      navtitle="Reentering a call with all people"
      format="dita" />
</topicref>
```

```
    <topicref href="Warnings.dita"/>
    <topicref href="http://www.comtech-serv.com/Comstar/"
       format="html" ></topicref>
    <topicref href="../../ComstarPricing.pdf"
       format="pdf" >
    </topicref>
    <topicref href="../GeneralTopic/Glossary.dita"
       format="DITA" />
</map>
```

Format attribute review questions

1. Can you reference non-DITA files using the *format* attribute?
2. What kinds of files can you reference using the *format* attribute?

LESSON 10

Scope Attribute

Use the *scope* attribute to indicate the location of your source topics relative to the DITA map. By setting this attribute, you indicate that a topic reference is a part of the immediate information set or that it points to an external topic.

In most cases, you want to set up your authoring environment so that maps point to topics in the same directory and subdirectories as the map. You should assign topic references the value of "local" to point to a file in the same directory or subdirectories. Any topics you process using this attribute value will output a file into your output directory. For any topic references you include in your map that you don't want the processor to copy to the output directory, you set the *scope* attribute to "peer". The third *scope* attribute value option is "external". Use the external value to point to topics or resources outside the immediate information set. The processor will not copy the external topic reference files to the output directory.

Local

Local topic references point to topics that are part of the immediate information set, meaning the topic reference is in the same directory or a subdirectory as the DITA map. When you set the *scope* attribute to "local", the processor builds an output file and copies the file into your output directory as part of the final deliverable. Most topic references in your DITA maps will use the local *scope* attribute. Therefore, the default value for the *scope* attribute is "local".

Peer

To reference topics that are in a larger information set but should not be individually copied to the output directory, set the *scope* attribute value to "peer". You might use "peer" if you have a central folder for boilerplate information, such as a company glossary or legal pages. The *href* value for a peer reference should be a relative path to another DITA topic depending on the map location. For a relative path in a file system, the *href* value should look like ../common/topic.dita. The ../common/ part of the path to the file tells the processor to back out of the directory where the map is located and go into the common folder to reference the topic.

Use the "peer" value when referencing a topic from a larger information set that you want to include in the navigation and linking as if it were part of your immediate information set. Keep in mind that when you assign a topic reference the "peer" value, your processor will generate an output topic but it will not copy it to the output directory. Setting the *scope* attribute value to "peer" ensures you don't create duplicate copies of the output file each time you produce your deliverable. This practice helps to keep your file system or repository uncluttered with commonly used topics and boiler plate information.

External

For any topics you reference that are outside your information set, set the topic reference *scope* attribute value to "external". In your map, any external topic reference should be an absolute URL or URI. An absolute path means you should include the full path and file name in the *href* value. By setting the *scope* to external, the topic you are referencing will open in its own content frame or application and not appear to be part of your information set.

You should not include topic references as children of an external topic reference in the map hierarchy. Normally, the processor includes links from parent topic references to children topic references in the hierarchy using the title and short description. The links cannot be added to an external topic during processing.

Figure 3.2 illustrates an example of a basic folder structure and topic files representing each of the values you might use in the *scope* attribute.

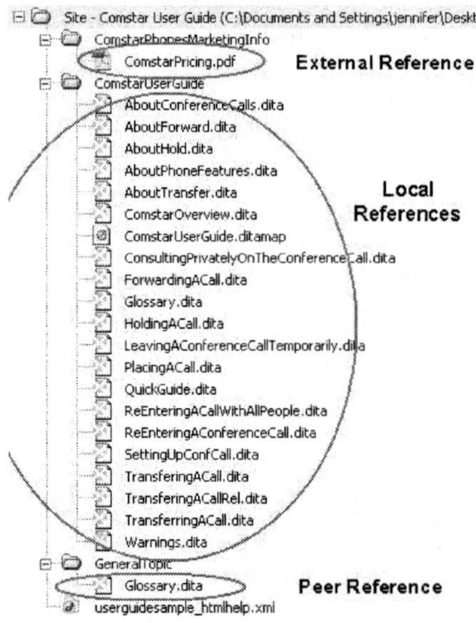

Figure 3.2 Folder structure of local, peer, and external references

Adding the *scope* attribute

This lesson explains the *scope* attribute and values you can use in your DITA map.

In this lesson, you learn to

- add the *scope* attribute to <topicref> elements
- identify when to use the *scope* attribute values "local", "peer", and "external"

1. Open your DITA map from Lesson 9: Format Attribute.

   Your DITA map at this point looks like the following example.

```
<map title="Comstar User Guide" id="Comstaruserguide">
   <topicref href="ComstarOverview.dita" format="dita" />
   <topicref href="QuickGuide.dita"
      navtitle="Quick guide" format="dita">
      <topicmeta>
         <author>Jennifer Linton</author>
         <author>Kylene Bruski</author>
         <publisher>Raven Printing</publisher>
         <copyright>
            <copyryear year="2006" />
            <copyrholder>Comtech Services, Inc.
            </copyrholder>
         </copyright>
         <audience audience="beginner" />
         <audience audience="intermediate" />
      </topicmeta>
   </topicref>
   <topicref href="AboutHold.dita" navtitle="Hold"
      format="dita" >
      <topicmeta>
         <author>John Parsens</author>
         <publisher>Comtech Services, Inc.</publisher>
         <copyright>
            <copyryear year="2006" />
            <copyrholder>Comstar Phones</copyrholder>
         </copyright>
         <audience audience="adminsitrator" />
      </topicmeta>
      <topicref href="HoldingACall.dita"
         navtitle="Putting a call on hold" format="dita" />
   </topicref>
   <topicref href="AboutTransfer.dita"
      navtitle="Transfer" format="dita" >
      <topicref href="TransferringACall.dita"
         navtitle="Transferring a call" format="dita" />
   </topicref>
   <topicref href="AboutForward.dita"
      navtitle="About forward" format="dita" >
      <topicref href="ForwardingACall.dita"
```

```
            navtitle="Forwarding a call" format="dita" />
      </topicref>
      <topicref href="AboutConferenceCalls.dita"
         navtitle="About conference calls" format="dita" >
         <topicref href="PlacingACall.dita"
            navtitle="Placing a conference call"
            format="dita" />
         <topicref href="
            LeavingAConferenceCallTemporarily.dita"
            navtitle="Leaving a conference call temporarily"
            format="dita" />
         <topicref href="ReEnteringAConferenceCall.dita"
            navtitle="Reentering a conference call"
            format="dita" />
         <topicref href="
            ConsultingPrivatelyOnTheConferenceCall.dita"
            format="dita" />
         <topicref href="ReEnteringACallWithAllPeople.dita"
            navtitle="ReEntering a call with all people"
            format="DITA" />
      </topicref>
      <topicref href="Warnings.dita"/>
      <topicref href="http://www.comtech-serv.com/Comstar/"
         format="html" ></topicref>
      <topicref href="../../ComstarPricing.pdf"
         format="pdf" ></topicref>
      <topicref href="../GeneralTopic/Glossary.dita"
         format="dita" />
   </map>
```

2. Add the *scope* attribute to your topic references.

   Because the PDF and HTML topic references are not DITA, you don't want to copy the referenced files to the output folder. Set the *scope* attribute values of the PDF and HTML topic references to "external" to ensure that the DITA processing pipeline doesn't process these topics.

   The Glossary topic reference points to a topic in a General Topics folder. The glossary in this example is a general topic that many deliverables use. Although the Glossary is a DITA topic and uses the DITA processing rules, you do not want to copy it to the output folder because you would have a duplicate copy to maintain. Set the *scope* attribute value for the Glossary topic reference to "peer".

   The following example illustrates the topic references mentioned in the step.

```
<map title="Comstar User Guide" id="Comstaruserguide">
   <topicref href="ComstarOverview.dita" format="dita"
      scope="local" />
```

```
    <topicref href="http://www.comtech-serv.com/Comstar/"
       format="html" scope="external"></topicref>
    <topicref href="../../ComstarPricing.pdf" format="pdf"
       scope="external"></topicref>
    <topicref href="../GeneralTopic/Glossary.dita"
       format="dita"  scope="peer"/>
</map>
```

3. Set the *navtitle* attribute value to a title DITA will process, and set the *locktitle* attribute value to "yes" for the http://www.comtech-serv.com/Comstar/ topic reference.

   If you don't provide the *navtitle* and *locktitle* attributes, the table of contents or navigation uses the entire value of the *href* http://www.comtech-serv.com/Comstar/ as the title.

   If you choose not to include the *navtitle* and *locktitle* attributes, you might consider excluding the HTML and PDF topic references in your table of contents or navigation by setting the *toc* attribute to "no". Processing will still include the topic in your output, but depending on your processing rules, the topics will only be accessible from their parent topic navigation.

   The example below illustrates each situation described in the step.

```
<topicref href="http://www.comtech-serv.com/Comstar/"
   scope="external" navtitle="Comtech Services:
   Comstar Phone Information" locktitle="yes"/>
<topicref href="../../ComstarPricing.pdf"
   scope="external"
   toc="no" />
```

4. Define the metadata for each topic reference in your map.

   Two attributes you can include in the metadata along with the author, publisher, and copyright are the link text and short description. The link text and short description override the information you include in your DITA topic, and they provide a navigation title and short description for any non-DITA topic references. It is especially important to define the link text and the short description for the external references. Since external topic references are not DITA XML files, they will most likely not have a title and short description. Including the link text and short description metadata for external references allows your users to search and retrieve external references more easily.

If you do not include link text for your external topic references, your processor uses the value provided in the *href* (i.e., the URL) as the text used to navigate through the topics. The link text replaces the URL in any navigation in your topics but does not replace the information in your *navtitle* attribute. Your link text provides alternative text to include in the topic to guide users as they navigate from one topic to another.

Comstaruserguide.ditamap

The following example shows a map using different *scope* attributes and values and additional information to enhance the *scope* attribute.

```
<map title="Comstar User Guide" id="Comstaruserguide">
   <topicref href="ComstarOverview.dita" format="dita"
      scope="local" />
   <topicref href="QuickGuide.dita"
      navtitle="Quick guide" format="dita"
      scope="local">
      <topicmeta>
         <author>Jennifer Linton</author>
         <author>Kylene Bruski</author>
         <publisher>Raven Printing</publisher>
         <copyright>
            <copyryear year="2006" />
            <copyrholder>Comtech Services, Inc.
            </copyrholder>
         </copyright>
         <audience audience="beginner" />
         <audience audience="intermediate" />
      </topicmeta>
   </topicref>
   <topicref href="AboutHold.dita"
      navtitle="Hold" format="dita" scope="local" >
      <topicmeta>
         <author>John Parsens</author>
         <publisher>Comtech Services, Inc.</publisher>
         <copyright>
            <copyryear year="2006" />
            <copyrholder>Comstar Phones</copyrholder>
         </copyright>
         <audience audience="adminsitrator" />
      </topicmeta>
      <topicref href="HoldingACall.dita"
         navtitle="Putting a call on hold" format="dita"
         scope="local" />
   </topicref>
   <topicref href="AboutTransfer.dita"
      navtitle="Transfer" format="dita"
      scope="local" >
```

```
    <topicref href="TransferringACall.dita"
       navtitle="Transferring a call" format="dita"
       scope="local" />
</topicref>
<topicref href="AboutForward.dita"
    navtitle="About forward" format="dita" >
    <topicref href="ForwardingACall.dita"
       navtitle="Forwarding a call" format="dita"
       scope="local" />
</topicref>
<topicref href="AboutConferenceCalls.dita"
    navtitle="About conference calls" format="dita"
    scope="local" >
    <topicref href="PlacingACall.dita"
       navtitle="Placing a conference call"
       format="dita" scope="local" />
    <topicref href="
       LeavingAConferenceCallTemporarily.dita"
    navtitle="Leaving a conference call temporarily"
       format="dita" scope="local" />
    <topicref href="ReEnteringAConferenceCall.dita"
    navtitle="Reentering a conference call"
       format="dita" scope="local" />
    <topicref href="
       ConsultingPrivatelyOnTheConferenceCall.dita"
       format="dita" scope="local" />
    <topicref href="ReEnteringACallWithAllPeople.dita"
    navtitle="Reentering a call with all people"
       format="dita" scope="local" />
</topicref>
<topicref href="Warnings.dita" scope="local" />
<topicref href="http://www.comtech-serv.com/Comstar/"
    format="html" navtitle="Comtech Services: Comstar
    Phone Information" locktitle="yes"
    scope="external">
<topicmeta>
       <linktext>Order Comstar Phones</linktext>
       <shortdesc>Online ordering for your choice
          of any Comstar phones.</shortdesc>
    </topicmeta>
</topicref>
```

```
    <topicref href="../../ComstarPricing.pdf" format="pdf"
       scope="external">
    <topicmeta>
          <linktext>Comstar Pricing List</linktext>
          <shortdesc>Comstar phones provide a variety of
             different plans you can purchase to use with
             your phone.</shortdesc>
       </topicmeta>
    </topicref>
    <topicref href="../GeneralTopic/Glossary.dita"
       format="dita"  scope="peer"/>
</map>
```

Scope attribute review questions

1. What is the purpose of the *scope* attribute?
2. What happens to the files in your browser when you set the *scope* attribute to external?
3. What is the difference between "peer" and "local"?

LESSON 11

Type Attribute

Use the *type* attribute to specify the information type of each topic reference. This attribute allows you to specify that a topic reference is a concept, task, reference, or some other kind of information.

The values you would most commonly use for the *type* attribute include "concept", "task", and "reference". Other options for *type* attribute values include "topic", "fig", "table", "li", "section", "fn" (footnote), and "other" (used for any other type of information referenced). You are more likely to assign these additional values to the *type* attribute for a cross reference <xref> element in your topics than a topic reference <topicref> element in your maps.

The purpose of the *type* attribute is to label each topic reference related-link group. When you create online DITA output, the processor automatically creates related links at the end of each topic using the collection-type and linking attribute rules. When the processor creates the related links, it uses the *type* attribute value assigned to each topic reference to group the related links for better usability. If you do not assign the *type* attribute to the topic reference, the processor groups the topic references using the root element of your information type. Figure 3.3 shows how processing would group topics into concepts, tasks, and references.

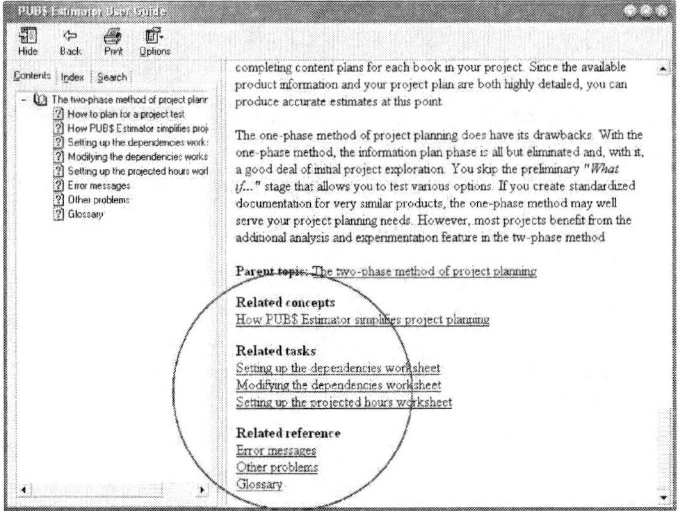

Figure 3.3 Example of related links

If you include a topic reference that you cannot categorize as a concept, task, or reference, you might assign the value "other" to the *type* attribute. Setting the *type* attribute value to "other" creates a 'Related Information' group label.

Adding the *type* attribute

This lesson explains the *type* attribute and values you can use in your DITA map.

In this lesson, you learn to

- add the *type* attribute to each <topicref> element
- assign values to the *type* attribute, such as "concept", "reference", "topic", or "other"

1. Open your DITA map from Lesson 10: Scope Attribute.

   Your DITA map at this point looks like the following example.

```
<map title="Comstar User Guide" id="Comstaruserguide">
   <topicref href="ComstarOverview.dita" format="dita"
      scope="local" />
   <topicref href="QuickGuide.dita"
      navtitle="Quick guide" format="dita" scope="local">
      <topicmeta>
         <author>Jennifer Linton</author>
         <author>Kylene Bruski</author>
         <publisher>Raven Printing</publisher>
         <copyright>
            <copyryear year="2006" />
```

```
         <copyrholder>Comtech Services, Inc.
         </copyrholder>
      </copyright>
      <audience audience="beginner" />
      <audience audience="intermediate" />
   </topicmeta>
</topicref>
<topicref href="AboutHold.dita" navtitle="Hold"
   format="dita" scope="local" >
   <topicmeta>
      <author>John Parsens</author>
      <publisher>Comtech Services, Inc.</publisher>
      <copyright>
         <copyryear year="2006" />
         <copyrholder>Comstar Phones</copyrholder>
      </copyright>
      <audience audience="adminsitrator" />
   </topicmeta>
   <topicref href="HoldingACall.dita"
      navtitle="Putting a call on hold" format="dita"
      scope="local" />
</topicref>
<topicref href="AboutTransfer.dita"
   navtitle="Transfer" format="dita" scope="local" >
   <topicref href="TransferringACall.dita"
      navtitle="Transferring a call" format="dita"
      scope="local" />
</topicref>
<topicref href="AboutForward.dita"
   navtitle="About forward" format="dita" >
   <topicref href="ForwardingACall.dita"
      navtitle="Forwarding a call" format="dita"
      scope="local" />
</topicref>
<topicref href="AboutConferenceCalls.dita"
   navtitle="About conference calls" format="dita"
   scope="local" >
   <topicref href="PlacingACall.dita"
      navtitle="Placing a conference call" format="dita"
      scope="local" />
   <topicref href="
      LeavingAConferenceCallTemporarily.dita"
      navtitle="Leaving a conference call temporarily"
      format="dita" scope="local" />
   <topicref href="ReEnteringAConferenceCall.dita"
      navtitle="Reentering a conference call"
      format="dita" scope="local" />
   <topicref href="
      ConsultingPrivatelyOnTheConferenceCall.dita"
      format="dita" scope="local" />
```

```
        <topicref href="ReEnteringACallWithAllPeople.dita"
           navtitle="ReEntering a call with all people"
           format="dita" scope="local" />
     </topicref>
     <topicref href="Warnings.dita" scope="local" />
     <topicref href="http://www.comtech-serv.com/Comstar/"
        format="html" navtitle="Comtech Services: Comstar
        Phone Information" locktitle="yes" scope="external">
        <topicmeta>
           <linktext>Order Comstar Phones</linktext>
           <shortdesc>Online ordering for your choice
              of any Comstar phones.</shortdesc>
        </topicmeta>
     </topicref>
     <topicref href="../../ComstarPricing.pdf" format="pdf"
        scope="external">
        <topicmeta>
           <linktext>Comstar Pricing List</linktext>
           <shortdesc>Comstar phones provide a variety of
              different plans you can purchase to use with
              your phone.</shortdesc>
        </topicmeta>
     </topicref>
     <topicref href="../GeneralTopic/Glossary.dita"
        format="dita"  scope="peer"/>
  </map>
```

2. Assign the *type* attribute to each topic reference.

   Assign the value for the QuickGuide.dita topic reference to "reference" because it uses the reference information type. The AboutHold.dita has the *type* value "concept" because it uses the concept information type. Assigning the two topic references a *type* provides the users knowledge about what kind of information to expect when they navigate or reference the topics. The *type* attribute provides a grouping mechanism for the related links and relationship table links so that the users can find all conceptual topics, task topics, and reference topics together in groups.

   ```
   <topicref href="QuickGuide.dita" type="reference" />
   <topicref href="AboutHold.dita" type="concept" />
   ```

Type attribute example

The example below shows parts of the map you created in the previous lessons. The markup illustrates the *type* attribute in different situations. The URL uses the *type* attribute value "topic" because it is not a task, concept, or reference; it is a general information type not assigned to a specific information type group. The Comstar Pricing List uses the value "other" to indicate that it is not an information type associated with DITA.

```
<map title="Comstar User Guide">
   <topicref href="QuickGuide.dita"
      navtitle="Quick start guide" type="reference">
   </topicref>
   <topicref href="AboutHold.dita" navtitle="Hold"
      type="concept"></topicref>
   <topicref href="HoldingACall.dita"
      navtitle="Putting a call on hold" type="task" />
   <topicref href="http://www.comtech-serv.com/Comstar/"
      type="topic"></topicref>
   <topicref href="../../ComstarPricing.pdf"
      type="other"></topicref>
</map>
```

Type attribute review questions

1. What is the purpose of the *type* attribute?
2. What are some of the common values that you would use for the *type* attribute in a topic rather than a map?

LESSON 12

Processing Attributes

In the DITA map, each topic reference can include two processing attributes, *toc* and *print*. The purpose of each of these attributes is to omit a topic reference and its child topic references from a particular output, such as print, or from the table of contents. Using these attributes is a way to process your deliverable for a particular output condition. Using the *toc* attribute customizes your table of contents or navigation for a specific audience or medium.

Both *toc* and *print* have "yes" and "no" as the possible values. For each attribute, the default value is "yes". Use these attributes if you create both an online and a print version of your deliverables. If you set the print attribute to "no" on any topic reference, you indicate that the topic should not be included in the print version of the deliverable.

In your DITA map hierarchy, you can use processing attributes on parent topic references to control the *print* and *toc* of the child topics. If you want to include one of the child topics in your table of contents or print output, you can use these same attributes to override the value it inherited from its parent topic. You should avoid using processing attributes on child topics because they make your content less likely to be reused.

This simple DITA map example illustrates the inheritance feature of the processing attributes and shows how to override the inherited values in child topics.

```
<topicref href="A.dita">
   <topicref href="B.dita" toc="no">
      <topicref href="C.dita">
         <topicref href="D.dita" toc="yes">
            <topicref href="E.dita" />
         </topicref>
      </topicref>
   </topicref>
</topicref>
```

When you create the output, the resulting table of contents will include the following topic references.

```
A.dita
D.dita
E.dita
```

B.dita is omitted because the *toc* attribute is set to "no". As a result, C.dita inherits the "no" value from B.dita. D.dita then overrides the inherited value from B.dita and sets the *toc* attribute back to "yes". E.dita inherits the value from D.dita.

Adding Processing Attributes

This lesson explains the processing attributes you can use to create custom deliverables from your DITA maps.

In this lesson, you learn to

- add the *print* attribute
- add the *toc* attribute

1. Open your DITA map from Lesson 11: Type Attribute.

   Your DITA map at this point looks like the following example.

```
<map title="Comstar User Guide" id="Comstaruserguide">
   <topicref href="ComstarOverview.dita" format="dita"
      scope="local" />
   <topicref href="QuickGuide.dita"
      navtitle="Quick guide" format="dita" scope="local"
      type="reference">
      <topicmeta>
         <author>Jennifer Linton</author>
         <author>Kylene Bruski</author>
         <publisher>Raven Printing</publisher>
         <copyright>
            <copyryear year="2006" />
            <copyrholder>Comtech Services, Inc.
            </copyrholder>
         </copyright>
         <audience audience="beginner" />
         <audience audience="intermediate" />
      </topicmeta>
   </topicref>
   <topicref href="AboutHold.dita" navtitle="Hold"
      format="dita" scope="local" type="concept">
      <topicmeta>
         <author>John Parsens</author>
         <publisher>Comtech Services, Inc.</publisher>
         <copyright>
            <copyryear year="2006" />
            <copyrholder>Comstar Phones</copyrholder>
         </copyright>
         <audience audience="adminsitrator" />
      </topicmeta>
      <topicref href="HoldingACall.dita"
         navtitle="Putting a call on hold" format="dita"
         scope="local" type="task" />
```

```
</topicref>
<topicref href="AboutTransfer.dita"
   navtitle="Transfer" format="dita" scope="local" >
   <topicref href="TransferringACall.dita"
      navtitle="Transferring a call" format="dita"
      scope="local" />
</topicref>
<topicref href="AboutForward.dita"
   navtitle="About forward" format="dita" >
   <topicref href="ForwardingACall.dita"
      navtitle="Forwarding a call" format="dita"
      scope="local" />
</topicref>
<topicref href="AboutConferenceCalls.dita"
   navtitle="About conference calls" format="dita"
   scope="local" >
   <topicref href="PlacingACall.dita"
      navtitle="Placing a conference call" format="dita"
      scope="local" />
   <topicref href="
      LeavingAConferenceCallTemporarily.dita"
      navtitle="Leaving a conference call temporarily"
      format="dita" scope="local" />
   <topicref href="ReEnteringAConferenceCall.dita"
      navtitle="Reentering a conference call"
      format="dita" scope="local" />
   <topicref href="
      ConsultingPrivatelyOnTheConferenceCall.dita"
      format="dita" scope="local" />
   <topicref href="ReEnteringACallWithAllPeople.dita"
      navtitle="ReEntering a call with all people"
      format="dita" scope="local" />
</topicref>
<topicref href="Warnings.dita" scope="local" />
<topicref href="
   http://www.comtech-serv.com/Comstar/" format="html"
   navtitle="Comtech Services: Comstar Phone
   Information" locktitle="yes" scope="external"
   type="topic">
   <topicmeta>
      <linktext>Order Comstar Phones</linktext>
      <shortdesc>Online ordering for your choice
      of any Comstar phones.</shortdesc>
   </topicmeta>
</topicref>
<topicref href="../../ComstarPricing.pdf"
   format="pdf" scope="external" type="other">
```

```
      <topicmeta>
         <linktext>Comstar Pricing List</linktext>
         <shortdesc>Comstar phones provide a variety
            of different plans you can purchase to use
            with your phone.</shortdesc>
      </topicmeta>
   </topicref>
   <topicref href="../GeneralTopic/Glossary.dita"
      format="dita"  scope="peer"/>
</map>
```

2. Add the *print* attribute to your http://www.comtech-serv.com/Comstar/ topic reference and assign a value of "no".

   Because this topic reference is an external web site, you do not want to include the web page in your PDF or print output. By setting the *print* attribute value to "no", you exclude the topic from your PDF.

```
<topicref href="http://www.comtech-serv.com/Comstar/"
   print="no">
</topicref>
```

3. Add the *toc* attribute for the Warnings.dita topic reference and set the value to "no".

   You may only want to link to your reference topics from inside the content of other topics. When you set the *toc* attribute to "no" on the Warnings.dita topic reference, you remove the hyperlink or topic reference from the hierarchical navigation and table of contents on output.

```
<topicref href="Warnings.dita" toc="no"/>
```

Comstaruserguide.ditamap

This example shows what a map looks like with the processing attributes.

```
<map title="Comstar User Guide" id="Comstaruserguide">
   <topicref href="ComstarOverview.dita" format="dita"
      scope="local" />
   <topicref href="QuickGuide.dita"
      navtitle="Quick guide" format="dita" scope="local"
      type="reference">
      <topicmeta>
         <author>Jennifer Linton</author>
         <author>Kylene Bruski</author>
         <publisher>Raven Printing</publisher>
         <copyright>
            <copyryear year="2006" />
            <copyrholder>Comtech Services, Inc.</copyrholder>
         </copyright>
```

```
            <audience audience="beginner" />
            <audience audience="intermediate" />
         </topicmeta>
      </topicref>
      <topicref href="AboutHold.dita" navtitle="Hold"
         format="dita" scope="local" type="concept">
         <topicmeta>
            <author>John Parsens</author>
            <publisher>Comtech Services, Inc.</publisher>
            <copyright>
               <copyryear year="2006" />
               <copyrholder>Comstar Phones</copyrholder>
            </copyright>
            <audience audience="adminsitrator" />
         </topicmeta>
         <topicref href="HoldingACall.dita"
            navtitle="Putting a call on hold" format="dita"
            scope="local" type="task" />
      </topicref>
      <topicref href="AboutTransfer.dita"
         navtitle="Transfer" format="dita" scope="local" >
         <topicref href="TransferringACall.dita"
            navtitle="Transferring a call" format="dita"
            scope="local" />
      </topicref>
      <topicref href="AboutForward.dita"
         navtitle="About forward" format="dita" >
         <topicref href="ForwardingACall.dita"
            navtitle="Forwarding a call" format="dita"
            scope="local" />
      </topicref>
      <topicref href="AboutConferenceCalls.dita"
         navtitle="About conference calls" format="dita"
         scope="local" >
         <topicref href="PlacingACall.dita"
            navtitle="Placing a conference call" format="dita"
            scope="local" />
         <topicref href="
            LeavingAConferenceCallTemporarily.dita"
            navtitle="Leaving a conference call temporarily"
            format="dita" scope="local" />
         <topicref href="ReEnteringAConferenceCall.dita"
            navtitle="Reentering a conference call"
            format="dita" scope="local" />
         <topicref href="
            ConsultingPrivatelyOnTheConferenceCall.dita"
            format="dita" scope="local" />
```

```
      <topicref href="ReEnteringACallWithAllPeople.dita"
        navtitle="ReEntering a call with all people"
        format="dita" scope="local" />
   </topicref>
   <topicref href="Warnings.dita" scope="local"
      toc="no" />
   <topicref href="http://www.comtech-serv.com/Comstar/"
      format="html" navtitle="Comtech Services: Comstar
      Phone Information" locktitle="yes" scope="external"
      type="topic" print="no">
      <topicmeta>
         <linktext>Order Comstar Phones</linktext>
         <shortdesc>Online ordering for your choice
            of any Comstar phones.</shortdesc>
      </topicmeta>
   </topicref>
   <topicref href="../../ComstarPricing.pdf" format="pdf"
      scope="external" type="other">
      <topicmeta>
         <linktext>Comstar Pricing List</linktext>
         <shortdesc>Comstar phones provide a variety of
            different plans you can purchase to use with
            your phone.</shortdesc>
      </topicmeta>
   </topicref>
   <topicref href="../GeneralTopic/Glossary.dita"
      format="dita" scope="peer"/>
</map>
```

Processing attribute review questions

1. What is the purpose of the processing attributes?
2. What are the processing attributes?

SECTION F

Understanding Map Linking

By creating parent and child relationships among the topic references in the hierarchy, you can easily create links between topics. When you nest one topic reference inside another, the nested topic reference is considered a child. When you process the output, you can automatically insert the titles and short descriptions of the child topics into the parent topic and hyperlink them for ease of navigation. The child topics, in turn, may include links back to the parent. You can control the direction of these links using the *linking* attribute.

Figure 3.4 shows how a parent topic has links automatically inserted for each child topic.

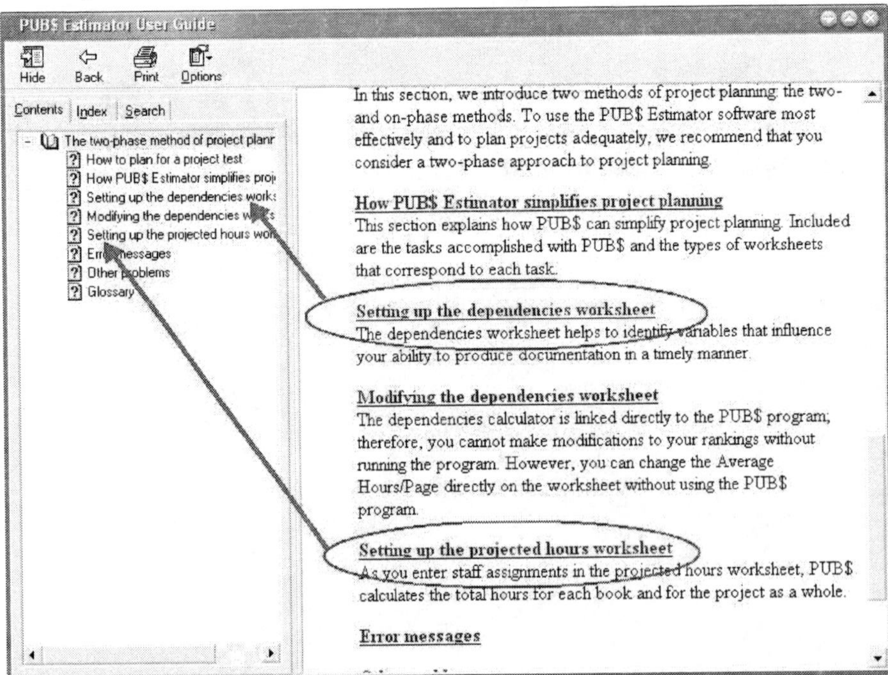

Figure 3.4 Parent topic linking

Figure 3.5 shows how each child topic automatically inserts a link back to the parent topic during processing.

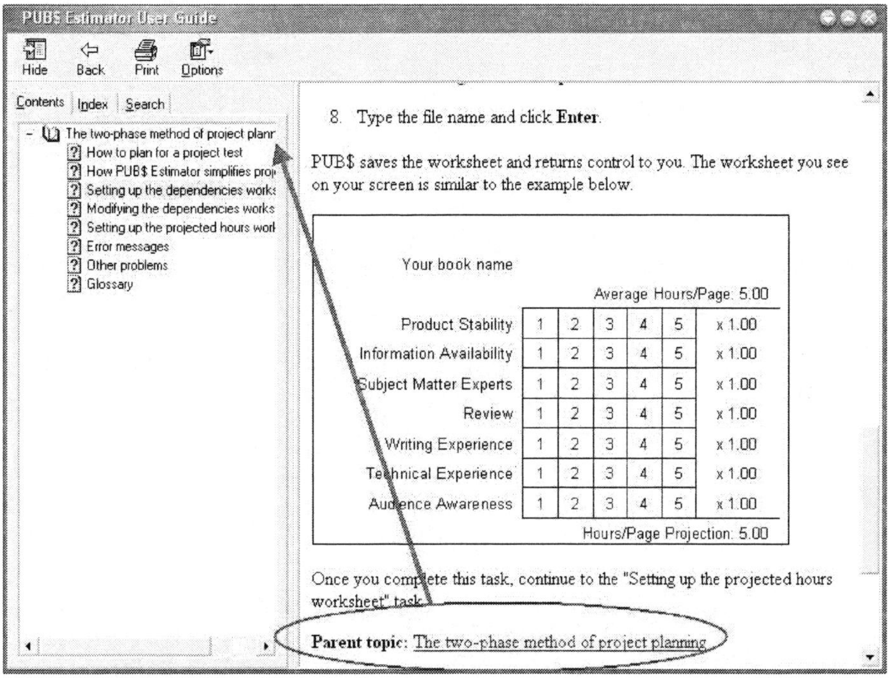

Figure 3.5 Child topic linking

You can also control linking with the *collection-type* attribute to display topic references in a family or sequence. Family linking is normally formatted to place links to related topics at the end of the topic content. Sequential linking puts the links in a numbered list, suggesting an order in which the user might read the topics.

There are several advantages to maintaining links in your map rather than in the topics. You can

- quickly add, remove, and change topic reference links. Editing groups, hierarchies, and tables is more efficient and effective than managing all the individual links in each topic.
- ensure accuracy and usability in one place, making it easier to identify patterns and holes in your information set.
- create customized information sets for specific audiences or product documentation. If you reuse information in a different context, you simply apply a different map without changing the topic content.

- continuously update topic content and easily recreate a map using additional or changed topics. You can incorporate links to topics throughout your information set without editing or hard coding the related-links content of each topic.

LESSON 13

Collection-type Attribute

Use the *collection-type* attribute to create relationships among topics that are closely associated. The purpose of the *collection-type* attribute is to group topics automatically, creating links in each topic for easier navigation and referencing. The two *collection-type* attribute values you will most likely use are "family" and "sequence". The other possible values you use more rarely are "unordered" and "choice". You can use any of the collection-type values to override a previously set collection-type. You will most likely use the unordered and choice values to override the family and sequence values.

A basic DITA map creates relationships by nesting topic references to create a hierarchy. These relationships are known as parent and child relationships. However, in some cases, you want to create a relationship between topics that are not related through the parent and child pair. Sibling topics are often written about similar subject matter, but the sibling topics generally do not have links to one another. The purpose of a *collection-type* attribute is to provide siblings with linking capabilities.

Collection-type family

Use the "family" value *collection-type* attribute if you have a set of closely related concepts, tasks, or references that you want to link together. These topics may all be siblings in a particular part of a map. If these sibling topic references are all at the second level of the hierarchy and have the same parent topic, you can assign a *collection-type* attribute to the parent topic that will link each of the sibling topics to one another.

For example, Figure 3.6 contains a collection-type attribute set to family on the primary topic reference which includes all other topic references. As a result, all of the topic references under this parent are considered siblings.

```
<?xml version="1.0" encoding="utf-8"?>
<!DOCTYPE map PUBLIC "-//OASIS//DTD DITA Map//EN"
 "../../../dtd/map.dtd">
<map title="Comstar User Guide" id="Comstaruserguide">
<topicref href="ComstarOverview.dita" collection-type="family">
        <topicref href="QuickGuide.dita"></topicref>
        <topicref href="AboutHold.dita" >
                <topicref href="HoldingACall.dita" />
        </topicref>
        <topicref href="AboutTransfer.dita" >
                <topicref href="TransferringACall.dita"/>
        </topicref>
        <topicref href="AboutForward.dita" >
                <topicref href="ForwardingACall.dita"/>
        </topicref>
        <topicref href="AboutConferenceCalls.dita"  collection-type="sequence" >
                <topicref href="PlacingACall.dita"/>
                <topicref href="LeavingAConferenceCallTemporarily.dita" />
                <topicref href="ReEnteringAConferenceCall.dita"  />
                <topicref href="ConsultingPrivatelyOnTheConferenceCall.dita" />
                <topicref href="ReEnteringACallWithAllPeople.dita"/>
        </topicref>
        <topicref href="AboutPhoneFeatures.dita"  />
        <topicref href="Warnings.dita"  />
</topicref>
</map>
```

Figure 3.6 Collection-type family map

Figure 3.7 illustrates links in each topic to each of the other topics according to the categories concept, task, or reference.

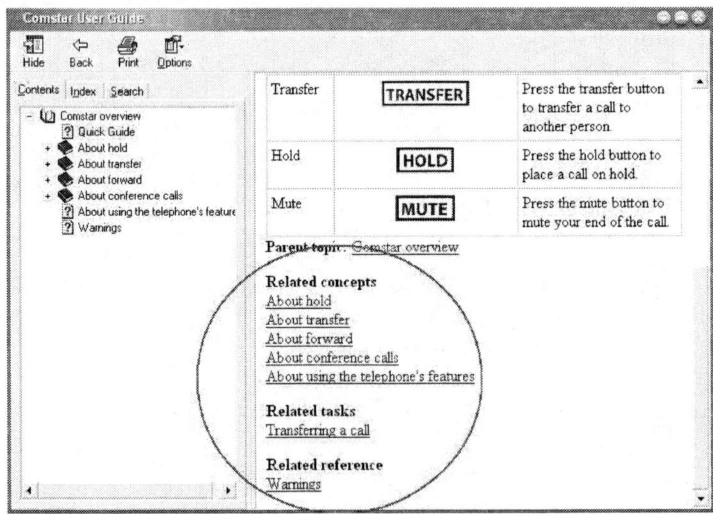

Figure 3.7 Collection-type family result

Collection-type sequence

Use the "sequence" value on the *collection-type* attribute to order your topics. You might use a "sequence" collection-type to present a series of tasks that the user must perform in a particular order or a series of concepts that the user must read in a particular order. The greatest benefit of the "sequence" attribute value is that you can place the topic references in different positions in the map, but when you create the deliverable, the processor will generate the sequence in the order you included the topic references in the map. You don't have to number anything. Using the "sequence" collection type also creates links in each topic to the next and previous topics in the sequence. It allows you to indicate pre-requisite and post requirement relationships automatically.

In Figure 3.8, all of the topics under the Conference call section are in a "sequence" collection-type.

```
<?xml version="1.0" encoding="utf-8"?>
<!DOCTYPE map PUBLIC "-//OASIS//DTD DITA Map//EN"
"../../../dtd/map.dtd">
<map title="Comstar User Guide" id="Comstaruserguide">
<topicref href="ComstarOverview.dita" collection-type="family">
      <topicref href="QuickGuide.dita"></topicref>
      <topicref href="AboutHold.dita" >
            <topicref href="HoldingACall.dita"  />
      </topicref>
      <topicref href="AboutTransfer.dita" >
            <topicref href="TransferringACall.dita"/>
      </topicref>
      <topicref href="AboutForward.dita" >
            <topicref href="ForwardingACall.dita"/>
      </topicref>
      <topicref href="AboutConferenceCalls.dita"  collection-type="sequence" >
            <topicref href="PlacingACall.dita"/>
            <topicref href="LeavingAConferenceCallTemporarily.dita" />
            <topicref href="ReEnteringAConferenceCall.dita"  />
            <topicref href="ConsultingPrivatelyOnTheConferenceCall.dita" />
            <topicref href="ReEnteringACallWithAllPeople.dita"/>
      </topicref>
      <topicref href="AboutPhoneFeatures.dita"  />
      <topicref href="Warnings.dita"  />
</topicref>
</map>
```

Figure 3.8 Collection-type sequence map

As a result, the processor generates normal links in the parent topic, AboutConferenceCalls.dita, except that the links are placed in the same order as the topic references in the map. In each of the sibling topics, the links at the end of the topic indicate the pre-requisite and post requirement topics, as illustrated in Figures 3.9 and 3.10.

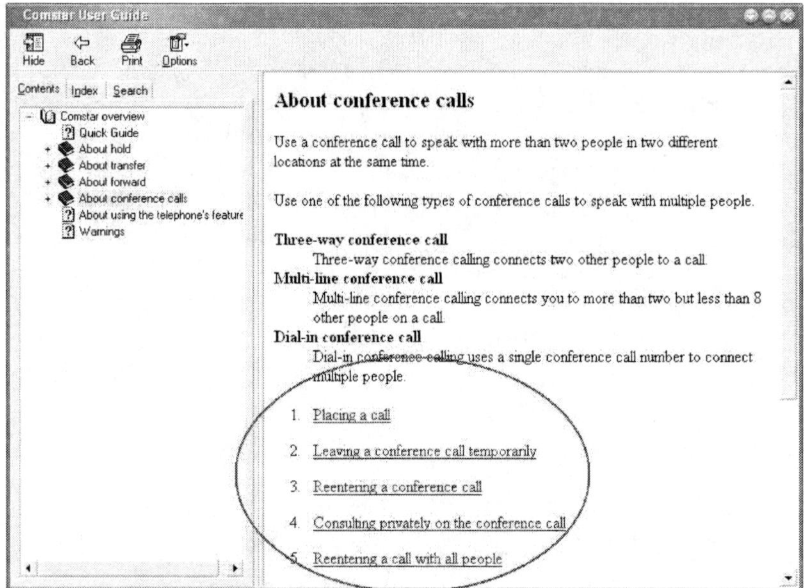

Figure 3.9 Collection-type sequence result for the parent topic

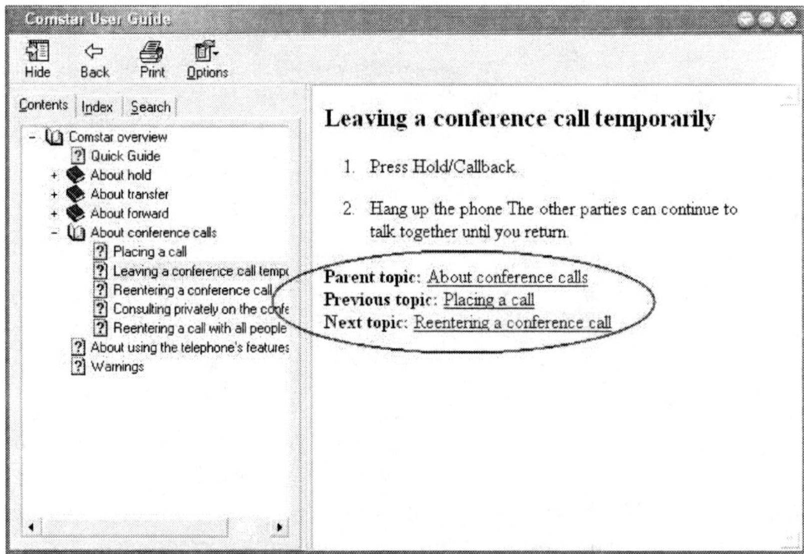

Figure 3.10 Collection-type sequence result for the child topic

Adding the *collection-type* attribute

This lesson explains the *collection-type* attribute and values you can use in your DITA map.

In this lesson, you learn to

- add the *collection-type* attribute to <topicref> elements
- add *collection-type* values, such as "family" and "sequence"

1. Start a new map and add a topic reference to your map that points to the ComstarOverview.dita topic.

   In this lesson, you start a new DITA map for easier learning. However, you can apply the same properties in your Comstaruserguide.ditamap example from previous lessons.

```
<?xml version="1.0" encoding="utf-8"?>
<!DOCTYPE map PUBLIC "-//OASIS//DTD DITA Map//EN"
   "map.dtd">
<map title="Comstar Phone Guide" id="ComstaruserguideV2">
   <topicref href="ComstarOverview.dita"></topicref>
</map>
```

2. Add five topic references as child topics of the ComstarOverview.dita topic reference.

   Point the new topic references to QuickGuide.dita, AboutHold.dita, AboutTransfer.dita, AboutForward.dita, and AboutConferenceCalls.dita topics respectively. If you are using the map from previous lessons, the five topic references shown below are the five second-level topic references in the hierarchy.

```
<map>
   <topicref href="ComstarOverview.dita">
      <topicref href="QuickGuide.dita" />
      <topicref href="AboutHold.dita" />
      <topicref href="AboutTransfer.dita" />
      <topicref href="AboutForward.dita" />
      <topicref href="AboutConferenceCalls.dita" />
   </topicref>
</map>
```

3. Add a *collection-type* attribute to the ComstarOverview.dita topic reference and assign the value "family".

   By default, the child topics of ComstarOverview.dita are unrelated except through their common parent. By adding the *collection-type* attribute with the value "family" on the parent topic reference, you create linking relationships among the sibling topic references. The sibling topic references in the example below are the five topic references you added in step 2.

```
<map>
   <topicref href="ComstarOverview.dita"
      collection-type="family">
      <topicref href="QuickGuide.dita" />
      <topicref href="AboutHold.dita" />
      <topicref href="AboutTransfer.dita" />
      <topicref href="AboutForward.dita" />
      <topicref href="AboutConferenceCalls.dita" />
   </topicref>
</map>
```

4. Create five more topic references as children of the AboutConferenceCalls.dita topic.

   Point the topic references to the following topics.

   - PlacingACall.dita
   - LeavingAConferenceCallTemporarily.dita
   - ReEnteringAConferenceCall.dita
   - ConsultingPrivatelyOnTheConferenceCall.dita
   - ReEnteringACallWithAllPeople.dita

   If you are using the map from previous lessons, the topic references in the example below are the children of the AboutConferenceCalls.dita topic already. The children of the AboutConferenceCalls.dita topic are third-level topic references.

```
<map>
   <topicref href="ComstarOverview.dita"
      collection-type="family">
      <topicref href="QuickGuide.dita" />
      <topicref href="AboutHold.dita" />
      <topicref href="AboutTransfer.dita" />
      <topicref href="AboutForward.dita" />
      <topicref href="AboutConferenceCalls.dita">
         <topicref href="PlacingACall.dita"/>
         <topicref href="
            LeavingAConferenceCallTemporarily.dita"/>
         <topicref href="
            ReEnteringAConferenceCall.dita"/>
         <topicref href="
            ConsultingPrivatelyOnTheConferenceCall.dita"/>
         <topicref
            href="ReEnteringACallWithAllPeople.dita"/>
   </topicref>
   </topicref>
</map>
```

For the next part of the lesson, imagine that you want the end user of the phone to do the tasks for conference calls in the order you included them in the map.

5. Add a *collection-type* attribute assigned to "sequence" to the AboutConferenceCalls.dita topic reference.

```
<map>
   <topicref href="ComstarOverview.dita"
      collection-type="family">
       <topicref href="QuickGuide.dita" />
       <topicref href="AboutHold.dita" />
       <topicref href="AboutTransfer.dita" />
       <topicref href="AboutForward.dita" />
       <topicref href="AboutConferenceCalls.dita"
          collection-type="sequence">
          <topicref href="PlacingACall.dita"/>
          <topicref href="
             LeavingAConferenceCallTemporarily.dita"/>
          <topicref href="
             ReEnteringAConferenceCall.dita"/>
          <topicref href="
             ConsultingPrivatelyOnTheConferenceCall.dita"/>
          <topicref href="
             ReEnteringACallWithAllPeople.dita"/>
       </topicref>
   </topicref>
</map>
```

Comstaruserguide.ditamap Version 2

The example below shows a topic reference hierarchy three levels deep, with two collection types, "sequence" and "family". Setting the *collection-type* attribute to "family" on the first topic reference results in each of the second-level topics linking to one another. The About Conference Calls overrides the inherited *collection-type* value and creates a sequential relationship for the sibling topics in the conference call section. The topics referenced after the conference call section are still part of the "family" *collection-type* group since they share a common parent. Your output includes Warnings.dita, http://www.comtech-serv.com/Comstar/, and ComstarPricing.pdf as related topics.

Note: If you want to create a collection-type for a group of topics that do not have a common parent, you can add a topic group container element <topicgroup> and assign the *collection-type* attribute without disrupting the desired hierarchy. See the *DITA Language Specification* for further information about the <topicgroup> element.

```
<map title="Comstar User Guide">
<topicref href="ComstarOverview.dita"
      navtitle="Comstar Overview"
      collection-type="family">
   <topicref href="QuickGuide.dita"
      navtitle="Quick guide"></topicref>
   <topicref href="AboutHold.dita" navtitle="Hold" >
      <topicref href="HoldingACall.dita"
         navtitle="Placing a call on hold" />
   </topicref>
   <topicref href="AboutTransfer.dita"
      navtitle="Transfer">
      <topicref href="TransferringACall.dita"
         navtitle="Transferring a call" />
   </topicref>
   <topicref href="AboutForward.dita" navtitle="Forward">
      <topicref href="ForwardingACall.dita"
         navtitle="Forwarding a call" />
   </topicref>
   <topicref href="AboutConferenceCalls.dita"
      navtitle="About conference calls"
      collection-type="sequence">
      <topicref href="PlacingACall.dita"
         navtitle="Placing a conference a call" />
      <topicref href="
         LeavingAConferenceCallTemporarily.dita"
         navtitle="Leaving a conference call temporarily" />
      <topicref href="ReEnteringAConferenceCall.dita"
         navtitle="Reentering a conference call" />
      <topicref href="
         ConsultingPrivatelyOnTheConferenceCall.dita"
         navtitle="Consulting with one party on the
         conference call privately" />
      <topicref href="ReEnteringACallWithAllPeople.dita"
         navtitle="ReEntering a call with all people" />
   </topicref>
   <topicref href="Warnings.dita" />
   <topicref href="http://www.comtech-serv.com/Comstar/">
   </topicref>
   <topicref href="../../ComstarPricing.pdf" >
   </topicref>
   <topicref href="Glossary.dita" />
</topicref>
</map>
```

Collection-type review questions

1. What is the purpose of the *collection-type* attribute?
2. What are the two main *collection-type* values?
3. What is the difference between the "family" and "sequence" values?
4. What values can you override with the *collection-type* attribute?
5. What happens to your output when you use a "sequence" collection type?

LESSON 14

Linking Attribute

Use the *linking* attribute to control the direction of the links between your topic references. In some situations, you will want to apply dynamic *linking* during your processing, but you don't necessarily want all the topics to link to each other.

For example, if you create a glossary, each topic reference should point to the glossary, but you will not want the glossary to point back to every other topic reference. You will want to control the direction of the links. Applying a *linking* attribute to your topic references provides unidirectional *linking*.

The *linking* attribute has four possible values. The two most commonly used values are "targetonly" and "sourceonly". The other two values are "normal" and "none".

Targetonly

When you set the *linking* attribute to "targetonly", topics can link to the topic reference with the "targetonly" *linking* attribute. However, the topic reference with the "targetonly" *linking* attribute will not link to any other topics. For example, add the "targetonly" *linking* attribute when a topic relates to many other topics in the map. When a topic links to many related topics, the processor generates links to all the related topics in the single topic. Too many links in a topic may overwhelm the reader.

Consider a case in which you have a common reference topic, such as a specification table that supports multiple tasks. The reference specification table should not include links back to all the tasks it supports. If you apply the *linking* attribute to the specification table topic and set the value to "targetonly", the processor will create hyperlinks from the tasks to the reference topic, but the reference topic will not include hyperlinks back to the task topics.

Sourceonly

When you set the *linking* attribute to "sourceonly", the topic reference with the "sourceonly" value can only link to other topics. Other topics cannot be linked to the topic marked as "sourceonly". "Sourceonly" *linking* is similar to "targetonly" *linking*.

For example, you may have several reference topics that you want to set to targetonly so that they do not link to a task topic. It is easier to assign the task topic "sourceonly" and omit the *linking* attribute from the reference topics. This way, you don't have to maintain all of the "targetonly" *linking* attributes on the reference topics in the map.

Normal
The default for the *linking* attribute is "normal". Normal means that a topic can be linked to or from any other topic. If you apply a "targetonly" or "sourceonly" *linking* attribute to a topic reference, all child topics in the map inherit this value. In some situations, you may need to override a "sourceonly" or "targetonly" link by assigning the "normal" *linking* attribute.

None
When you set the *linking* attribute to "none" for a topic reference, the topic can neither be linked from nor link to any other topic. You may set the *linking* attribute to "none" for several reasons:

- You don't want the topic to affect your *linking* for print output.
- You want to craft the links yourself in the DITA source files.
- You have a topic that you want to include for the table of contents or introductory boilerplate information, but you don't want it to link to other topics.

Setting the *linking* attribute to "none" doesn't mean that you won't be able to access the topic from the table of contents, site map, or navigation; it just means that the topic will not have links in it to other topics and other topics will not link to it. For example, you may have a central content reuse topic file to hold your *conref* (content reference) items. If you don't want to include the central file in your navigation, you can set the *linking* attribute to "none".

Adding the *linking* attribute

This lesson explains the *linking* attribute and values you can use in your DITA map.

In this lesson, you learn to

- add the *linking* attribute to <topicref> elements
- add the values "sourceonly", "targetonly", and "normal" to your *linking* attribute

1. Open the DITA map you created in Lesson 13: Collection-type Attribute.

   At this point your DITA map looks like the following example.

```
<map title="Comstar User Guide">
   <topicref href="ComstarOverview.dita"
      navtitle="Comstar Overview" collection-type="family">
   <topicref href="QuickGuide.dita"
      navtitle="Quick guide"></topicref>
   <topicref href="AboutHold.dita" navtitle="Hold" >
      <topicref href="HoldingACall.dita"
         navtitle="Placing a call on hold" />
   </topicref>
   <topicref href="AboutTransfer.dita"
      navtitle="Transfer">
      <topicref href="TransferringACall.dita"
      navtitle="Transferring a call" />
   </topicref>
   <topicref href="AboutForward.dita" navtitle="Forward">
      <topicref href="ForwardingACall.dita"
         navtitle="Forwarding a call" />
   </topicref>
   <topicref href="AboutConferenceCalls.dita"
      navtitle="About conference calls"
      collection-type="sequence">
      <topicref href="PlacingACall.dita"
         navtitle="Placing a conference a call" />
      <topicref href="
         LeavingAConferenceCallTemporarily.dita"
         navtitle="Leaving a conference call temporarily" />
      <topicref href="ReEnteringAConferenceCall.dita"
         navtitle="Reentering a conference call" />
      <topicref href="
        ConsultingPrivatelyOnTheConferenceCall.dita"
        navtitle="Consulting with one party on the
        conference call privately" />
      <topicref href="ReEnteringACallWithAllPeople.dita"
         navtitle="Reentering a call with all people" />
   </topicref>
   <topicref  href="Warnings.dita" />
   <topicref href="http://www.comtech-serv.com/Comstar/">
   </topicref>
   <topicref href="../../ComstarPricing.pdf" >
   </topicref>
   <topicref href="Glossary.dita" />
   </topicref>
</map>
```

2. Add a *linking* attribute to the QuickGuide.dita topic reference, and set the value to "sourceonly".

   Setting the QuickGuide.dita topic reference to "sourceonly" means the topic output contains links to other topics, but other topics cannot link to it.

```
<topicref href="AboutHold.dita"
   linking="sourceonly" />
```

3. Set the *linking* attribute for the HoldingACall.dita topic reference to "normal".

   Setting the topic reference to "normal" *linking* disables the inherited "sourceonly" linking from the AboutHold.dita topic reference.

```
<topicref href="AboutHold.dita" linking="sourceonly">
   <topicref href="HoldingACall.dita"
      linking="normal" />
</topicref>
```

Figure 3.11 illustrates a scenario for linking multiple topics in a DITA map. Following the example is the map markup needed to create the linking.

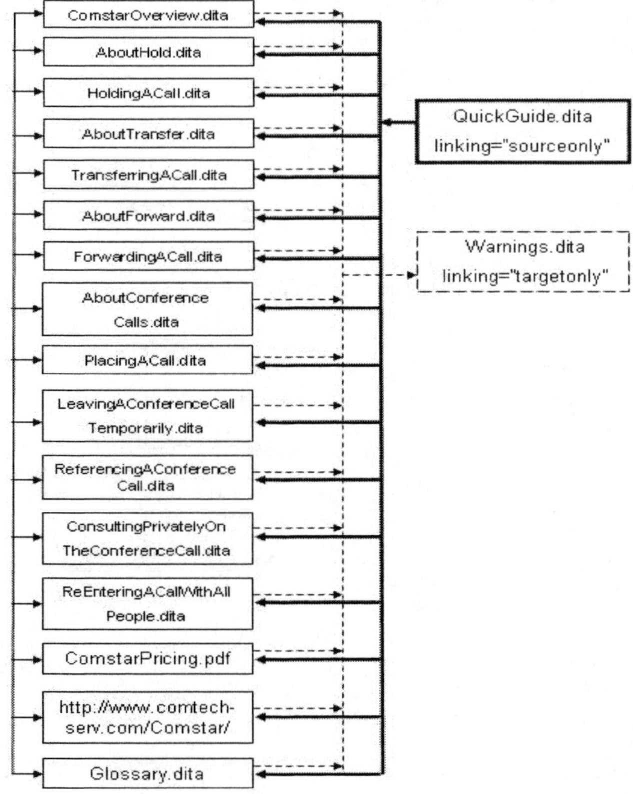

Figure 3.11 Linking visual representation

The following example shows the code used to produce the Comstar User Guide map.

```
<map title="Comstar User Guide">
<topicref href="ComstarOverview.dita"
   navtitle="Comstar Overview" collection-type="family"
   linking="normal">
   <topicref href="QuickGuide.dita"
      navtitle="Quick guide" linking="sourceonly">
   </topicref>
   <topicref href="AboutHold.dita"
      navtitle="About hold" linking="normal">
      <topicref href="HoldingACall.dita"
         navtitle="Holding a call" />
   </topicref>
   <topicref href="AboutTransfer.dita"
      navtitle="About transfer">
      <topicref href="TransferringACall.dita"
      navtitle="Transferring a call" />
   </topicref>
   <topicref href="AboutForward.dita"
      navtitle="About forward" >
      <topicref href="ForwardingACall.dita"
         navtitle="Forwarding a call" />
   </topicref>
   <topicref href="AboutConferenceCalls.dita"
      navtitle="About conference calls"
      collection-type="sequence">
      <topicref href="PlacingACall.dita"
         navtitle="Placing a conference a call" />
      <topicref href="
         LeavingAConferenceCallTemporarily.dita"
         navtitle="Leaving a conference call
         temporarily" />
      <topicref href="ReEnteringAConferenceCall.dita"
         navtitle="Reentering a conference call" />
      <topicref href="
         ConsultingPrivatelyOnTheConferenceCall.dita"
         navtitle="Consulting with one party on the
         conference call privately" />
      <topicref href="
         ReEnteringACallWithAllPeople.dita"
         navtitle="ReEntering a call with all people" />
   </topicref>
   <topicref href="Warnings.dita"
      linking="targetonly" />
   <topicref href="http://www.comtech-serv.com/Comstar/">
   </topicref>
```

```
        <topicref href="../../ComstarPricing.pdf">
        </topicref>
        <topicref href="Glossary.dita" />
    </topicref>
    </map>
```

Linking attribute review questions

1. What is the purpose of the *linking* attribute?
2. What are the possible values you can use in a *linking* attribute?
3. What attributes produce one-way links?
4. What is the default *linking* attribute?
5. What happens when you set the *linking* attribute to "none"?

SECTION G

Understanding Relationship Tables

DITA relationship tables free you from the burden of creating and maintaining links in your topics or in your maps.

Users are often frustrated when they find task information that has no supporting concept information or tasks that refer to reference data that is in another book or set of information that they don't have. By creating a relationship table, you can identify and correct relationship problems in your information set.

Using a relationship table to plan your topics helps you find information gaps that need to be filled. For example, you may find a task that is accurate and complete, but your users lack the background information they need to complete the task. You may also discover topics that don't seem to fit with the rest of the topics. For example, you may have concept topics that were added by product developers but add little to the user's understanding. If you choose to pursue a minimalist agenda, you will remove unnecessary topics from your information set.

Relationship tables enable you to create a well-defined, systematic linking structure for your topics and modify that structure in response to user needs. For example, you could use a relationship table to define an entire web site or help system by defining all the links to connect your topics without ever having to hardcode them. Hyperlinks hardcoded from topic to topic are usually hard to maintain and often break whenever you move or delete the target topic. If you maximize the features provided with relationship tables, you can create links for your topics without ever having to verify every hyperlink to make sure it works correctly for each release of your information.

DITA relationship tables, a feature exclusive to the DITA model, helps you create dynamic and complete information sets. Using a set of topic references to build a table, you can easily link from concepts to tasks and back again, link reference information to multiple tasks, and link task information to supporting information needed to complete the task.

LESSON 15

Relationship Tables

In this lesson, you learn how relationship tables define the relationships or links among topics in a DITA map.

Relationship tables are created using a complex table of rows and columns to define links. Each column in the table groups similar information type together, such as concept, task and reference. Each row in the table represents a relationship, which is generally rendered as a link, and each cell lists participants in the relationship. Each topic reference in a cell links to the topic references in the other cells in the same row.

Because relationship tables render as hyperlinks, you may not use relationship tables to create PDFs. You can create a stylesheet to include lists of related topics and create hyperlinks in your PDF, but adding related links in your PDF is not usual.

To build a simple relationship table, consider linking three topics: simpleconcept.dita, simpletask.dita, and simplereference.dita. The relationship table will look like the one in Figure 3.12.

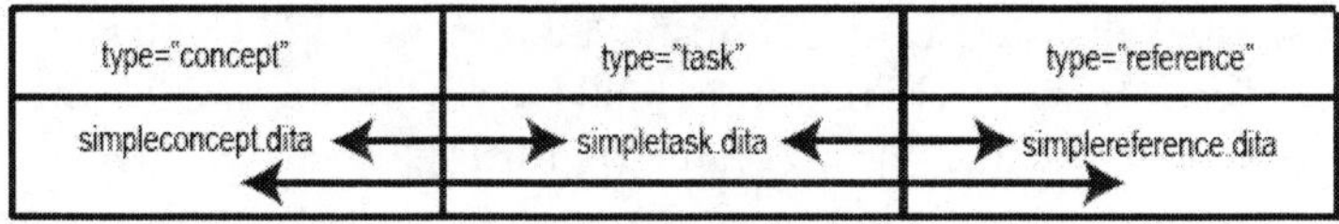

Figure 3.12 Simple relationship table

In practice, relationship tables are more complex than this simple example. When creating a more complex relationship table, you must consider the following guidelines:

- Each row in the table represents a separate set of relationships and links.
- No relationships exist between the rows in a table.
- Topic references are not needed in every cell in a row.
- Each cell can contain multiple topic references.
- Topic references can be repeated in multiple rows.

In the complex relationship table in Figure 3.13, each arrow represents a link that is created between topics. Upon rendering, each link created in the table is placed at the end of each topic .

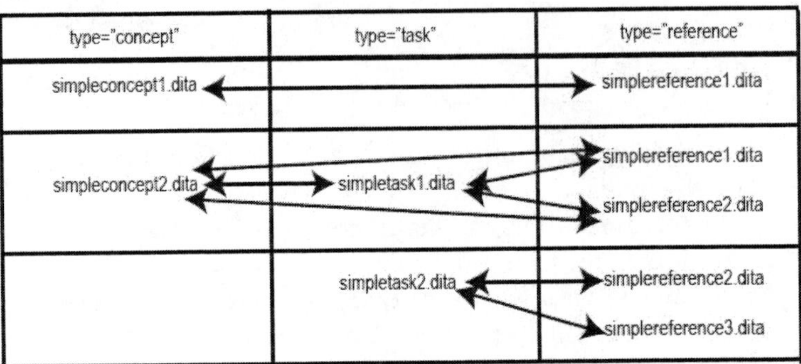

Figure 3.13 Complex relationship table

In a relationship table, topic references in a cell are often not linked together. However, there are instances when they should be linked. Applying the *collection-type* attribute in the <topicgroup> element allows you to link topic references inside a cell.

The *collection-type* attribute is added to give additional functionality to related topics. The *collection-type* attribute only affects the relationships among topic in a cell. The *collection-type* attribute does not affect relationships across cells. The most common *collection-type* value used in a relationship table is "family". If you have a set of closely related concepts or tasks that need links or relationships, other than a parent/child relationship, use the "family" value for the *collection-type* attribute. For example, in the table in Figure 3.14, the simplereference1.dita and simplereference2.dita are related using the collection-type="family".

Use the *linking* attribute to create one-way links in a relationship table. The *linking* attribute values are "sourceonly" and "targetonly". The "sourceonly" value creates a link in the source topic to the target topic. The target topic will not contain a link back to the source topic. For example, the simpletask1.dita *linking* attribute value is set to "sourceonly". Therefore, the link to simplereference1.dita and simplereference2.dita appears only in the simpletask1.dita. The simplereference1.dita and simplereference2.dita do not contain a link back to the simpletask1.dita. These links do not affect the linking between simplereference1.dita and simplereference2.dita. The "targetonly" value creates a link in the target topic to the source topic, which means that the source topic will not contain a link to the target topic.

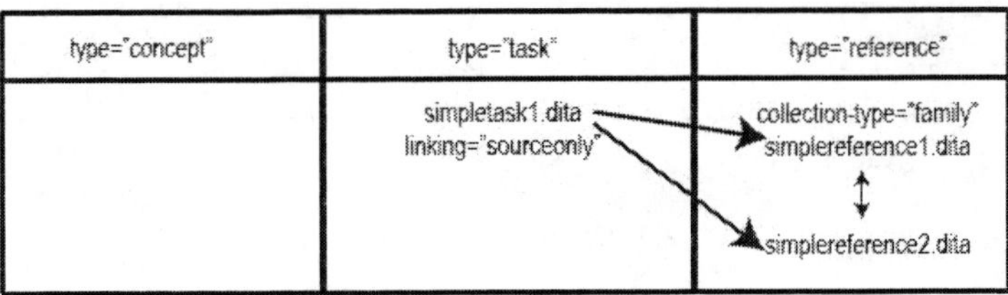

Figure 3.14 Collection-type linking in relationship table

Creating a relationship table

This lesson explains how to build a relationship table in your DITA map.

In this lesson, you learn to

- add the required elements needed to build a relationship table, such as <reltable>, <relrow>, and <relcell>
- add optional elements to enhance your relationship table, such as <relheader>, <relcolspec>, and the relcolspec *type* attribute
- add topic references to your relationship table using the <topicref> element
- control linking capabilities in your relationship table using the *linking* attribute

1. Open your Comstaruserguide.ditamap you created in Lesson 8: DITA Map Structure.

   At this point, your DITA map looks like the following example.

   ```
   <?xml version="1.0" encoding="utf-8"?>
   <!DOCTYPE map PUBLIC "-//OASIS//DTD DITA Map//EN"
      "map.dtd">
   <map title="Comstar Phone Guide" id="Comstaruserguide">
      <topicref href="ComstarOverview.dita" />
      <topicref href="QuickGuide.dita" />
      <topicref href="AboutHold.dita" navtitle="Hold"
         locktitle="yes"></topicref>
   </map>
   ```

2. Add <reltable> element start and end tags between the <map> element start and end tags after your last topic reference.

   The relationship table element is the container for the entire relationship table.

   ```
   <reltable>
   </reltable>
   ```

3. Add <relheader> element start and end tags between the <reltable> element start and end tags.

   The relationship table head is the container element for the column heads in the relationship table.

```
<reltable>
   <relheader>
   </relheader>
</reltable>
```

4. Add three empty <relcolspec> elements between the <relheader> element start and end tags.

   In a relationship table, the relationship column specification groups your topics using the type attribute. The relationship column specification allows you to add a column head to each of your columns.

```
<reltable>
   <relheader>
      <relcolspec/>
      <relcolspec/>
      <relcolspec/>
   </relheader>
</reltable>
```

5. Add the *type* attribute to each <relcolspec> element, and set the attribute values to "concept", "task", and "reference" respectively.

   The value for the *type* attribute is a common group name for the topics you include in the column. Each topic reference in a column cell must fit into the type category. You can use concept, task, and reference as your values, but you can also specify your own values.

```
<reltable>
   <relheader>
      <relcolspec type="concept"/>
      <relcolspec type="task"/>
      <relcolspec type="reference"/>
   </relheader>
</reltable>
```

6. Add <relrow> element start and end tags after the <relheader> element end tag.

   Each relationship row <relrow> start and end tag creates a new row in the relationship table. Each row defines a new set of linking relationships among the topic references in that row.

```
<reltable>
   <relheader>
      <relcolspec type="concept"/>
      <relcolspec type="task"/>
      <relcolspec type="reference"/>
   </relheader>
   <relrow></relrow>
   <relrow></relrow>
   <relrow></relrow>
   <relrow></relrow>
   <relrow></relrow>
   <relrow></relrow>
   <relrow></relrow>
   <relrow></relrow>
</reltable>
```

7. Add <relcell> element start and end tags between the <relrow> element start and end tags.

   The number of <relcell> elements in each <relrow> element must match the number of <relcolspec> elements used in the <relhead>.

```
<relrow>
   <relcell>
   </relcell>
   <relcell>
   </relcell>
   <relcell>
   </relcell>
</relrow>
```

8. Add <topicref> element start and end tags between the <relcell> element start and end tags.

   The processing does not generate a link among the topics located in the same relationship cell. Instead, processing generates links among all topics located in the other cells in the same row. You can add multiple topic references to each cell.

```
<relrow>
   <relcell>
      <topicref/>
   </relcell>
   <relcell>
      <topicref/>
   </relcell>
   <relcell>
   </relcell>
</relrow>
```

9. Add the *href* attribute to point to the file location of the target topics for every <topicref> element.

   Use the *href* attribute in the topic reference container to point to the topic you want to add to the relationship cell.

```
<relrow>
   <relcell>
      <topicref href="AboutHold.dita"/>
   </relcell>
   <relcell>
      <topicref href="HoldingACall.dita"/>
   </relcell>
   <relcell>
   </relcell>
</relrow>
```

10. Add <topicgroup> element start and end tags surrounding the topic references in the <relcell> element.

    The topic group element groups topics located in the same cell to create relationships among topics of the same information type.

```
<relrow>
   <relcell>
   </relcell>
   <relcell>
   </relcell>
   <relcell>
      <topicgroup>
         <topicref href="QuickGuide.dita"/>
         <topicref href="Warnings.dita"/>
      </topicgroup>
   </relcell>
</relrow>
```

11. Add the *collection-type* attribute and set the value to "family" in the <topicgroup> element.

    Adding the *collection-type* attribute to the topic group element container allows you to create links among topics in the same relationship cell.

```
<relrow>
   <relcell>
   </relcell>
   <relcell>
   </relcell>
   <relcell>
```

```
        <topicgroup collection-type="family">
            <topicref href="QuickGuide.dita"/>
            <topicref href="Warnings.dita"/>
        </topicgroup>
    </relcell>
</relrow>
```

12. Add the *linking* attribute to the Glossary.dita <topicref> element container and set the value to "targetonly".

    By assigning the Glossary.dita topic reference the *linking* value of "targetonly", you can create a one-way link during processing. For more information about the *linking* attribute, see Lesson 14: Linking Attribute.

```
<relrow>
    <relcell>
        <topicref href="AboutHold.dita"/>
        <topicref href="AboutTransfer.dita"/>
        <topicref href="AboutForward.dita"/>
        <topicref href="AboutConferenceCalls.dita"/>
    </relcell>
    <relcell>
        <topicref href="HoldingACall.dita"/>
        <topicref href="TransferringACall.dita"/>
        <topicref href="ForwardingACall.dita"/>
        <topicref href="PlacingACall.dita"/>
        <topicref href="ReEnteringAConferenceCall.dita"/>
        <topicref href="
            ConsultingPrivatelyOnTheConferenceCall.dita"/>
        <topicref href="
            ReEnteringACallWithAllPeople.dita"/>
    </relcell>
    <relcell>
        <topicref href="Glossary.dita"
            linking="targetonly"/>
    </relcell>
</relrow>
```

13. Save the Comstaruserguide.ditamap.

    Figure 3.15 shows a more complex relationship table.

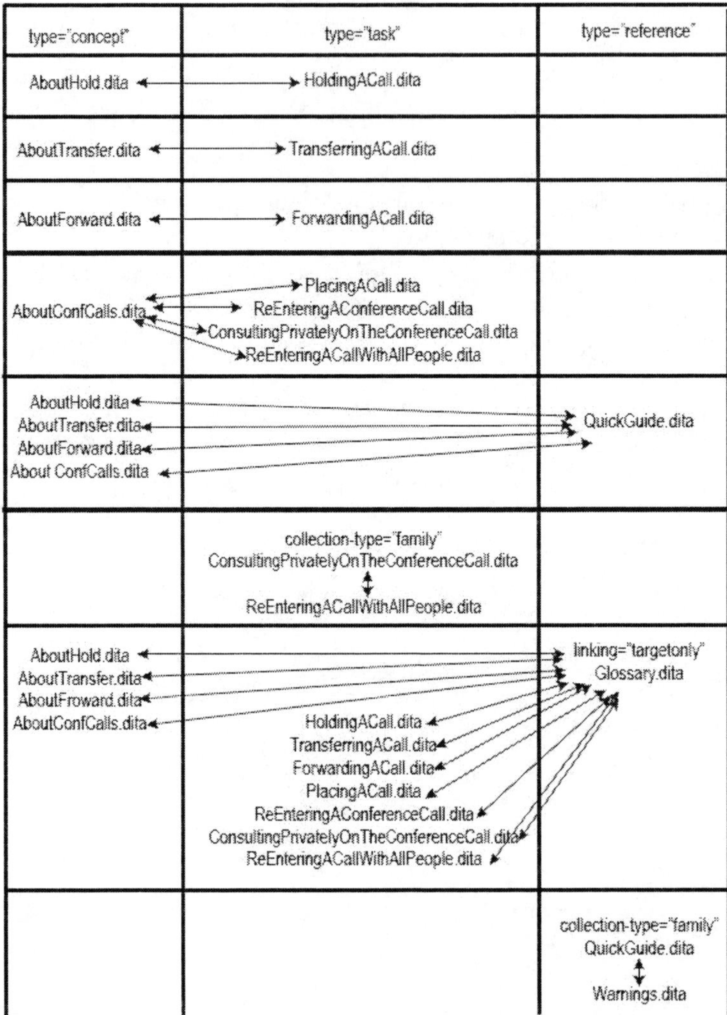

Figure 3.15 Comstar user guide relationship table

Below is the markup for the relationship table illustrated above.

```
<?xml version="1.0" encoding="utf-8"?>
<!DOCTYPE map PUBLIC "-//OASIS//DTD DITA Map//EN"
   "map.dtd">
<map title="ComstarUserGuide" id="Sample" toc="yes">
   <reltable>
      <relheader>
         <relcolspec type="concept"/>
```

```
    <relcolspec type="task"/>
    <relcolspec type="reference"/>
 </relheader>
 <relrow>
    <relcell>
       <topicref href="AboutHold.dita"/>
    </relcell>
    <relcell>
       <topicref href="HoldingACall.dita"/>
    </relcell>
    <relcell>
    </relcell>
 </relrow>
 <relrow>
    <relcell>
       <topicref href="AboutTransfer.dita"/>
    </relcell>
    <relcell>
       <topicref href="TransferringACall.dita"/>
    </relcell>
    <relcell>
    </relcell>
 </relrow>
 <relrow>
    <relcell>
       <topicref href="AboutForward.dita"/>
    </relcell>
    <relcell>
       <topicref href="ForwardingACall.dita"/>
    </relcell>
    <relcell>
    </relcell>
 </relrow>
 <relrow>
    <relcell>
       <topicref href="AboutConferenceCalls.dita"/>
    </relcell>
    <relcell>
       <topicref href="PlacingACall.dita"/>
       <topicref href="
          ReEnteringAConferenceCall.dita"/>
       <topicref href="
         ConsultingPrivatelyOnTheConferenceCall.dita"/>
       <topicref href="
          ReEnteringACallWithAllPeople.dita"/>
    </relcell>
    <relcell>
    </relcell>
 </relrow>
 <relrow>
```

```
      <relcell>
         <topicref href="AboutHold.dita"/>
         <topicref href="AboutTransfer.dita"/>
         <topicref href="AboutForward.dita"/>
         <topicref href="AboutConfCalls.dita"/>
      </relcell>
      <relcell>
      </relcell>
      <relcell>
         <topicref href="QuickGuide.dita"/>
      </relcell>
   </relrow>
   <relrow>
      <relcell>
      </relcell>
      <relcell>
         <topicgroup collection-type="family">
            <topicref href="ConsultingPrivatelyOn
               TheConferenceCall.dita"/>
            <topicref href="
               ReEnteringACallWithAllPeople.dita"/>
         </topicgroup>
      </relcell>
      <relcell>
      </relcell>
   </relrow>
   <relrow>
      <relcell>
         <topicref href="AboutHold.dita"/>
         <topicref href="AboutTransfer.dita"/>
         <topicref href="AboutForward.dita"/>
         <topicref href="AboutConferenceCalls.dita"/>
      </relcell>
      <relcell>
         <topicref href="HoldingACall.dita"/>
         <topicref href="TransferringACall.dita"/>
         <topicref href="ForwardingACall.dita"/>
         <topicref href="PlacingACall.dita"/>
         <topicref href="
            ReEnteringAConferenceCall.dita"/>
         <topicref href="ConsultingPrivatelyOnThe
            ConferenceCall.dita"/>
         <topicref href="
            ReEnteringACallWithAllPeople.dita"/>
      </relcell>
      <relcell>
         <topicref href="Glossary.dita"
            linking="targetonly"/>
      </relcell>
   </relrow>
```

```
        <relrow>
            <relcell>
            </relcell>
            <relcell>
            </relcell>
            <relcell>
                <topicgroup collection-type="family">
                    <topicref href="QuickGuide.dita"/>
                    <topicref href="Warnings.dita"/>
                </topicgroup>
            </relcell>
        </relrow>
    </reltable>
</map>
```

Relationship table elements

Relationship table elements are found only in maps. The relationship table elements are listed here in the order that you may use them when creating a relationship table in a map.

<reltable> relationship table

Use the <reltable> element to create the framework for the relationship table. Add all elements in the relationship table between the beginning and ending tags of the <reltable> element.

<relheader> relationship head

Use the <relheader> element as the container for defining the column categories. The relationship header element is the first element in the relationship table and can only occur once.

<relcolspec> relationship column specification

Use the <relcolspec> element to define the category for each column in the relationship table. At least two <relcolspec> elements must be added to the relationship table. The categories in the <relcolspec> element are defined using the *type* attribute. You may use three <relcolspec> elements to categorize your topics as concept, task, and reference. You do not have to use task, concept, and reference as the values for the *type* attribute. However, all topic references in the column of the relationship table must fit into the category specified in the relationship column <relcolspec> element.

<relrow> relationship table row

Use the <relrow> element to define the relationships among the topics in each relationship row. Each <relrow> element defines a new set of relationships. More than one <relrow> element can be added to each relationship table.

<relcell> relationship table cell

Use the <relcell> element to define the topic references. These topic references will be linked during processing. By default, the topic references in the same relationship cell are not linked. However, you can add the <topicgroup> element and *type* attribute to create a relationship among the topic references in a relationship cell. For more information about the <topicgroup> and *type* attribute, see Lesson 8: DITA Map Structure.

The number of <relcell> elements has to match the number and order of <relcolspec> elements. Most authors set up their relationship tables with three columns and three relationship cells for each relationship row. They usually put the columns in the order of concept, task, and reference. If you do not want to include a topic reference for one of the cells in a row, you must still add <relcell>start and end tags. Do not include topic references in the <relcell>.

Relationship table review questions

1. What is the purpose of a relationship table?
2. Why do you need multiple rows in a relationship table?
3. Can a topic reference appear in more than one row?
4. What attribute do you use to create relationships between topic references within the same cell?
5. What are the recommended column heads of a relationship table?

Content Reuse

DITA offers many opportunities for information developers to use content in multiple contexts, reducing duplication of effort and improving productivity. DITA topics, carefully typed according to the content they contain, provide the foundation for content reuse. You can reference the same topics in multiple DITA maps to build content assemblies that meet the needs of many user communities. You can use the same topic more than once in a DITA map, reducing maintenance costs and improving accuracy and consistency. But topic reuse is not the only mechanism that DITA provides to optimize your information-development resources.

Using the DITA model, you can select individual content units, defined by XML elements, for multiple use. Information developers can identify warnings, cautions, legal statements, repetitive sets of steps, and other content snippets that are common to many deliverables. By storing this content separately and referencing it through the DITA *conref* (content reference) mechanism, you can easily and consistently maintain common content.

By developing topics and smaller content units once, you

- improve accuracy and consistency. When you use the same topic in different contexts, you reduce redundancy and eliminate inaccuracies. When authors follow DITA-supported authoring guidelines to develop topics, you reduce the time required for editing and rewriting. DITA topic standards, whether you use the core information types or create your own specializations, enforce business rules for content development and ensure consistency. When topics are consistently written, they are more amenable to be used in multiple contexts.

- increase efficiency. When one information developer authors a topic so that it can be used effectively in multiple contexts, you increase the productivity of all your information developers. When information developers create format-free XML source content, you reduce the time required for final production in multiple media. You also increase the productivity of reviewers and approvers. You reduce the confusion that results when reviewers repeatedly comment on the same content in different contexts, often recommending contradictory changes.
- streamline processes. By authoring topics that are free of proprietary format code, you reduce the time required for final production in multiple media. Deliverables in PDF, HTML, help systems, and other formats can be produced quickly and easily. Styling is consistent because style sheets are added at the end of the production cycle rather than during authoring.
- simplify updating. Topic-based authoring and content reuse helps information developers provide updated and improved content to customers as soon as it is approved.

SECTION H

Understanding DITA Content Reuse

In DITA, there are several ways to define and output content to multiple deliverables.

Five primary methods of reusing content are to

- reference the same topic more than once in a DITA map. For example, you may have a topic that includes instructions for performing a basic task that is used repeatedly in several task sequences. In the DITA map, you point to the same topic in your repository every time you want it to appear in the final deliverable.
- reference the same topic in more than one map. For example, you might use a task in two deliverables created for different audiences or for different versions of a product. Reusing topics in multiple maps is the core reuse functionality of DITA.
- output deliverables to different media types using the same map. For example, you can use a single map to produce both an online or a print deliverable simply by applying different stylesheets to the XML content.
- reference smaller parts of topics in multiple contexts and deliverables. For example, you can use a common warning statement in different task topics. You use the *conref* attribute to reuse the same warning element wherever it is needed.
- use maps in other maps. For example, you can build groups of topics that usually work together into component-, chapter-, or section-level maps. Then, you can reuse these maps by reference in the large map you develop to organize your books, help systems, or web sites. You use the *conref* attribute to reuse smaller maps in larger maps.

Through content reuse mechanisms, you can minimize the number of topics you create, maintain, and manage, and you can deliver more consistent and accurate content to your user community.

Topic reuse

The topic is the fundamental reusable structure in DITA. DITA topics should be carefully designed so that they can be read and used independently of other topics. The lessons in the Topic section of this guide demonstrate how to structure your content so that it follows the standard DITA information typing architecture.

If you plan at the beginning of your projects both the topics you need to author and the maps that outline your final deliverables, you will maximize your reuse potential. Many DITA information architects advocate setting up your DITA maps, outlining the topics needed in each map, and identifying topics that will appear in multiple maps before assigning topic authoring to your team.

Map reuse

To create your deliverables, you must reference your topics in DITA maps. When you process the maps, you specify the stylesheets to use to format the content. In the DITA toolkit, you can choose to apply an HTML stylesheet for web delivery, a PDF stylesheet for print delivery, or stylesheets that produce Microsoft, Java, or Eclipse help. You can also use a single map to output deliverables to different audiences or for different products. To develop maps that produce multiple deliverables, see Lesson 20: .ditaval File.

Content unit reuse

To reuse smaller parts of topics, you need to identify those content units that are better managed as individual elements than as content units embedded in topics. Many information architects create a file of content units that are used in multiple contexts and deliverables. Admonishments, legal information, or other frequently repeated information are all candidates for your collection of common-to-all content units.

Use a DITA base topic to store your reusable content units. A DITA base topic can contain task, concept, and reference root elements in the same topic, but it is neither a task, concept, nor reference. The DITA base topic allows you to gather content units that you may want to use in tasks, concepts, and references. Each reusable content unit is still a standalone element, but all the content units are stored in a single file so that they can be more easily maintained. For example, if you have a warning that will be used frequently, create a concept root element in a DITA base topic and assign it a unique identifier. We suggest using the concept topic because warnings, which are defined by an attribute on the note element, are easiest to add to a concept. To reuse the warning, you reference the warning content unit with a *conref* attribute in the appropriate position in a task.

Component reuse

You use the conref attribute to insert component-level maps into larger maps. Component-level maps reference a group of related topics that are most often used together rather than separately. You can also define smaller maps as chapters or sections of books.

LESSON 16

Conref Attribute

The purpose of the *conref* attribute is to reference a content unit that you want to reuse.

When you use the *conref* attribute in a topic or map, you point to another content unit in another topic or map. When you use a *conref*, the referenced text appears in place in your topic, as if you copied it. However, when you update the element that is *conref*-ed, it changes everywhere it is referenced.

To use the *conref* attribute, you must ensure that the content unit you reference will work in the new context. For example, you cannot *conref* a <note> element in a <p> element. You must reference the information in a note element <note> only in another <note> container element.

The *conref* attribute uses unique *id* attributes to identify the content unit you want to reuse. If you want to use a <note> from one concept in another topic, you must add an *id* attribute to the original note.

Use the *conref* attribute as you would the *href* attribute. You point to the topic and *id* of the content unit you want to reuse. The value of the *conref* attribute must be an absolute or relative path to the topic and *id* of the source content. For example, if you are working in a file system and you want to reference a step from one topic to another, the typical format for the *conref* attribute is systempathandfilname.dita # topicid / elementid .

You can also use a *conref* attribute in a DITA map by adding a *conref* attribute on any topic reference. In this way, you can reference smaller maps in larger maps by pointing to the first topic reference in the smaller map. If you want to use the *conref* attribute in a map, the syntax you use for a *conref* attribute value on a <topicref> element is systempathandfilname.dita # topicrefid.

If you use a content management system, you need only point to the unique *id* of the content unit you want to *conref*. You do not use file paths and file names in the *conref* attribute value because content management systems usually do not use file paths.

Because you can assign an *id* attribute to any element in DITA, you can reuse any piece of information.

Adding the *conref* attribute to a topic

This lesson explains the *conref* attribute in a DITA topic.

In this lesson, you learn to

- create a chunk of information you wish to reuse
- add a *conref* attribute
- reference a tip from an central content reuse file

1. Copy the example of a DITA base topic below and save it as DITAreuse.dita.

   For more information about creating a DITA base topic, see the *DITA Language Specification*. As you can see in this example, each smaller topic in the DITA base topic is assigned an*id*, and each element in the topic has an *id*. You can assign an *id* to any DITA element.

```
<?xml version="1.0" encoding="UTF-8"?>
<!DOCTYPE DITA PUBLIC "-//OASIS//DTD DITA Composite//EN"
   "../../DITAbase.dtd">
<dita>
   <concept id="reusableconcept">
      <title></title>
      <conbody>
         <p>
            <note id="hangupphone" type="tip">You must
               hang up your phone before you can make
               another call.</note>
         </p>
      </conbody>
   </concept>
   <task id="reusabletask">
      <title></title>
      <taskbody>
         <steps>
            <step id="turnonphone"><cmd>Turn on your
               phone.</cmd></step>
         </steps>
      </taskbody>
   </task>
</dita>
```

2. Open the TransferringaCall.dita file you created in Lesson 2: Task Information Type.

   At this point, your TransferringACall.dita topic looks like the example below.

```
<?xml version="1.0" encoding="utf-8"?>
<!DOCTYPE task PUBLIC "-//OASIS//DTD DITA Task//EN"
   "task.dtd">
<task id="TransferringACall" xml:lang="en-us">
```

```
<title>Transferring a call</title>
<shortdesc>When you transfer a call to another
   person in your office, you have two ways of handling
   the transfer.</shortdesc>
<prolog>
   <author>John Smith
   </author>
</prolog>
<taskbody>
   <context>
      <p> When you transfer the call without speaking
         to the person, it is an unannounced transfer.
         When you speak to the person receiving the
         transferred call, it is an announced transfer.
      </p>
   </context>
   <steps>
      <step>
         <cmd>Press the transfer button.</cmd>
      </step>
      <step>
         <cmd>Dial the number.</cmd>
         <info>Dial the number manually or using your
            pre-defined speed dial keys. </info>
      </step>
      <step>
         <cmd>Transfer the call.</cmd>
         <choicetable>
            <chhead>
               <choptionhd>Type of Announcement
               </choptionhd>
               <chdeschd>Steps to complete
                  announcement</chdeschd>
            </chhead>
            <chrow>
               <choption>Announce a call transfer
               </choption>
               <chdesc>
                  <ol>
                     <li>Speak to the person</li>
                     <li>Hang up the phone</li>
                  </ol>
               </chdesc>
            </chrow>
            <chrow>
               <choption>Transfer a call unannounced
               </choption>
               <chdesc>
```

```
                    <ul>
                       <li>Hang up the phone</li>
                    </ul>
                 </chdesc>
              </chrow>
           </choicetable>
           <info>
              <note>If you announce a call and the
                 person refuses the transfer, do not hang
                 up the phone. Press the transfer button
                 again to retrieve the call on your phone
                 station.</note>
           </info>
        </step>
     </steps>
     <result>The call is transferred.</result>
  </taskbody>
     <related-links>
        <link href="AboutTransfer.dita" scope="local"/>
     </related-links>
</task>
```

3. Add <postreq> element start and end tags after the <result> element container.

   In your <postreq> container, add a <note> container.

```
  </steps>
  <result>The call is transferred.</result>
  <postreq><note></note></postreq>
</taskbody>
```

4. Add a *conref* attribute on the note element and assign the value.

   The value for the *conref* attribute should point to the file and *id* in the DITAreuse.dita topic. When adding a *conref* attribute, the value must have the following syntax, systempathandfilname.dita # topicid / elementid . In this example, assume the DITAreuse.dita topic is in the same folder as TransferringACall.dita. Notice that you don't include any content in the start and end tags for the note. If you did include content in this container, the content in the *conref* would overwrite any content you include in the referencing topic.

```
  </steps>
  <result>The call is transferred.</result>
  <postreq>
     <note conref="DITAreuse.dita#reusableconcept/
        hangupphone"></note>
  </postreq>
</taskbody>
```

5. Save the TransferringACall.dita topic.

   When processing the TransferringACall.dita topic, the content reused from the DITAbase.dita topic replaces the <note> element container referencing the reusable note.

TransferringACall.dita with a *conref*

Your topic should now look like the example below.

```
<?xml version="1.0" encoding="utf-8"?>
<!DOCTYPE task PUBLIC "-//OASIS//DTD DITA Task//EN"
   "../../dtd/task.dtd">
<task id="TransferringACall" xml:lang="en-us">
   <title>Transferring a call</title>
   <shortdesc>When you transfer a call to another person
      in your office, you have two ways of handling the
      transfer.</shortdesc>
   <prolog>
      <author>John Smith</author>
   </prolog>
   <taskbody>
      <context>
         <p> When you transfer the call without speaking
            to the person, it is an unannounced transfer.
            When you speak to the person receiving the
            transferred call, it is an announced transfer.
         </p>
      </context>
      <steps>
         <step>
            <cmd>Press the transfer button.</cmd>
         </step>
         <step>
            <cmd>Dial the number.</cmd>
            <info>Dial the number manually or using your
               pre-defined speed dial keys. </info>
         </step>
         <step>
            <cmd>Transfer the call.</cmd>
            <choicetable>
               <chhead>
                  <choptionhd>Type of Announcement
                  </choptionhd>
                  <chdeschd>Steps to complete announcement
                  </chdeschd>
               </chhead>
               <chrow>
                  <choption>Announce a call transfer
                  </choption>
                  <chdesc>
```

```
                    <ol>
                        <li>Speak to the person</li>
                        <li>Hang up the phone</li>
                    </ol>
                </chdesc>
            </chrow>
            <chrow>
                <choption>Transfer a call unannounced
                </choption>
                <chdesc>
                    <ul>
                        <li>Hang up the phone</li>
                    </ul>
                </chdesc>
            </chrow>
        </choicetable>
        <info>
            <note>If you announce a call and the
               person refuses the transfer, do not hang
               up the phone. Press the transfer button
               again to retrieve the call on your phone
               station.</note>
        </info>
    </step>
  </steps>
  <result>The call is transferred.</result>
  <postreq>
     <note conref="DITAreuse.dita#reusableconcept/
        hangupphone"></note>
  </postreq>
 </taskbody>
</task>
```

Adding the *conref* attribute to a map

This lesson explains how to add the *conref* attribute to a DITA map.

In this lesson, you learn to

- add a *conref* attribute to a topic reference
- reference a group of topics from one map into another map

To create this guide, we used the *conref* attribute in the master map. We authored the information needed for smaller section maps first and then combined all of the maps into a master book map. Because the examples used until this point have been simple, we chose to show the example of building this guide.

1. Copy the ContentReuse.ditamap example shown below.

   The example map below encompasses the Content Reuse section of this guide. By creating a Content Reuse map, you can print out only the Content Reuse section for review and editing during the information-development workflow. Providing your editors and reviewers with parts of your book before you finish the final deliverable allows you to simultaneously author and edit/review.

Notice the *ID* on the first topic reference. You use the *ID* to reference the group of topic references in your master map. You must ensure that the first topic reference surrounds the other topic references because the *conref* only reuses the topic reference and its children.

```
<?xml version="1.0" encoding="utf-8"?>
<!DOCTYPE map PUBLIC "-//OASIS//DTD DITA Map//EN"
   "../../../dtd/map.dtd">
<map title="Content Reuse">
   <topicref href="ContentReuse.dita"
      id="contentreusechapter" navtitle="Content reuse">
      <topicref href="AddingConrefAttributeTopic.dita"
         navtitle="
         Adding the conref attribute to a topic" />
      <topicref href="AddingConrefAttributeMap.dita"
         navtitle="Adding the conref attribute to a map" />
   </topicref>
</map>
```

2. Copy the DITAUserGuide.ditamap shown below to begin a new DITA map.

```
<?xml version="1.0" encoding="utf-8"?>
<!DOCTYPE map PUBLIC "-//OASIS//DTD DITA Map//EN"
   "../../dtd/map.dtd">
<map id="DITAuserguide" rev="Version 1.0"
   title="DITA User Guide">
</map>
```

3. Add a <topicref> element start and end tag between your map start and end tags.

```
<?xml version="1.0" encoding="utf-8"?>
<!DOCTYPE map PUBLIC "-//OASIS//DTD DITA Map//EN"
   "../../dtd/map.dtd">
<map id="DITAuserguide" rev="Version 1.0"
   title="DITA User Guide">
   <topicref></topicref>
</map>
```

4. Add a *conref* attribute and assign the value to point to the file and *id* of the first topic reference in the Content Reuse map.

   In this topic reference, you do not include the *href* attribute but only the *conref* attribute.

When adding a *conref* attribute to a map, the value must have the following syntax, systempathandfilname.dita # topicrefid. In the example below, assume that the ContentReuse.ditamap file is in a ContentReuse folder in the same location as the DITAUserGuide.ditamap file.

```
<?xml version="1.0" encoding="utf-8"?>
<!DOCTYPE map PUBLIC "-//OASIS//DTD DITA Map//EN"
   "../../dtd/map.dtd">
<map id="DITAuserguide" rev="Version 1.0" title="DITA
   User Guide">
   <topicref conref="ContentReuse/
      ContentReuse.ditamap#contentreusechapter">
   </topicref>
</map>
```

5. Save the DITAUserGuide.ditamap file

During processing, the topics you reference from the ContentReuse.ditamap appear as part of your final deliverable.

You may notice a reference to the *navref* or *mapref* attribute in the DITA Language Specification. Note that neither attribute is currently supported in the DITA Open Toolkit. If you choose to use these attributes, you must customize your processing to use them correctly.

If you try to *conref* a content unit that contains another *conref*, you may have errors processing your deliverable with the DITA Open Toolkit. For example, if your map *conrefs* another map, which in turn*conrefs* a third smaller map, it is possible that the *conrefs* will not work correctly. It is important to test your processing if you choose to nest *conrefs*.

6. Repeat the steps above for each map you want to reuse in the master map.

DITA User Guide ditamap

The following example illustrates the final deliverable map for this guide, which uses multiple *conrefs* in the map.

```
<?xml version="1.0" encoding="utf-8"?>
<!DOCTYPE map PUBLIC "-//OASIS//DTD DITA Map//EN"
   "../../dtd/map.dtd">
<map  id="DITAuserguide" rev="Version 1.0"
   title="DITA User Guide">
   <topicref href="Introduction/AboutDITA.dita"
      navtitle="About this Guide" />
   <topicref conref="Introduction/
      Introduction.ditamap#introductionchapter" />
   <topicref conref="Topics/
      Topics.ditamap#topicchapter" />
   <topicref conref="Maps/
      DITAmaps.ditamap#DITAmapschapter" />
```

```
    <topicref conref="ContentReuse/
       ContentReuse.ditamap#contentreusechapter" />
    <topicref conref="Specialization/
       specialization_map.ditamap#specializationchapter"/>
    <topicref conref="Processing/
       Processing_map.ditamap#processingchapter" />
    <topicref conref="Appendix/
       Appendix.ditamap#appendix"></topicref>
</map>
```

Conref attribute review questions

1. What is the purpose of the *conref* element?
2. What is the benefit of using the *conref* element?
3. Can you use a sub-step as a step using the *conref* element?
4. What is the syntax for the *conref* attribute value used in a map, and how is it different from the syntax used in the *conref* attribute value for a topic?

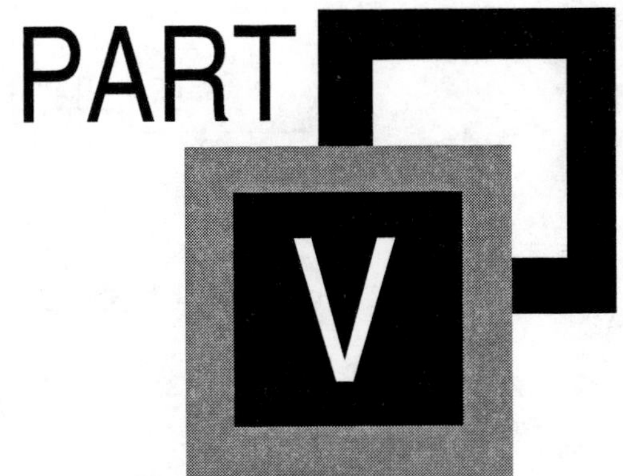

PART V Specialization

Specialization is the process of using existing structures from the base DITA structure to create new information types that better fit your needs. DITA specialization drastically simplifies the process of creating new DTDs for your unique information types. An average DTD may contain hundreds of lines of code. A DITA specialized DTD can be written with just a few lines of code because a specialized DITA DTD inherits all the structure, semantics, and processing rules of the parent DITA DTD.

The basic DITA package consists of six DTDs: map.dtd, topic.dtd, concept.dtd, task.dtd, reference.dtd, and ditabase.dtd. The task.dtd, concept.dtd, and reference.dtd describe the core DITA information types. Each of these information types, as you have learned earlier, have the same basic structure (title, short description, prolog, body, and related links). The source of this basic structure is the topic.dtd. Each of the core information type DTDs are specializations on the basic structure of the topic.dtd, as illustrated in Figure 5.1.

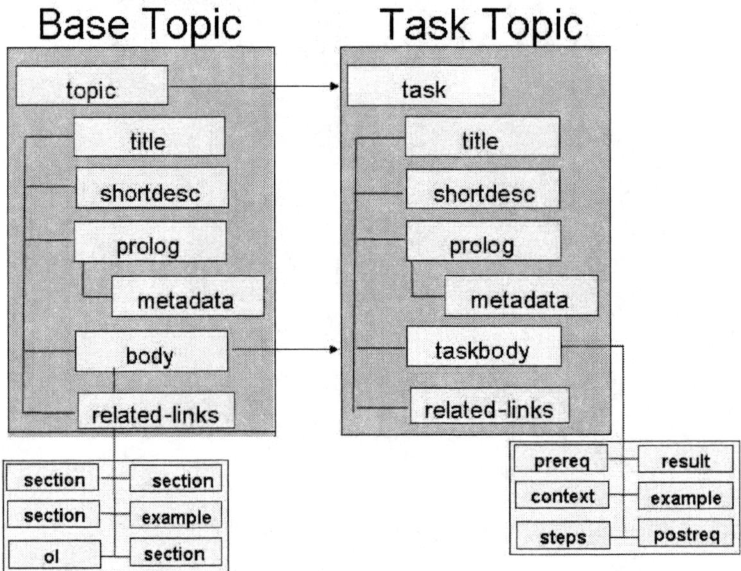

Figure 5.1 Specialization of task topic

In DITA, the task, concept, and reference specializations of the base topic information type are included in the DITA package. They represent the specialized structures that the DITA developers considered essential to define technical content. The DITA package also includes specialized domain elements that describe content required to write about product user interfaces, software development, and programming. By using the specialization mechanism at the core of the DITA architecture, you can create additional specializations to better define the structure of your information and more precisely name the elements in your subject domain. You may decide, for example, that you need a specialized information type to define the structure and semantics of a glossary of terms, an installation task, and a process description.

SECTION I

Understanding DITA Specialization

To define your special information types, you begin with the basic structure and semantics of the topic, task, concept, and reference information types. You create new DTDs with specialized structure and element names to meet your needs. The goal is to use the same structures provided in the DITA package to create your new information types. The DITA information architects strongly recommend that you never make changes to the six core DTDs themselves. If you change the core DTDs and their corresponding mod or ent files, your information architecture will no longer be DITA compatible.

One of the most important principles of DITA specialization is inheritance. The inheritance principle enables you to create new information types with only a few lines of code, effectively single sourcing your DTD set and greatly simplifying their maintenance. Inheritance means that you can use the structures and semantics already defined in the base DITA DTD and the core DITA information types. For example, the <steps> element that is the heart of the task information type is specialized from the ordered list <ol> in the base information type. The steps inherit the structure already defined for the ordered list. Because the base structure is already established for the ordered list in a DITA stylesheet, you do not have to create a new style to account for <steps> in the task. Each <step> in the <steps> container element is formatted using your stylesheet with the sequential numbers already defined for list items <li> inside the <ol> container element.

Inheritance provides a mechanism so that you can use a *class* attribute to map a parent element to the specialized element you want to create.

For example, the *class* attribute value for steps is " - topic/ol task/steps" in which <topic> maps to <task> and ordered list <ol> maps to steps <steps>. The attribute value creates a relationship from the topic information type to the task information type and the ordered list content unit to the steps content unit. The *class* attribute value tells your processor that when it finds a <steps> container element, it should find and follow the ordered list processing rules.

When you create a specialization, you do not have to redefine a style in your stylesheet or write new structure rules in your DTD because your new elements inherit the styles and structure rules from the parent elements in the information type you are specializing from. As a result, you can generalize your specialized information type or content unit back to the parent structures or elements.

Generalizing means to revert to the base structures and more generic content units. If you generalized the steps content unit, you would revert to an ordered list. Generalization, part of the inheritance principle, means that you can exchange DITA content with organizations that have different specializations than yours. For example, you may work closely with an original equipment manufacturer (OEM) or a supplier that provides you with content. The OEM or supplier can deliver DITA content to you that includes their own specialized information types and content units. You can generalize the content to the base DITA information type and process it as part of your information set.

Deciding to specialize

When information architects or information developers first learn about DITA specialization, they often assume that they will have to create specialized information types for all of their content. After studying the core information types (concept, task, and reference), they soon learn that most of their content matches quite well. Only when they delve in the details of their information structures do they identify requirements for specializations.

Some information architects find the need for one or two specializations to define the specific structures and semantics required by their content. Others develop 10 to 20 specializations to account for their unique content. As you analyze the underlying structures of your content and define the semantic elements to best describe your subject domain, you will identify opportunities for specialization.

To build a new structure for an information type, you create a structural specialization. To create new elements that name your content units more accurately than the standard DITA element names, you create a domain specialization. In the following scenario, we introduce an information type that requires a structural specialization and we semantically rename the elements to easily identify the specialization.

Structural specialization

With a structural specialization, you expand, limit, or rearrange the elements that are used to author your topics. Information architects use structural specializations to customize the authoring environment so that authors have only the elements they need in the order they should be written. They remove many of the elements in the core DITA information types because those elements are not needed. For example, if you want to restrict tasks to steps only with no additional content units, you can create a specialization that excludes elements, such as the <example>, <result>, <prereq>, and <postreq>.

Information architects can remove elements using specialization. The simple task structural specialization eliminates some elements not needed to create a simple task.Figure 5.3 shows the simple task topic specialization.

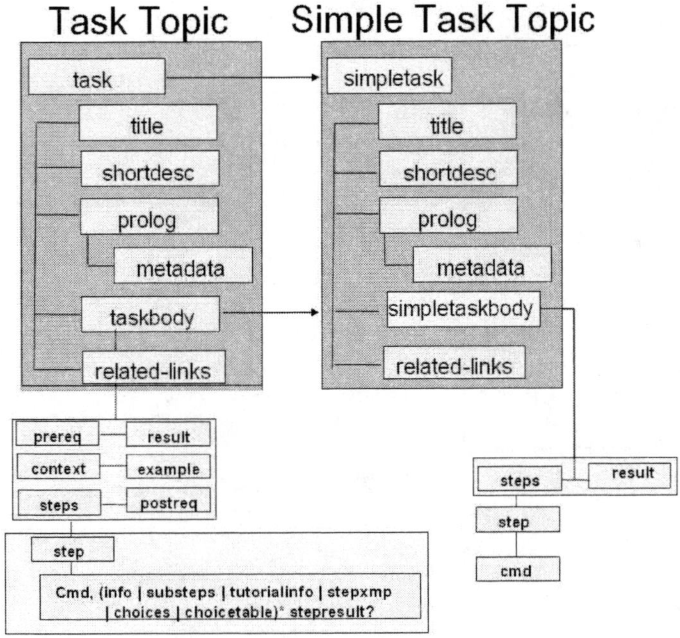

Figure 5.2 Simple task structural specialization

Information architects also find that they need to define structures that are not included in the core information types. For example, a hardware manufacturer may want to define a hardware installation task that follows a pre-requisite element with an element that defines a list of required equipment. In a standard DITA task, you cannot have two pre-requisites. You can add a second list using a structural specialization. Figure 5.2 shows the task topic specialization with an additional pre-requisite element for an equipment list.

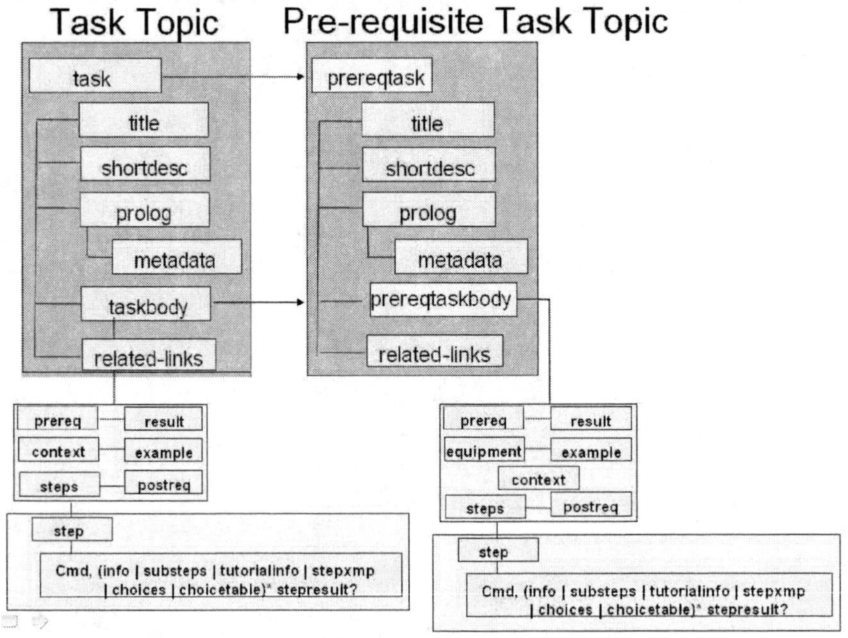

Figure 5.3 Pre-requisite structural specialization

Domain specialization

With a domain specialization, you create elements that allow your authors to define your content units more precisely. Information architects refer to precise element names as semantic elements because they more accurately describe the content and make the content easier to search and retrieve by authors and users. There are many opportunities for domain specialization. You may develop domain specializations to describe the content developed for domains such as semiconductor, aerospace, transportation, telecommunications, and medical equipment. Industry specializations allow you to standardize and share information among companies and to create consistent and searchable content for end users. Figure 5.4 illustrates information types developed for specific industries.

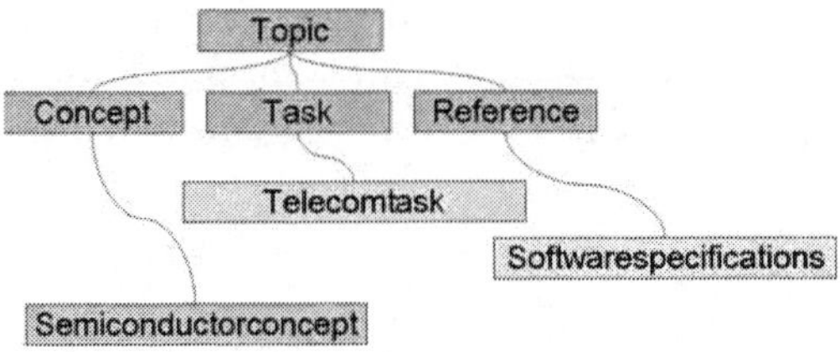

Figure 5.4 Industry domain specialization

You may also develop domain specializations to describe information specific to a particular department, information type, or product. Companies may create domain specializations for Application Programming Interfaces (APIs) because the content is significantly different from the previously defined user interface, programming, and software domains. Figure 5.5 illustrates the relationships between domain specializations for departments or deliverables and their parent information type.

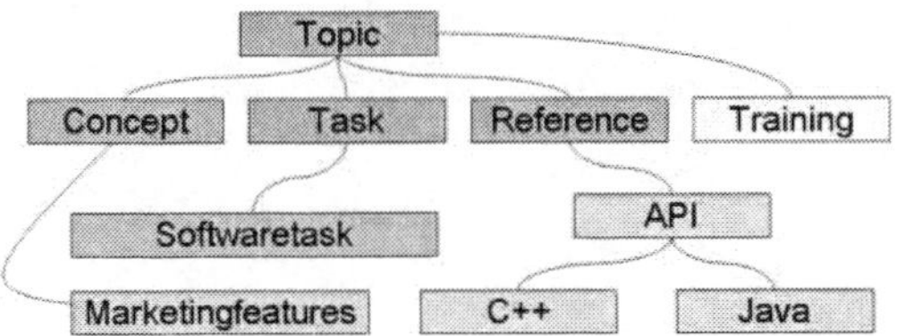

Figure 5.5 Department and information type domain specialization

IBM has created domain specializations to structure training content by adding information types for learning objectives, instructor notes, learning summaries, laboratory exercises, and learning assessments (tests).

.DTD, .MOD, and .ENT files

In the following specialization lesson, you learn to reuse the DITA base topic information type structure to create a glossary information type specialization. You modify two files, the .mod file and the .dtd file. The DITA .mod (modification) file contains the definitions of the elements, attributes, and entities. The .dtd (Document Type Definition) file formally defines the XML structure and references the .mod file for the element and structure definitions. In the lesson, you learn that the element changes you make to the .mod file are what you see when you author a DITA glossary topic. Because the DTD is the standard file used to define and validate your XML structure, you must reference the .mod file containing your element definitions in your .dtd file. If you choose to create a domain specialization, use the .ent file. Because the glossary specialization in this lesson is primarily structural, we will not use the .ent file. You can open all of the files in any text editor. However, you should never modify the original DITA .dtd, .mod and .ent files. Make copies of these files and modify the copies for your specializations.

LESSON 17

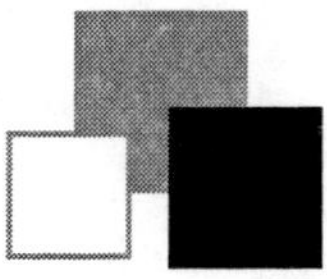

Glossary Specialization

Most information-development organizations create glossaries to define key terms used in product documentation. A glossary specialization provides your information developers with a standard structure and semantic elements to facilitate maintaining a list of glossary terms and definitions.

When you inventory your content, you may find that you need a standard structure to create a glossary of your product and industry terminology. You want to use the glossary definitions as popups in your help system so that users can easily understand the terms in your help topics. You also want to add a glossary to your PDFs that lists only the terms found in each manual. You would like to point to a specific glossary file in your DITA maps and related-links.

You decide that the best approach is to create a new information type that will explicitly define a glossary structure and semantically named glossary elements. You learn that the structure of the base DITA topic includes a block element called a definition list. However, you do not need the column heads in a standard definition list because all the entries in your glossary have the same structure: term and definitions.

You also want to delete all the content units in the base DITA topic that are not needed in a glossary. You define the structure you want for your glossary in the following example.

Example structure for a glossary information type

```
<glossary>
   <title></title>
      <titlealts></titlealts>
   <shortdesc></shortdesc>
   <prolog></prolog>
   <glossarybody>
      <glossarylist>
         <glossaryentry>
            <glossaryterm></glossaryterm>
            <glossarydefinition></glossarydefinition>
         </glossaryentry>
```

```
            <glossaryentry>
               <glossaryterm></glossaryterm>
               <glossarydefinition></glossarydefinition>
               <glossarydefinition></glossarydefinition>
            </glossaryentry>
         </glossarylist>
      </glossarybody>
   </glossary>
```

Specializing the .mod file

This lesson explains how to specialize a .mod file to create a glossary information type from a base information type.

For this lesson you should have some experience working with document type definitions (DTDs).

In this lesson, you learn to

- duplicate the topic.mod file
- delete any elements you do not want to use in your new structure
- rename and change the structure of some elements
- add the entity declarations for each of the elements you create
- add the class attribute value to map the new elements to the parent elements

1. Copy the topic.mod file and name the new file glossary.mod.

   Close the topic.mod file; you will not work with it again. You should never modify the topic.mod that is part of the base DITA package. You enter content changes only in the new glossary.mod file.

2. Delete everything in the glossary.mod file except the element definitions for topic, body, dl, dlentry, dt, and dd.

   The example shows the elements you modify to create your glossary information type.

```
<!--=========================================-->
<!--          ELEMENT NAME ENTITIES        -->
<!--=========================================-->

<!--   Definitions of declared elements    -->
<!ENTITY %topicDefns PUBLIC
         "-//OASIS//ENTITIES DITA Topic Definitions//EN"
         "topicDefn.ent"       >
%topicDefns;

<!ENTITY %term.cnt        "#PCDATA|%basic.ph;|%image;">
<!ENTITY %defn.cnt        "%listitem.cnt;">
```

```
<!--==========================================-->
<!--          ELEMENT DECLARATIONS          -->
<!--==========================================-->

<!--          LONG NAME: Topic          -->
<!ELEMENT topic   (%title;,(%titlealts;)?,(%shortdesc;)?,
                  (%prolog;)?,(%body;)?,
                  (%related-links;)?,
                  (%topic-info-types;)*)>
<!ATTLIST topic
    id              ID          #REQUIRED
    conref          CDATA       #IMPLIED
    %select-atts;
    outputclass     CDATA       #IMPLIED
    xml:lang        NMTOKEN     #IMPLIED
    %arch-atts;
    domains         CDATA       "&included-domains;">

<!--          LONG NAME: Body          -->
<!ELEMENT body   (%body.cnt;|(%section;)|(%example;)*   >
<!ATTLIST body
    %id-atts;
    translate      (yes|no)       #IMPLIED
    %select-atts;
    xml:lang        NMTOKEN     #IMPLIED
    outputclass     CDATA       #IMPLIED
    >

<!--          LONG NAME: Definition List          -->
<!ELEMENT dl   ((%dlhead;)?,(%dlentry;)+)   >
<!ATTLIST dl
    compact        (yes|no)       #IMPLIED
    spectitle      CDATA          #IMPLIED
    %univ-atts;
    outputclass     CDATA       #IMPLIED
    >

<!--          LONG NAME: Definition List Entry          -->
<!ELEMENT dlentry   ((%dt;)+,(%dd;)+)   >
<!ATTLIST dlentry
    %univ-atts;
    outputclass     CDATA       #IMPLIED
    >

<!--          LONG NAME: Definition Term          -->
<!ELEMENT dt   (%term.cnt;)*   >
<!ATTLIST dt
    keyref          CDATA       #IMPLIED
    %univ-atts;
    outputclass     CDATA       #IMPLIED   >
```

```
<!--          LONG NAME: Definition Description        -->
<!ELEMENT dd    (%defn.cnt;)*    >
<!ATTLIST dd
    %univ-atts;
    outputclass       CDATA        #IMPLIED
    >
```

3. Modify the topic definition by renaming topic to glossary, renaming the body to glossarybody, and removing the related-links and topic-info-types elements.

   Removing the related-links and topic-info-types modifies the information type structure creating a structural specialization. By removing the related-links and topic-info-types elements, you cannot include the <related-links> element at the end of the topic. However, it is unlikely that you would place related links in a glossary. If you need related links, you can use a relationship table in the map to create links among related topics.

   By removing the topic-info-types element, you can no longer embed other information types (i.e., concepts, tasks, or references) in the glossary information type. The question marks after the titlealts, shortdesc, and prolog indicate that these elements are optional, and you can only have one of each (i.e., non-repeatable). By removing the question mark associated with the glossarybody, you require your authors to enter a glossary body. If you keep the question mark associated with glossarybody, authors have the option to include the glossarybody or not. Removing elements from the glossary is a structural specialization.

```
<!--          LONG NAME: Glossary          -->
<!ELEMENT glossary    (%title;,(%titlealts;)?,
   (%shortdesc;)?,(%prolog;)?,(%glossarybody;))>
<!ATTLIST glossary
    id                ID           #REQUIRED
    conref            CDATA        #IMPLIED
    %select-atts;
    outputclass       CDATA        #IMPLIED
    xml:lang          NMTOKEN      #IMPLIED
    %arch-atts;
    domains           CDATA        "&included-domains;">
```

4. Modify the body definition by renaming it glossarybody and include only the glossarylist in the list of allowed elements for a glossarybody.

   Within the glossary information type, you will specialize the definition list and eliminate sections and examples.

```
<!--          LONG NAME: Glossary Body          -->
<!ELEMENT glossarybody   (%glossarylist;)>
<!ATTLIST glossarybody
    %id-atts;
    translate       (yes|no)        #IMPLIED
    %select-atts;
    xml:lang        NMTOKEN       #IMPLIED
    outputclass     CDATA         #IMPLIED>
```

5. Modify the definition list by renaming it glossarylist so that the name matches the name you used in the glossarybody definition in step 4.

   In the element definition, remove the %dlhead reference to restrict the structure slightly. Removing the %dlhead eliminates the need to include column heads in your glossary terms and definitions list.

   The plus sign next to glossaryentry indicates that authors can add one or more glossary entry elements to the glossarylist. The glossaryentry element is repeatable.

```
<!--          LONG NAME: Glossary List          -->
<!ELEMENT glossarylist((%glossaryentry;)+)>
<!ATTLIST glossarylist
    compact         (yes|no)        #IMPLIED
    spectitle        CDATA          #IMPLIED
    %univ-atts;
    outputclass      CDATA          #IMPLIED
    >
```

6. Modify the definition entry by renaming it glossaryentry.

   The glossaryentry name must match the glossaryentry element name created in the glossarylist definition in step 5. Remove the plus signs next to glossaryterm to ensure that each glossary entry has only one term. The plus sign next to the glossarydescription allows your author to include more than one description for each glossaryterm.

```
<!--          LONG NAME: Glossary List Entry          -->
<!ELEMENT glossaryentry(%glossaryterm;),
   (%glossarydescription;)+)    >
<!ATTLIST glossaryentry
    %univ-atts;
    outputclass      CDATA         #IMPLIED    >
```

7. Rename defnition term (dt) to glossaryterm.

   You must rename the glossaryterm name to match the element name you included in the glossaryentry definition in step 6. You do not need to modify the %term.cnt value. The %term.cnt is an entity that points to a definition in the topic DTD you still want to reference. The %term.cnt entity allows you to include an inline phrase elements such as keyword, xref, term, tm, image, and so on. If you wanted the author to enter only text in the glossaryterm container, you would replace the %term.cnt with "#PCDATA". #PCDATA is the XML term used to indicate text-only entry in a DTD.

```
<!--          LONG NAME: Glossary Term            -->
<!ELEMENT glossaryterm    (%term.cnt;)*    >
<!ATTLIST glossaryterm
    keyref            CDATA        #IMPLIED
    %univ-atts;
    outputclass       CDATA        #IMPLIED
    >
```

8. Rename the definition description (dd) to glossarydescription

   You must rename the glossarydescription to match the element you included in the glossaryentry definition in step 6. You do not need to modify the %defn.cnt value. The %defn.cnt is an entity that points to a definition in the topic DTD you still want to reference. The %defn.cnt entity allows you to include phrase and block elements, such as image, note, paragraph, definition list, simple table, lists, and so on. If you wanted the author to enter only text in the glossarydescription container, you would replace the %defn.cnt with "#PCDATA". #PCDATA is the XML term used to indicate a text-only entry in a DTD.

```
<!--          LONG NAME: Glossary Description            -->
<!ELEMENT glossarydescription    (%defn.cnt;)*    >
<!ATTLIST glossarydescription
    %univ-atts;
    outputclass       CDATA        #IMPLIED
    >
```

9. Add entity declarations for each of the terms you have redefined.

   Assigning entity values to each of the new terms creates reusable elements you can include in future information type specializations. Entities also declare your element definitions. If you need to change an element definition in the future, you need only to change the definition in one location because all other specializations use the same entities. If you decide to reuse one of the new elements defined in the glossary specialization in another specialization, you need only to include the entity value. Then, if you decide to change the name or structure of any glossary terms, all other references also change. Retain the entity declarations for the term and defn entities from the previous topic.mod file. Leave the term and defn entities in the glossary.mod file to use the existing topic element definitions for your glossaryterm and glossarydescription entries.

```
<!--==========================================-->
<!--          ELEMENT NAME ENTITIES          -->
<!--==========================================-->

<!--    Definitions of declared elements    -->
<!ENTITY %topicDefns PUBLIC
         "-//OASIS//ENTITIES DITA Topic Definitions//EN"
         "topicDefn.ent"      >
%topicDefns;

<!ENTITY %term.cnt          "#PCDATA|%basic.ph;|%image;">
<!ENTITY %defn.cnt          "%listitem.cnt;">

<!ENTITY %glossary          "glossary">
<!ENTITY %glossarybody          "glossarybody">
<!ENTITY %glossarylist          "glossarylist">
<!ENTITY %glossaryentry          "glossaryentry">
<!ENTITY %glossaryterm          "glossaryterm">
<!ENTITY %glossarydescription "glossarydescription">
```

10. Using the ATTLIST definitions, add the class attribute declarations for each element you redefined or introduced.

    You can include ATTLIST definitions at the end of your .mod file after your individual element definitions. The class attribute in the DITA model enforces the inheritance structure from the parent element to the specialized element you create. By including the element inheritance in the class attribute, you can reuse the stylesheets created for the original DITA information types because your new elements inherit the styles of the parent element. You can override the styles for your new elements if you wish.

    In the example below, each ATTLIST renames the new element's class attribute value with the information in quotes.

    Each ATTLIST class attribute value defines the association between the parent information type and content unit and the specialized information type and content unit.

    Remember that you must map each element you add to a previously defined element from the DITA base architecture for inheritance to work correctly. You can map different specialized elements to the same parent element if the structure is the same. For example, if you want a paragraph-like structure for two new elements, the new elements' class attribute value can use topic/p in the ATTLIST definition. If you decide to create an entirely new element with a new structure that doesn't map to a previous DITA element, you must account for the new element in your stylesheet.

```
<!ATTLIST glossary %global-atts; class CDATA
 "- topic/topic glossary/glossary ">
<!ATTLIST glossarybody %global-atts; class CDATA
 "- topic/body glossary/glossarybody ">
<!ATTLIST glossarylist %global-atts; class CDATA
 "- topic/dl glossary/glossarylist ">
<!ATTLIST glossaryentry %global-atts; class CDATA
 "- topic/dlentry glossary/glossaryentry ">
<!ATTLIST glossaryterm %global-atts; class CDATA
 "- topic/dt glossary/glossaryterm ">
<!ATTLIST glossarydescription %global-atts; class CDATA
 "- topic/dd glossary/glossarydescription ">
```

glossary.mod

The following example illustrates a complete .mod file for the glossary specialization.

```
<!--========================================-->
<!--          ELEMENT NAME ENTITIES         -->
<!--========================================-->

<!--   Definitions of declared elements    -->
<!ENTITY %topicDefns PUBLIC
         "-//OASIS//ENTITIES DITA Topic Definitions//EN"
         "topicDefn.ent"      >
%topicDefns;

<!ENTITY %term.cnt        "#PCDATA|%basic.ph;|%image;">
<!ENTITY %defn.cnt        "%listitem.cnt;">

<!ENTITY %glossary        "glossary">
<!ENTITY %glossarybody        "glossarybody">
<!ENTITY %glossarylist        "glossarylist">
<!ENTITY %glossaryentry        "glossaryentry">
<!ENTITY %glossaryterm        "glossaryterm">
<!ENTITY %glossarydescription "glossarydescription">
```

```
<!--=========================================-->
<!--          ELEMENT DECLARATIONS         -->
<!--=========================================-->

<!--          LONG NAME: Glossary          -->
<!ELEMENT glossary   (%title;,(%titlealts;)?,
   (%shortdesc;)?,(%prolog;)?,(%glossarybody;)) >
<!ATTLIST glossary
    id              ID          #REQUIRED
    conref          CDATA       #IMPLIED
    %select-atts;
    outputclass     CDATA       #IMPLIED
    xml:lang        NMTOKEN     #IMPLIED
    %arch-atts;
    domains         CDATA       "&included-domains;">

<!--          LONG NAME: Glossary Body         -->
<!ELEMENT glossarybody   (%glossarylist;)>
<!ATTLIST glossarybody
    %id-atts;
    translate      (yes|no)       #IMPLIED
    %select-atts;
    xml:lang        NMTOKEN     #IMPLIED
    outputclass     CDATA       #IMPLIED
    >

<!--          LONG NAME: Glossary List         -->
<!ELEMENT glossarylist((%glossaryentry;)+)>
<!ATTLIST glossarylist
    compact        (yes|no)       #IMPLIED
    spectitle       CDATA         #IMPLIED
    %univ-atts;
    outputclass     CDATA         #IMPLIED
    >

<!--          LONG NAME: Glossary List Entry         -->
<!ELEMENT glossaryentry((%glossaryterm;),
   (%glossarydescription;))   >
<!ATTLIST glossaryentry
    %univ-atts;
    outputclass     CDATA       #IMPLIED
    >

<!--          LONG NAME: Glossary Term         -->
<!ELEMENT glossaryterm   (%term.cnt;)*   >
<!ATTLIST glossaryterm
    keyref          CDATA       #IMPLIED
    %univ-atts;
    outputclass     CDATA       #IMPLIED
    >
```

```
<!--          LONG NAME: Glossary Description          -->
<!ELEMENT glossarydescription    (%defn.cnt;)*    >
<!ATTLIST glossarydescription
    %univ-atts;
    outputclass       CDATA        #IMPLIED    >
<!ATTLIST glossary %global-atts; class CDATA
 "- topic/topic glossary/glossary ">
<!ATTLIST glossarybody %global-atts; class CDATA
 "- topic/body glossary/glossarybody ">
<!ATTLIST glossarylist %global-atts; class CDATA
 "- topic/dl glossary/glossarylist ">
<!ATTLIST glossaryentry %global-atts; class CDATA
 "- topic/dlentry glossary/glossaryentry ">
<!ATTLIST glossaryterm %global-atts; class CDATA
 "- topic/dt glossary/glossaryterm ">
<!ATTLIST glossarydescription %global-atts; class CDATA
 "- topic/dd glossary/glossarydescription ">
```

Specializing the .dtd file

This lesson explains how to specialize a .dtd file to create a glossary information type from a base information type.

In this lesson, you learn to

- duplicate the topic.dtd file
- delete any unnecessary code
- add a reference to the glossary.mod file that defines the glossary elements

1. Duplicate the topic.dtd file and rename it glossary.dtd.

   Close the topic.dtd file; you will not work with it again. You should never modify the topic.dtd that is part of the base DITA package. You enter content changes only in the new glossary.dtd file.

2. Delete everything in the glossary.dtd except for the markup in the example below.

   You want to include the topic.mod reference because you will use some entities from the topic.mod element definitions, such as %term.cnt and %defn.cnt. You want to include all the domain element integration to use the domain specific elements, such as programming, user interface, and software.

```
<!--========================================-->
<!--     DOMAIN ENTITY DECLARATIONS     ==-->
<!--========================================-->

<!ENTITY %ui-d-dec PUBLIC
"-//OASIS//ENTITIES DITA User Interface Domain//EN"
"uiDomain.ent">
%ui-d-dec;

<!ENTITY %hi-d-dec PUBLIC
"-//OASIS//ELEMENTS DITA Highlight Domain//EN"
"highlightDomain.ent">
%hi-d-dec;

<!ENTITY %pr-d-dec PUBLIC
"-//OASIS//ELEMENTS DITA Programming Domain//EN"
"programmingDomain.ent">
%pr-d-dec;

<!ENTITY %sw-d-dec PUBLIC
"-//OASIS//ELEMENTS DITA Software Domain//EN"
"softwareDomain.ent">
%swhi-d-dec;

<!ENTITY %ut-d-dec PUBLIC
"-//OASIS//ELEMENTS DITA Utilities Domain//EN"
"utilitiesDomain.ent">
%ut-d-dec;

<!--=======================================-->
<!--       DOMAIN EXTENSIONS             -->
<!--=======================================-->
<!--        One for each extended base
            element, with the name of the
            domain(s) in which the extension
            was declared                -->

<!ENTITY % pre     "pre  | %pr-d-pre;  |%sw-d-pre;    |
                    %ui-d-pre;"          >
<!ENTITY % keyword "keyword  | %pr-d-keyword;
   |%sw-d-keyword;    | %ui-d-keyword;"          >
<!ENTITY % ph     "ph  | %pr-d-ph;  |%sw-d-ph;    |
                    %hi-d-ph;      |    %ui-d-ph;"          >
<!ENTITY % fig     "fig  | %pr-d-fig;  |%ut-d-fig;    >
<!ENTITY % dl     "dl  | %pr-d-dl;"          >
```

```
<!--=====================================-->
<!--      DOMAINS ATTRIBUTE OVERRIDE     -->
<!--=====================================-->
<!--   Must be declared ahead of the DTDs,
       which puts @domains first in order -->

<!ENTITY included-domains
        "&ui-d-att; &hi-d-att; &pr-d-att;
         &sw-d-att; &ut-d-att;"    >

<!--=====================================-->
<!--     TOPIC ELEMENT INTEGRATION     ==-->
<!--=====================================-->

<!--     Embed topic to get generic elements       -->
<!ENTITY %topic-type PUBLIC
"-//OASIS//ELEMENTS DITA Topic//EN"
"topic.mod">
%topic-type;

<!--=====================================-->
<!--     DOMAIN ELEMENT INTEGRATION    ==-->
<!--=====================================-->

<!ENTITY %ui-d-def PUBLIC
"-//OASIS//ELEMENTS DITA User Interface Domain//EN"
"uiDomain.mod">
%ui-d-def;

<!ENTITY %hi-d-def PUBLIC
"-//OASIS//ELEMENTS DITA Highlight Domain//EN"
"highlightDomain.mod">
%hi-d-def;

<!ENTITY %pr-d-def PUBLIC
"-//OASIS//ELEMENTS DITA Programming Domain//EN"
"programmingDomain.mod">
%pr-d-def;

<!ENTITY %sw-d-def PUBLIC
"-//OASIS//ELEMENTS DITA Software Domain//EN"
"softwareDomain.mod">
%swhi-d-def;

<!ENTITY %ut-d-def PUBLIC
"-//OASIS//ELEMENTS DITA Utilities Domain//EN"
"utilitiesDomain.mod">
%ut-d-def;
```

3. Add an entity declaration for the glossary.mod file.

   When you add the entity declaration, you reference the elements needed to create your glossary topic. Add the entity declaration after the topid.mod reference. In order to keep your specializations path distinct from the OASIS specializations, change the PUBLIC identifier. In this example, use "MYSPECIALIZATIONS."

```
<!--========================================-->
<!--     TOPIC ELEMENT INTEGRATION      ==-->
<!--========================================-->

<!--     Embed topic to get generic elements       -->
<!ENTITY %topic-type PUBLIC
"-//MYSPECIALIZATIONS//ELEMENTS DITA Topic//EN"
"topic.mod"                      >
%topic-type;

<!-- Embed glossary to get glossary elements     -->
<!ENTITY %glossary PUBLIC "-//MYSPECIALIZATIONS//ELEMENTS DITA
   Glossary//EN" "glossary.mod"                    >
%glossary;
```

glossary.dtd

In the glossary.dtd file, you define the public and system document type declarations using an entity called %glossary. Your final .dtd file should look like the markup illustrated below.

```
<!--========================================-->
<!--     DOMAIN ENTITY DECLARATIONS     ==-->
<!--========================================-->

<!ENTITY %ui-d-dec PUBLIC
"-//OASIS//ENTITIES DITA User Interface Domain//EN"
"uiDomain.ent">
%ui-d-dec;

<!ENTITY %hi-d-dec PUBLIC
"-//OASIS//ELEMENTS DITA Highlight Domain//EN"
"highlightDomain.ent">
%hi-d-dec;

<!ENTITY %pr-d-dec PUBLIC
"-//OASIS//ELEMENTS DITA Programming Domain//EN"
"programmingDomain.ent">
%pr-d-dec;

<!ENTITY %sw-d-dec PUBLIC
"-//OASIS//ELEMENTS DITA Software Domain//EN"
```

```
"softwareDomain.ent">
%swhi-d-dec;

<!ENTITY %ut-d-dec PUBLIC
"-//OASIS//ELEMENTS DITA Utilities Domain//EN"
"utilitiesDomain.ent">
%ut-d-dec;

<!--========================================-->
<!--         DOMAIN EXTENSIONS             -->
<!--========================================-->
<!--         One for each extended base
             element, with the name of the
             domain(s) in which the extension
             was declared                     -->

<!ENTITY % pre      "pre  | %pr-d-pre;  |%sw-d-pre;    |
                     %ui-d-pre;"          >
<!ENTITY % keyword "keyword  | %pr-d-keyword;
   |%sw-d-keyword;   |  %ui-d-keyword;"         >
<!ENTITY % ph      "ph  | %pr-d-ph;  |%sw-d-ph;   |
                    %hi-d-ph;     |   %ui-d-ph;"           >
<!ENTITY % fig      "fig  | %pr-d-fig;  |%ut-d-fig;    >
<!ENTITY % dl      "dl  | %pr-d-dl;"          >

<!--========================================-->
<!--       DOMAINS ATTRIBUTE OVERRIDE      -->
<!--========================================-->
<!--    Must be declared ahead of the DTDs,
        which puts @domains first in order -->

<!ENTITY included-domains
         "&ui-d-att; &hi-d-att; &pr-d-att;
          &sw-d-att; &ut-d-att;"    >

<!--========================================-->
<!--     TOPIC ELEMENT INTEGRATION       ==-->
<!--========================================-->

<!--     Embed topic to get generic elements       -->
<!ENTITY %topic-type PUBLIC
"-//OASIS//ELEMENTS DITA Topic//EN"
"topic.mod"                 >
%topic-type;

<!-- Embed glossary to get glossary elements     -->
<!ENTITY %glossary PUBLIC "-//OASIS//ELEMENTS DITA
   Glossary//EN" "glossary.mod" >
%glossary;
```

```
<!--========================================-->
<!--    DOMAIN ELEMENT INTEGRATION    ==-->
<!--========================================-->

<!ENTITY %ui-d-def PUBLIC
"-//OASIS//ELEMENTS DITA User Interface Domain//EN"
"uiDomain.mod"                    >
%ui-d-def;

<!ENTITY %hi-d-def PUBLIC
"-//OASIS//ELEMENTS DITA Highlight Domain//EN"
"highlightDomain.mod"                    >
%hi-d-def;

<!ENTITY %pr-d-def PUBLIC
"-//OASIS//ELEMENTS DITA Programming Domain//EN"
"programmingDomain.mod"                 >
%pr-d-def;

<!ENTITY %sw-d-def PUBLIC
"-//OASIS//ELEMENTS DITA Software Domain//EN"
"softwareDomain.mod"                    >
%swhi-d-def;

<!ENTITY %ut-d-def PUBLIC
"-//OASIS//ELEMENTS DITA Utilities Domain//EN"
"utilitiesDomain.mod"                  >
%ut-d-def;
```

Using specializations

This lesson explains how to use your glossary DTD to create a DITA glossary topic.

In this lesson, you learn to

- include a document type declaration in your DITA topic file
- add content to your glossary information type

1. Start a new glossary topic.

   You can open a new topic in your XML editor or you can start a new glossary topic in a text editor. You must start with an XML declaration and a document type declaration. The XML editor usually adds the declarations for you automatically.

If you are using an XML editor	XML editors usually allow you to browse to the DTD you want to use. In an XML editor, select the glossary.dtd you created in the Specializing the .dtd file lesson.
If you are using a text editor	In the text editor, you must insert in an XML declaration and a document type declaration pointing to your glossary DTD. Your glossary document type declaration must look like the markup example below. The only content you need to modify is the relative path to the location of your glossary DTD. `<?xml version="1.0" encoding="UTF-8"?> <!DOCTYPE glossary PUBLIC "-//MYSPECIALIZATIONS//ELEMENTS DITA Glossary//EN" "../dtd/glossary.dtd" >`

2. Add <glossary> element start and end tags after the document type declaration.

   Because glossary is the first element defined in your specialization, you must use the <glossary> element as the root or topic element like the root <task>, <concept>, or <reference> elements.

```
<?xml version="1.0" encoding="UTF-8"?>
<!DOCTYPE glossary PUBLIC "-//OASIS//ELEMENTS DITA
   Glossary//EN" "../dtd/glossary.dtd" >
<glossary>
</glossary>
```

3. Add the standard *id* attribute, <title>, and <shortdesc> element start and end tags.

   In your specialization, you didn't delete the title and short description from your glossary element definition, so the title and short description containers are the same as they are in the core information types: topic, task, concept, and reference.

   For a glossary specialization, you may not need a short description. In the specialization, the short description element remains optional. A short description is illustrated in the example below.

```
<?xml version="1.0" encoding="UTF-8"?>
<!DOCTYPE glossary PUBLIC "-//OASIS//ELEMENTS DITA
   Glossary//EN" "../dtd/glossary.dtd" >
<glossary id="phoneglossary">
   <title>Phone Glossary</title>
```

```
   <shortdesc>Below are definitions to help guide you
      through the Phone User Guide</shortdesc>
</glossary>
```

4. Add the <glossarybody>, <glossarylist>, <glossaryentry>, <glossaryterm>, and <glossarydescription> element start and end tags to add a new glossary entry.

   The example illustrates the structure explained in the scenario in which you can have multiple glossary entries. For each glossary entry, you can have one term with multiple definitions.

```
<?xml version="1.0" encoding="UTF-8"?>
<!DOCTYPE glossary PUBLIC "-//OASIS//ELEMENTS DITA
   Glossary//EN" "../dtd/glossary.dtd" >
<glossary id="phoneglossary">
   <title>Phone Glossary</title>
   <shortdesc>Below you should find definitions to help
      guide you through the Phone User Guide</shortdesc>
   <glossarybody>
      <glossarylist>
         <glossaryentry>
            <glossaryterm>Call Waiting</glossaryterm>
            <glossarydescription>If your line is busy,
               callers are asked to wait while you are
               alerted to their incoming call.
            </glossarydescription>
         </glossaryentry>
         <glossaryentry>
            <glossaryterm>AC</glossaryterm>
            <glossarydescription>Access Carrier: Refers
               to the underlying carrier.
            </glossarydescription>
            <glossarydescription>Account Codes: Also
               known as Project Codes or Bill-Back Codes.
               Account Codes are additional digits dialed by
               the calling party that provide information
               about the call. Typically used by hourly
               professionals (accountants, lawyers, etc.) to
               track and bill clients, projects, etc.
            </glossarydescription>
         </glossaryentry>
      </glossarylist>
   </glossarybody>
</glossary>
```

Specialization review questions

1. When is specialization appropriate?
2. What is the difference between structural and domain specialization?
3. How do the .mod and .dtd work together?
4. How do you reference a specialized DTD after you create it?
5. Should you ever make changes to the DITA .dtd or .mod files?

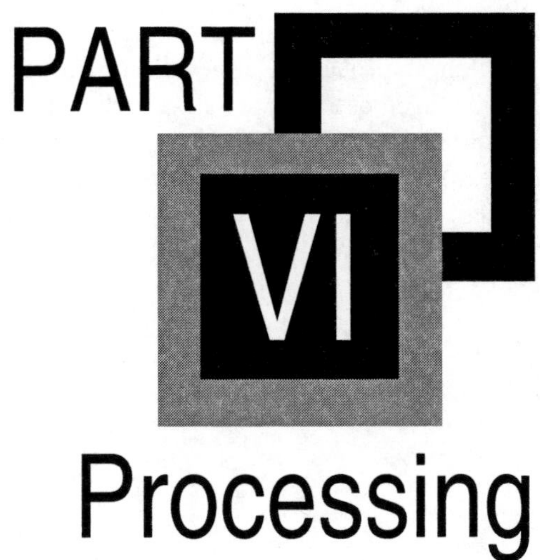

Processing

Processing your DITA topics and maps requires a suite of tools. To process and produce your final deliverables, consider using either commercial-off-the-shelf products or a group of open source applications.

To create XHTML, HTML, or something that compiles HTML output, you will need to look into a product that uses an XML parser and an XSLT processor. If you are interested in creating PDF or print output, you will need to use an XML parser as well as an XSL-FO processor. Some of the commercial products bundle each of these pieces into a single processing unit with a wizard to walk you through the production options.

Many people currently use the DITA Open Toolkit to process their DITA deliverables. Many vendors are also using or planning to use the Open Toolkit as the production tool in the background of their products. The open toolkit is an open source version of each of the pieces listed above. With this suite of tools, you can produce output for your users.

Using XML as a tool to author your information allows you to separate creating content from styling and formatting. By separating the formatting from the content, you ensure more consistency in your output. In the DITA Open toolkit, you will find stylesheets already built for DITA. All the effort you once had to put into creating XSLT, XSL-FO, and CSS stylesheets is already done for you in DITA. You can take time to configure and manipulate the styles to better fit your needs, but you don't have to work through all of the processing rules needed for adequate output.

You handle your processing rules using build files. Build files allow you to point to your stylesheet, processing applications, and source content. The build files pull everything together to create a single deliverable or a set of deliverables. If you don't use build files, you will find that your processing tools will prompt you to enter the same information every time you want to create a deliverable. The DITA Open Toolkit provides functionality to create build files that you can use to process your information quickly and easily.

SECTION J

Understanding the DITA Open Toolkit

The DITA Open Toolkit is an implementation of the OASIS DITA Technical Committee's specification for Darwin Information Typing Architecture (DITA) DTDs and schemas. The Toolkit transforms DITA XML source content into deliverable formats such as PDF, HTML, and help systems.

Installation Requirements

To successfully install the DITA Open Toolkit using these installation instructions, you must have a Windows operating system running on your workstation. If you are using a Linux system, please see the DITA Open Toolkit installation instructions for that platform on the Sourceforge.com web site.

You can install the items in any order. If you already have some of the items (JavaHelp, SAXON, etc.) installed on your computer, skip to another section and proceed until all required items are installed.

LESSON 18

DITA Open Toolkit

To process your DITA topics and maps into deliverables, you can use a suite of tools provided on www.sourceforge.com.

The DITA Open Toolkit and all applications needed to run the DITA Open Toolkit are all open source, free to download and use. The DITA Open Toolkit does not include an authoring tool. However, you can author in DITA using tools, such as Arbortext Editor, Syntext Serna, oXygen, XMetaL and some others. These tools provide an easy-to-use, WYSIWIG, graphical user interface for authoring structured content. Other XML authoring tools, such as Altova XML Suite, Microsoft Word, or any text editor can also be used to author information in DITA.

The following items are included in the DITA Open Toolkit:

- the six DTDs (base topic, concept, task, reference, map, and bookmap)
- the stylesheets for HTML, HTML Help, Java Help, and PDF output

The following six applications are all open source and needed by the DITA Open Toolkit to produce HTML, HTML Help, Java Help, and PDF output.

Java Development Kit (JDK)

The Java processor is needed to produce each output. All of the tools are tied together through Java.

Java Help

The compiler used to generate the Java Help files during the build process

HTML Help

The compiler used to generate the HTML Help files during the build process.

Apache FOP

The Formatting Objects Processor (FOP) used to pull all style and information together for PDF outputs.

SAXON XSLT processor

The processor used to create HTML output using XSLT stylesheets.

Ant

The system that pulls all of the tools together and builds the final outputs.

DITA Open Toolkit Contents

The information in the table describes the file structure and content of the DITA Open Toolkit directory (DITAOT) after installation.

Folder	Contents
ant	all build templates
css	the styles for displaying XML source files in editors or browsers
demo	demonstrations and experiments for DITA capabilities
doc	documentation for DITA and the Open Toolkit
dtd	the document type definitions for the DITA vocabulary
lib	the Java implementation for advanced processing
out	the formatted output Note: This file is generated the first time a document is processed, not when the DITA Open Toolkit is installed.
resource	the styles and other resources for XHTML and other output
samples	example DITA content for testing the processing
schema	the XML Schema definitions for the DITA vocabulary
temp	the intermediate files created during processing **Note:** This file is generated the first time a document is processed, not when the DITA Open Toolkit is installed.
xsl	the XSLT files for XHTML and PDF processing.

Installing the DITA Open Toolkit

The DITA Open Toolkit is downloaded from the SourceForge web site. For this installation, you access the web sites for each of the required installation items, including Ant, Java Development Toolkit, JavaHelp, Apache FOP, SAXON XSLT Processor, and Microsoft HTML Help.

1. Enter the URL: http://sourceforge.net/projects/DITA-ot
2. Click on the green box that says **Download DITA Open Toolkit.**
3. Scroll to the latest release shown in the table.

   The latest release will have a title that looks like **dita ot 1.2**.
4. Select the green Download box next to the release you want to download.
5. Click on the latest release with the title that looks like**DITA-OT1.2_bin.zip**.

   Another page opens with `download options` for you to choose from.
6. Select any of the images to start the download.

   If the DITA Open Toolkit does not appear to be downloading, wait a few minutes before selecting another image. You may have to select more than one image until you find one that works.

   Note: If you are an Internet Explorer user and a yellow bar appears at the top of the screen with the message, "To help protect your security, Internet Explorer blocked this site from downloading files to your computer. Click here for options,"click on the bar and select "Download File".
7. Click **Save** to unzip the DITA-OT1.2_bin.zip file and save it to your C:\ directory as `DITAOT`.

Because there are regularly updated releases to the DITA Open Toolkit, you may find that a different release is available. Please download the latest release and follow any additional instructions provided with the DITA Open Toolkit installation.

Installing Ant

Apache Ant is a Java-based build tool that uses Java classes. Ant configuration files are XML based. You can use them to build output files such as HTML, PDF, and help systems.

1. Enter the URL: http://ant.apache.org/bindownload.cgi
2. On the Apache Ant Project page, find the heading **Current Release of Ant**.
3. Select **apache-ant-1.6.5-bin.zip [PGP] [SHA1] [MD5]**.
4. Click **Save** to unzip the apache-ant-1.6.5-bin.zip [PGP] [SHA1] [MD5] file and save it to your C:\ directory as `ant`.
5. Add the `bin` directory to your Path environment variable.
6. Add the ANT_HOME environment variable.

If you see a different version of Ant as an option, download the latest version.

If you need instructions for installing Ant on your Linux system, see the DITA Open Toolkit installation instructions on the Sourceforge web site.

Installing JDK (Java Development Kit)

The Java Development Kit (JDK) is a Sun product targeted for Java developers. You use it to write, compile, debug, and run Java applets and applications.

1. Enter the URL: http://java.sun.com/j2se/1.4.2/download.html
2. From the Sun Developer Network page, scroll to find the heading **J2SE v 1.4.2_10 SDK**
3. Select **Download J2SE SDK**
4. From the Sun Developer Network page, accept the license agreement and scroll to the heading "Windows Platform - Java(TM) 2 SDK, Standard Edition 1.4.2_10"
5. Select **Windows Installation, Multi-language**.
6. Click **Run**.
7. If prompted, install the JDK to the C:\ directory as `j2sdk1.4.2_10`
8. Set the environment variable for JAVA_HOME.

   If you do not see `j2sdk1.4.2_10` as an option to download, download the latest version of the J2SE SDK.

Installing JavaHelp

Use JavaHelp to incorporate online help in applications, components, operating systems, applets, and devices.

1. Enter the URL:
   http://java.sun.com/products/javahelp/download_binary.html
2. From the Sun Developer Network page, scroll to find the heading **JavaHelp 2.0_02** (Zip).
3. Select **Download**.
4. From the Sun Developer Network page, accept the license agreement and scroll to the heading "Platform - JavaHelp API 2.0_02 FCS".
5. Select **javahelp-2_0_02.zip, 6.49 MB**.

   The `File Download` window opens.
6. Click **Save** to unzip the javahelp-2_0_02.zip file and save it to the C:\ directory as `javahelp`.
7. Set the JHHOME environment variable.

   If you would like instructions for installing Java Help on your Linux system, please see the DITA Open Toolkit installation instructions on the Sourceforge web site.

Installing Apache FOP

The Formatting Objects Processor (FOP) is a print formatter. It uses XSL formatting objects (XSL-FO) to produce the Portable Document Format (PDF) files. You can use it to format and produce PDF output from XML.

1. Enter the URL: http://apache.tradebit.com/pub/xml/fop/
2. From the FOP page, in the Name column, select **"fop-0.20.5-bin.zip"**.
3. Click **Save** to unzip the fop-0.20.5-bin.zip file and save it to the C:\ directory as `fop-0.20.5`.
4. Set the CLASSPATH environment variable for the following jar files:
   \build\fop.jar
   \lib\batik.jar
   \lib\avalon-framework-cvs-20020806.jar

If you would like instructions for installing FOP on your Linux system, see the DITA Open Toolkit installation instructions on the Sourceforge web site.

Installing SAXON XSLT Processor

Use the SAXON XSLT Processor to import stylesheets and queries into an XML schema, validate XML data against a schema, and select the elements and attributes in your XML documents according to their schema-defined type.

1. Enter the URL: http://saxon.sourceforge.net/
2. From SAXON: The XSLT and XQuery Processor page, scroll to find the heading **Saxon 6.5.5**.
3. Select **Download (3265 Kbytes)**.

   The SourceForge.net page opens with a list of download options.
4. Select any of the images to start the download.

   If SAXON does not appear to be downloading, wait a few minutes before selecting another image. You may have to select more than one image until you find one that works.

   Note: If you are an Internet Explorer user and a yellow bar appears at the top of the screen with the message, "To help protect your security, Internet Explorer blocked this site from downloading files to your computer. Click here for options," click on the bar and select "Download File".
5. Click **Save** to unzip the saxon 6-5-5.zip file and save it to the C:\ directory as `saxon`.
6. Set the CLASSPATH environment variable for the saxon.jar file.

If you see a different version of Saxon as an option, download the latest version.

If you need instructions for installing Saxon on your Linux system, see the DITA Open Toolkit installation instructions on the Sourceforge web site.

Installing Microsoft HTML Help

Microsoft HTML Help is an online help authoring tool. You use it to develop and author online help for software applications or web sites.

1. Enter the URL: http://msdn.microsoft.com/library/default.asp?url=/library/en-us/htmlhelp/html/hwmicrosofthtmlhelpdownloads.asp
2. From the MSDN page, scroll to find the heading **HTML Help Workshop**.
3. Select **Download Htmlhelp.exe.**
4. Click **Run** and navigate to an appropriate directory.
5. Follow the steps in the HTML Help install wizard to complete the installation.

If you need instructions for installing Microsoft HTML Help on your Linux system, see the DITA Open Toolkit installation instructions on the Sourceforge web site.

Setting Environment Variables

Use this information to find and set your environment variables. Set your system environment variables after all DITA Open Toolkit items are installed. The environment variables must be set for each item installed in this guide.

The steps below assume you are working on a Windows 2003 platform. If you have another version of Windows or a different operating system, see your computer documentation about setting environment variables.

1. From the Start Menu, select **Start** > **Settings** > **Control Panel.**
2. Double-click System to open the System Properties window.
3. On the Advanced tab, select environmental variables .
4. Modify each environmental or system variable.

Set the Path environment variable to include the directory where you installed the Ant bin directory.	1. Find the Path environment variable in the list. If Path is not listed, click on **New** under the System variables section. 2. Type `%ANT_HOME%\bin` **Important:** If there are other variables listed, create a new variable separated by a semicolon. Ensure there are no spaces before or after the semicolon.
Set the ANT_HOME environment variable to the directory where you installed Ant.	1. Click on **New** under the System variables section. 2. Type `ANT_HOME` in the variable name field. 3. Type `C:\ant` in the variable value field.
Set the JAVA_HOME environment variable to the directory where you installed the J2SE SDK application.	1. Click on **New** under the System variables section. 2. Type `JAVA_HOME` in the variable name field. 3. Type `C:\j2sdk1.4.2_10` in the variable value field.
Set the JHHOME environment variable to the directory where you installed the JavaHelp application.	1. Click on **New** under the System variables section. 2. Type `JHHOME` in the variable name field. 3. Type `C:\javahelp\jh2.0\javahelp\bin` in the variable value field.
Set the CLASSPATH environment variable to include the .jar files from the Apache FOP application.	1. Find the CLASSPATH environment variable in the list. If CLASSPATH is not listed, click on **New** under the System variables section. 2. Type `C:\fop-0.20.5\build\fop.jar;C:\fop-0.20.5\lib\batik.jar;C:\fop-0.20.5\lib\avalon-framework-cvs-20020806.jar` **Important:** If there are other variables listed, create a new variable separated by a semicolon. Ensure there are no spaces before or after the semicolon.

Set the CLASSPATH environment variable to include the directory where you installed Saxon.	1. Find the CLASSPATH environment variable in the list. If CLASSPATH is not listed, click on **New** under the System variables section. 2. Type `c:\saxon\saxon.jar` **Important:** If there are other variables listed, create a new variable separated by a semicolon. Ensure there are no spaces before or after the semicolon.

Testing DITA Installation

This lesson presents the tests you should run to ensure correct DITA Open Toolkit installation.

1. From the toolbar, click **Start** > **Run** .
2. In the Open field, type `cmd`.
3. Change the command prompt according to the following table.

If this prompt displays,	type the following command
D:\	`c:`
H:\	`c:`
C:\My Documents\...	`cd \`

4. At the prompt, type `cd DITAOT`

   The command prompt changes to `c:\DITAOT>`
5. Type java -version.

   Your command prompt displays something similar to the example message below. If your command prompt does not display the information below, double check your environment variables. If you still cannot display the information below, reinstall the java SDK.

```
java version "1.5.0_06"
Java(TM) 2 Runtime Environment, Standard Edition
   (build 1.5.0_06-b05)
Java HotSpot(TM) Client VM (build 1.5.0_06-b05,
mixed mode, sharing)
```

6. Type ant -version.

   Your command prompt displays something similar to the example below. If your command prompt does not display the information below, double check your environment variables. If you still cannot display the information below, reinstall Ant.

```
Apache Ant version 1.6.2 compiled on July 16 2004
```

7. Type `ant all` and press Enter to begin testing.

   If you see an Out of Memory Error, perform the following steps.

   a. In the command prompt under the DITA Open Toolkit directory (DITAOT), type `set ANT_OPTS=-Xmx256M`
   b. Test the DITA installation process again by typing `ant all` in the command prompt.

   The processing finishes after a few minutes depending on the speed of your computer and how large your project is. When testing completes, the command prompt displays the confirmation message "BUILD SUCCESSFUL". If you do not see "BUILD SUCCESSFUL", look through the error messages on the command prompt to research the problem or reinstall the DITA Open Toolkit and other applications.

   Note: To read more about the DITA Open Toolkit options and functions, see C:\DITAOT\doc\DITA-readme.html on your local hard drive.

Another method you can use to create the samples and test your installation is to type only `ant` in your command prompt. When you type `ant`, you also have the option of putting in your own .ditamap file as a source and creating your own outputs. Your command prompt displays the following information requests:

- `Please enter the filename for the DITA map you want to build including the path (if any). The filename must have the .ditamap extension.`
  `Note that the relative paths that climb (../) are not supported yet. To build the sample, press return without entering anything. The DITA map filename:`
- `Please enter the name of the output directory or press return to accept the default. The output directory (out):`
- `Please enter the type of output to generate. Options include eclipse, htmlhelp, javahelp, PDF, or web. Use lowercase letters. The output type: (eclipse, htmlhelp, javahelp, PDF, web, dokbook)`
- `Continue? (Y,y,N,n)`

You can also create Ant build scripts so that you don't have to answer the same questions at the command prompt each time you want to create your output.

DITA Open Toolkit review questions

1. Where do you find the DITA Open Toolkit?
2. What is the purpose of the Ant file in the DITA Open Toolkit?
3. What kind of outputs can you create using the DITA Open Toolkit?
4. What applications are required to use the DITA Open Toolkit?

LESSON 19

Build Files

When you use the DITA Open Toolkit to produce your deliverable, you will create an Ant build file to make processing easier. Use the Ant application to identify your source files, stylesheets, and the other applications needed to create your deliverables.

After you download the DITA Open Toolkit, you will find an ant folder that contains several build file templates. Figure 6.1 shows a sample of one build file template.

```
<?xml version="1.0" encoding="UTF-8" ?>
<!-- (c) Copyright IBM Corp. 2004, 2005 All Rights Reserved. -->
<!-- revise @PLACEHOLDER@ names and values-->
<project name="@PROJECT.NAME@_htmlhelp" default="all" basedir="..">
  <path id="dost.class.path">
    <pathelement location="${basedir}${file.separator}lib${file.separator}dost.jar"/>
  </path>

  <taskdef name="integrate" classname="org.dita.dost.platform.IntegratorTask">
    <classpath refid="dost.class.path"/>
  </taskdef>
  <target name="all" depends="integrate, @DELIVERABLE.NAME@2htmlhelp"></target>
  <target name="integrate">
    <integrate ditadir="${basedir}"/>
  </target>

  <target name="@DELIVERABLE.NAME@2htmlhelp">
    <ant antfile="${basedir}${file.separator}conductor.xml" target="init">
      <property name="args.input" value="@DITA.INPUT@"/>
      <property name="output.dir" value="@OUTPUT.DIR@"/>
      <property name="transtype" value="htmlhelp"/>
    </ant>
  </target>
</project>
```

Figure 6.1 Example of the htmlhelp template file in the ant folder

The purpose of the ANT build file is to

- set project and import properties to indicate where the tools are in your processing environment.
- define targets for the output type you want to build by indicating the stylesheet you want to use. The stylesheets in the Open Toolkit output PDF, HTML Help (.chm), XHTML, Java Help, or Eclipse.
- invoke a property to identify your DITA map source file and your output directory.

The Ant build file connects the source files (DITA map and stylesheets) and the production processes together.

A build file can be complex or simple depending upon your needs. The basic build file defines where the map is located, which stylesheets you want to use to process your output (i.e., XHTML, PDF, HTML Help, Java Help, or Eclipse), and the directory where the output should be placed.

Because the Open Toolkit uses different processes and files to define each output type, you may want to create a new build file for each output. If you use the template provided in the Open Toolkit ant folder, you will need to create one build file to produce HTML Help and another build file to produce PDF. If you want to create one build file to produce HTML and PDF output simultaneously, see the Invoking Multiple Builds exercise in this lesson.

This lesson contains eight exercises that lead you through the DITA processing procedures.

Creating a build file

This exercise explains the process to create a build file for PDF output. All output build files are created in the same way; they just use different templates. The output template files are located in the DITAOT directory in the ant folder.

In this exercise, you learn to

- start a build file for a specific project and deliverable
- point to a .ditamap file as your input
- add a folder location for your output files

1. Open the template_pdf.xml file in a text editor such as notepad or EditPad Lite.

   The template_pdf.xml file is in the DITAOT directory in the ant folder.

   The template_pdf.xml looks like the example below.

```
<?xml version="1.0" encoding="UTF8" ?>
<!-- (c) Copyright IBM Corp. 2004, 2005 All Rights
   Reserved. -->
<project name="@PROJECT.NAME@_xhtml" default="all"
   basedir="..">
   <path id="dost.class.path">
      <pathelement location="${basedir}${file.separator}
         lib${file.separator}dost.jar"/>
   </path>
   <taskdef name="integrate" classname="org.dita.dost.
      platform.IntegratorTask">
      <classpath refid="dost.class.path"/>
   </taskdef>
```

```
    <target name="all" depends="integrate,
      @DELIVERABLE.NAME@2xhtml"></target>
    <target name="integrate">
      <integrate ditadir="${basedir}"/>
    </target>
    <target name="@DELIVERABLE.NAME@2xhtml">
      <ant antfile="${basedir}${file.separator}
        conductor.xml" target="init">
        <property name="args.input"
          value="@DITA.INPUT@"/>
        <property name="output.dir"
          value="@OUTPUT.DIR@"/>
        <property name="transtype" value="xhtml"/>
        <property name="dita.extname" value=".dita"/>
      </ant>
     </target>
</project>
```

2. Replace all @placeholders@, including the @ symbol, in the template.
    a. Change the @PROJECT.NAME@ to ComstarUserGuide, the name of your project.
    b. Change the @DELIVERABLE.NAME@ to ComstarUserGuide, the unique name for your deliverable.

       Because you can include multiple targets in a single build file, you need to create a specific deliverable name for each target element. For more information about creating multiple deliverables with a single build file, see the Invoking Multiple Builds exercise in this lesson.
    c. Change the @DITA.INPUT@ to myprojects/ComstarUserGuide/ComstarUserGuide.ditamap, the file path and file name of the DITA map you want to process.
    d. Change the @OUTPUT.DIR@ to out/myprojects/ComstarUserGuide/web.

       The output directory is the file path to the folder where you want your output files to be stored after processing completes.

   The template creates a build file for your custom project.
3. Save the build file as ComstarUserGuide_xhtml.xml in the ant folder under the DITAOT directory.

   The name of the build file must match the project name (@PROJECT.NAME@) you assigned in your build file.

Figure 6.2 shows you what to change in your build file.

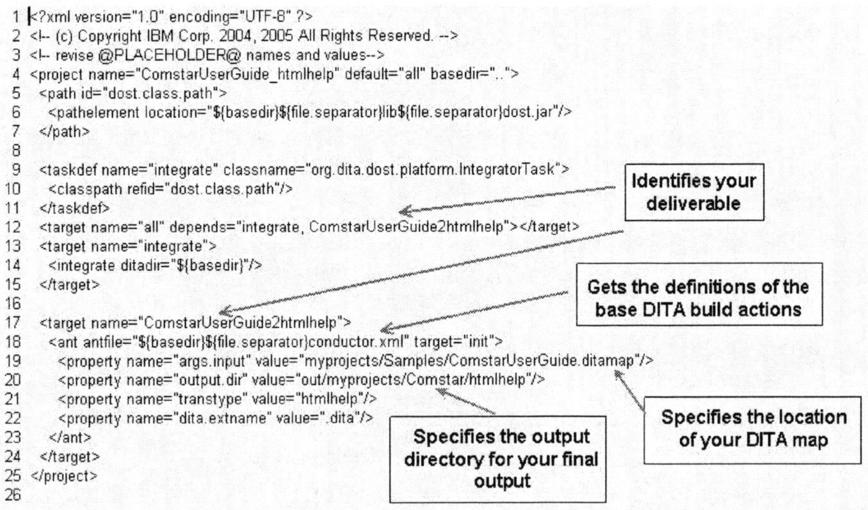

```
<?xml version="1.0" encoding="UTF-8" ?>
<!-- (c) Copyright IBM Corp. 2004, 2005 All Rights Reserved. -->
<!-- revise @PLACEHOLDER@ names and values-->
<project name="ComstarUserGuide_htmlhelp" default="all" basedir="..">
  <path id="dost.class.path">
    <pathelement location="${basedir}${file.separator}lib${file.separator}dost.jar"/>
  </path>

  <taskdef name="integrate" classname="org.dita.dost.platform.IntegratorTask">
    <classpath refid="dost.class.path"/>
  </taskdef>
  <target name="all" depends="integrate, ComstarUserGuide2htmlhelp"></target>
  <target name="integrate">
    <integrate ditadir="${basedir}"/>
  </target>

  <target name="ComstarUserGuide2htmlhelp">
    <ant antfile="${basedir}${file.separator}conductor.xml" target="init">
      <property name="args.input" value="myprojects/Samples/ComstarUserGuide.ditamap"/>
      <property name="output.dir" value="out/myprojects/Comstar/htmlhelp"/>
      <property name="transtype" value="htmlhelp"/>
      <property name="dita.extname" value=".dita"/>
    </ant>
  </target>
</project>
```

Identifies your deliverable
Gets the definitions of the base DITA build actions
Specifies the output directory for your final output
Specifies the location of your DITA map

Figure 6.2 ComstarUserGuide_xhtml.xml build file

Processing a build file

To create output, you must know how to process an Ant build file.

1. From your toolbar, click **Start** > **Run** .
2. In the Open field, type `cmd`.
3. Change your command prompt to your C: directory using the rules provided in the table below.

If this prompt displays,	type the following command
D:\	`c:`
H:\	`c:`
C:\My Documents\...	`cd \`

4. In your command prompt, type `cd DITAOT`

   Your command prompt should change to `c:\DITAOT>`
5. In your command prompt, type ant -f ant\ComstarUserGuide_xhtml.xml and press enter to begin processing.

   The file name located after ant\ is the name of the build file you created.

The processing finishes after a few minutes depending on the speed of your computer and how large your project is. When the processing completes, the confirmation message "BUILD SUCCESSFUL" displays on your command prompt. If the build is not successful and displays "BUILD FAILED", look through the error messages on the command prompt to identify the problem. If you cannot find the problem, contact a DITA Open Toolkit developer.

Modifying Ant build files

In the DITA Open Toolkit, Ant allows you to add custom functionality to create your output. You can use properties to extend the build functionality. In this lesson, you learn to modify your Ant build files to

- copy external files from your immediate information set to a different resource directory
- invoke multiple build actions in one build file
- add a customized cascading stylesheet to your output
- insert an automatically generated header in each of your HTML output files

Some other options you can include using customized Ant build files include invoking additions to the XSL stylesheets and overriding the DITA element processing with custom XSL stylesheets. You can learn more about Ant build options from the DITA-antscript.html file in the DITA Open Toolkit doc folder.

Copying files

When you process your DITA deliverables, you may want to add content that was not created with DITA. For example, you might want to reference an HTML or a PDF file in your DITA map. In most instances, you will not want to make duplicate copies of the external non-DITA files in your output folder. You might want to create a duplicate if you create a CD for your content and want to add all content to the CD. By using the Ant build process, you can copy the external references to your output folder automatically.

You may also want to copy a file to your output directory to create a custom frameset for your deliverable. A frameset uses HTML functionality to produce an output displaying a left hand navigation frame with the topic content on the right. You can find an example frameset in the resource directory of the DITA Open Toolkit.

In this exercise, you copy the index.html file into your output directory to create the frameset. If you don't copy the html file, your output is a plain toc site map. Figure 6.3 shows a sample output without a frameset added to a build file. Figure 6.4 shows a sample output with a frameset added to the build file.

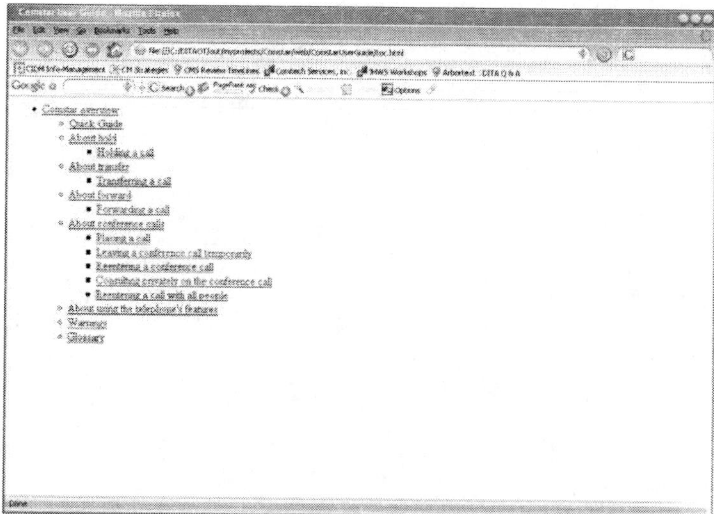

Figure 6.3 Example output without frameset

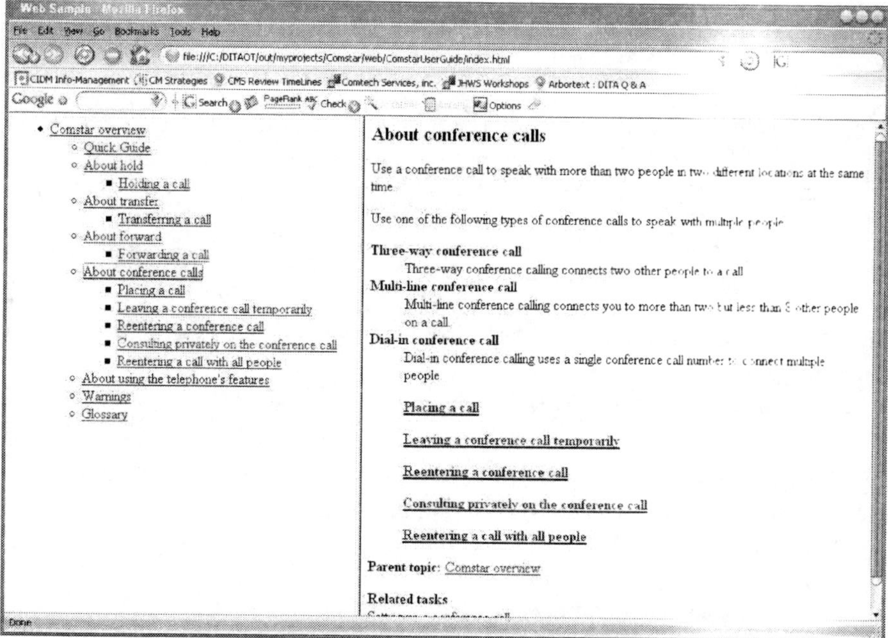

Figure 6.4 Example output with frameset

1. Create a new build file for your deliverable.

   Your build file should look like the following example:

```
<?xml version="1.0" encoding="UTF8" ?>
<!-- (c) Copyright IBM Corp. 2004, 2005 All Rights
   Reserved. -->
<project name="ComstarUserGuide_xhtml" default="all"
   basedir="..">
   <path id="dost.class.path">
      <pathelement location="${basedir}${file.separator}
         lib$ {file.separator}dost.jar"/>
   </path>
   <taskdef name="integrate" classname="org.dita.dost.
      platform.IntegratorTask">
      <classpath refid="dost.class.path"/>
   </taskdef>
   <target name="all" depends="integrate,
      ComstarUserGuide2xhtml"></target>
   <target name="integrate">
      <integrate ditadir="${basedir}"/>
   </target>
   <target name="ComstarUserGuide2xhtml">
      <ant antfile="${basedir}${file.separator}
        conductor.xml" target="init">
         <property name="args.input" value="myprojects/
            ComstarUserGuide/ComstarUserGuide.ditamap"/>
         <property name="output.dir" value="out/
            myprojects/ComstarUserGuide/web"/>
         <property name="transtype" value="xhtml"/>
         <property name="dita.extname" value=".dita"/>
      </ant>
   </target>
</project>
```

2. Add a property to create a table of contents page within your <ant> element container.

```
<property name="args.xhtml.toc" value="toc"/>
```

3. Add a copy element to specify the file to copy to your output folder.

   Add the example <copy> element container after your <ant> element block.

```
</ant>
<copy todir="out/myprojects/Comstar/web/
      ComstarUserGuide">
      <fileset dir="${basedir}${file.separator}resource"
         includes="index.html"/>
</copy>
```

Your final build file looks like this example.

```
<?xml version="1.0" encoding="UTF8" ?>
<!-- (c) Copyright IBM Corp. 2004, 2005 All Rights
   Reserved. -->
<project name="ComstarUserGuide_xhtml" default="all"
   basedir="..">
   <path id="dost.class.path">
      <pathelement location="${basedir}${file.separator}
         lib$ {file.separator}dost.jar"/>
   </path>
   <taskdef name="integrate" classname="org.dita.dost.
      platform.IntegratorTask">
      <classpath refid="dost.class.path"/>
   </taskdef>
   <target name="all" depends="integrate,
      ComstarUserGuide2xhtml"></target>
   <target name="integrate">
      <integrate ditadir="${basedir}"/>
   </target>
   <target name="ComstarUserGuide2xhtml">
      <ant antfile="${basedir}${file.separator}
         conductor.xml" target="init">
         <property name="args.input" value="myprojects/
            ComstarUserGuide/ComstarUserGuide.ditamap"/>
         <property name="output.dir" value="out/
            myprojects/ComstarUserGuide/web"/>
         <property name="transtype" value="xhtml"/>
         <property name="dita.extname" value=".dita"/>
      <property name="args.xhtml.toc" value="toc"/>
      </ant>
      <copy todir="out/myprojects/Comstar/web/
         ComstarUserGuide">
         <fileset dir="${basedir}${file.separator}
            resource" includes="index.html"/>
      </copy>
   </target>
</project>
```

If you want to copy a file such as index.html, use the <copy> element and replace the first example with the second example.

Example 1:

```
<copy todir="out/myprojects/Comstar/web/
   ComstarUserGuide">
   <fileset dir="${basedir}${file.separator}resource"
      includes="index.html"/>
</copy>
```

Example 2:

```
<copy file="${basedir}${file.separator}resource$
   {file.separator}index.html" todir="out/myprojects/
   Comstar/web/ComstarUserGuide" />
```

Invoking multiple builds

Use the multiple builds feature when creating different types of media output or processing different DITA maps at one time. You can include multiple targets for creating your output in one build file. Doing so decreases the time to run multiple build files.

1. Create a new build file for your deliverable.

   Your build file should look like the following example:

```
<?xml version="1.0" encoding="UTF8" ?>
<!-- (c) Copyright IBM Corp. 2004, 2005 All Rights
   Reserved. -->
<project name="ComstarUserGuide_xhtml" default="all"
   basedir="..">
   <path id="dost.class.path">
      <pathelement location="${basedir}${file.separator}
         lib$ {file.separator}dost.jar"/>
   </path>
   <taskdef name="integrate" classname="org.dita.dost.
      platform.IntegratorTask">
      <classpath refid="dost.class.path"/>
   </taskdef>
   <target name="all" depends="integrate,
      ComstarUserGuide2xhtml"></target>
   <target name="integrate">
      <integrate ditadir="${basedir}"/>
   </target>
   <target name="ComstarUserGuide2xhtml">
      <ant antfile="${basedir}${file.separator}
        conductor.xml" target="init">
         <property name="args.input" value="myprojects/
            ComstarUserGuide/ComstarUserGuide.ditamap"/>
         <property name="output.dir" value="out/
            myprojects/ComstarUserGuide/web"/>
         <property name="transtype" value="xhtml"/>
         <property name="dita.extname" value=".dita"/>
      </ant>
   </target>
</project>
```

2. Create a new target definition for one or more projects.

   You can create another target for the same map with a different media type, or you can create a target to a completely different map.

```
<target name="ComstarUserGuide_pdf2pdf">
   <ant antfile="${basedir}${file.separator}
      conductor.xml" target="init">
      <property name="args.input" value="myprojects/
        Samples/ComstarUserGuide/ComstarUserGuide.ditamap"/>
      <property name="output.dir" value="out/myprojects/
        Comstar/pdf"/>
      <property name="transtype" value="pdf"/>
      <property name="dita.extname" value=".dita"/>
      <property name="args.xhtml.toc" value="toc"/>
   </ant>
</target>

<target name="ComstarUserGuideRevTwo2xhtml">
   <ant antfile="${basedir}${file.separator}
      conductor.xml" target="init">
      <property name="args.input" value="myprojects/
         Samples/ComstarUserGuide/
         ComstarUserGuideRevTwo.ditamap"/>
      <property name="output.dir" value="out/myprojects/
         Comstar/rev2"/>
      <property name="transtype" value="xhtml"/>
      <property name="dita.extname" value=".dita"/>
      <property name="args.xhtml.toc" value="toc"/>
   </ant>
</target>
```

3. Modify your target with the *name* attribute value set to "all" to include new targets.

   When you run the build file in the toolkit, your processor uses the information in the "all" target and runs the targets listed in the *depends* attribute value.

```
<target name="all" depends="integrate, ComstarUserGuide2xhtml,
   ComstarUserGuide_pdf2pdf,
   ComstarUserGuideRevTwo2xhtml">
</target>
```

When you run the build file, it creates three output folders. The first output is an XHTML file, the second output is a PDF using the same DITA map, and the third output is an XHTML file using a new DITA map.

```
<?xml version="1.0" encoding="UTF8" ?>
<!-- (c) Copyright IBM Corp. 2004, 2005 All Rights
   Reserved. -->
<project name="ComstarUserGuide_xhtml" default="all"
   basedir="..">
   <path id="dost.class.path">
      <pathelement location="${basedir}${file.separator}
         lib$ {file.separator}dost.jar"/>
   </path>
   <taskdef name="integrate" classname="org.dita.dost.
      platform.IntegratorTask">
      <classpath refid="dost.class.path"/>
   </taskdef>
   <target name="all" depends="integrate,
      ComstarUserGuide2xhtml,
      ComstarUserGuide_pdf2pdf,
      ComstarUserGuideRevTwo2xhtml">
   </target>
   <target name="integrate">
      <integrate ditadir="${basedir}"/>
   </target>
   <target name="ComstarUserGuide2xhtml">
      <ant antfile="${basedir}${file.separator}
        conductor.xml" target="init">
         <property name="args.input" value="myprojects/
            ComstarUserGuide/ComstarUserGuide.ditamap"/>
         <property name="output.dir" value="out/
            myprojects/ComstarUserGuide/web"/>
         <property name="transtype" value="xhtml"/>
         <property name="dita.extname" value=".dita"/>
      </ant>
   </target>
   <target name="ComstarUserGuide_pdf2pdf">
      <ant antfile="${basedir}${file.separator}
         conductor.xml" target="init">
         <property name="args.input" value="myprojects/
            Samples/ComstarUserGuide/
            ComstarUserGuide.ditamap"/>
         <property name="output.dir" value="out/
            myprojects/Comstar/pdf"/>
         <property name="transtype" value="pdf"/>
         <property name="dita.extname" value=".dita"/>
         <property name="args.xhtml.toc" value="toc"/>
      </ant>
   </target>
```

```
    <target name="ComstarUserGuideRevTwo2xhtml">
       <ant antfile="${basedir}${file.separator}
          conductor.xml" target="init">
          <property name="args.input" value="myprojects/
             Samples/ComstarUserGuide/
             ComstarUserGuideRevTwo.ditamap"/>
          <property name="output.dir" value="out/
             myprojects/Comstar/rev2"/>
          <property name="transtype" value="xhtml"/>
          <property name="dita.extname" value=".dita"/>
          <property name="args.xhtml.toc" value="toc"/>
       </ant>
    </target>
</project>
```

Adding a cascading stylesheet

When you create your HTML-based outputs, you may want to override some styles defined in the stylesheets. If you created your own XSLT stylesheets, creating a cascading stylesheet is not critical because you have already designed your XSLT stylesheets. If you want to customize a deliverable to have a different look and feel, use a cascading stylesheet. If you choose to use the stylesheets provided out-of-the-box with the DITA Open Toolkit, you might find yourself adding a custom cascading stylesheet more often. Figure 6.5 shows the default output you get for your HTML.

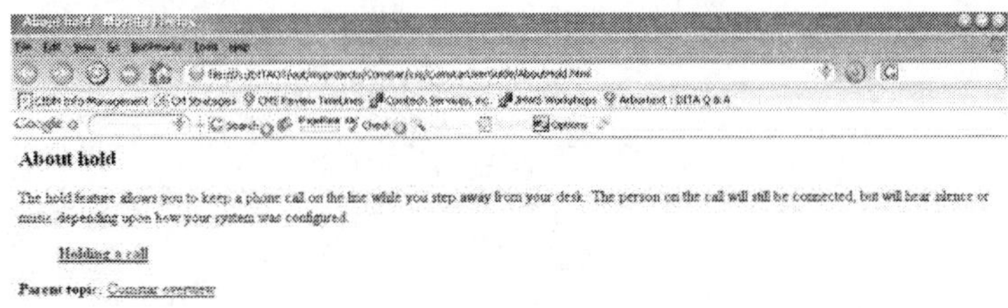

Figure 6.5 Default HTML output from open toolkit

After applying the CSS stylesheet, your output is customized. In Figure 6.6, the background changes to black and the title Answering a Call changes to white and c the font changes to Verdana, Arial, Helvetica, sans-serif.

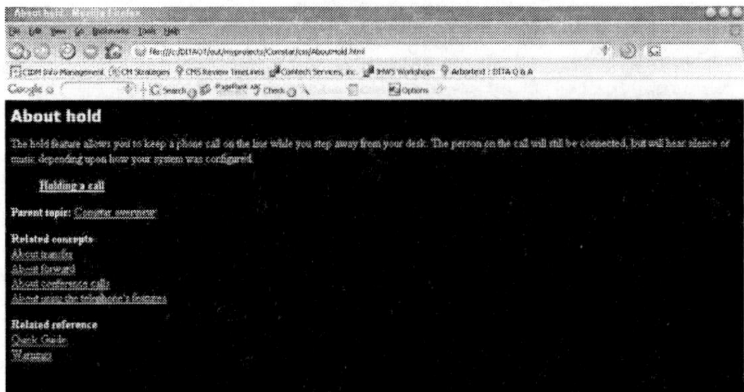

Figure 6.6 Example output with CSS applied

1. Save the example cascading stylesheet in a file called phones.css in a resources folder under your ComstarUserGuide directory.

```
body {
   background: black; color: white;
 }

 a {
   color: yellow;
 }

h1.topictitle1 {
   font-family:  Verdana, Arial, Helvetica, sans-serif;
 }
```

2. Create a new build file for your deliverable.

   Your build file should look like the following example:

```
<?xml version="1.0" encoding="UTF8" ?>
<!-- (c) Copyright IBM Corp. 2004, 2005 All Rights
   Reserved. -->
<project name="ComstarUserGuide_xhtml" default="all"
   basedir="..">
   <path id="dost.class.path">
      <pathelement location="${basedir}${file.separator}
         lib$ {file.separator}dost.jar"/>
   </path>
   <taskdef name="integrate" classname="org.dita.dost.
      platform.IntegratorTask">
      <classpath refid="dost.class.path"/>
   </taskdef>
   <target name="all" depends="integrate,
      ComstarUserGuide2xhtml"></target>
   <target name="integrate">
```

```
      <integrate ditadir="${basedir}"/>
   </target>
   <target name="ComstarUserGuide2xhtml">
      <ant antfile="${basedir}${file.separator}
        conductor.xml" target="init">
         <property name="args.input" value="myprojects/
            ComstarUserGuide/ComstarUserGuide.ditamap"/>
         <property name="output.dir" value="out/
            myprojects/ComstarUserGuide/web"/>
         <property name="transtype" value="xhtml"/>
         <property name="dita.extname" value=".dita"/>
      </ant>
   </target>
</project>
```

3. Add three new property definitions for args.css, args.csspath, and args.copycss.

   You can either point to a file locally on your computer or to a web site URL to specify the CSS. If you point to a local file, the args.csspath allows you to create a special folder for the css file. **Note:** Make sure you do not have spaces, tabs, or soft returns in your build file.

```
<property name="args.css" value="${basedir}${file.separator}myproje
cts${file.separator}Samples${file.separator}ComstarUserGuide${file.
separator}phones.css" />
<property name="args.csspath" value="ComstarUserGuide/resources" />
<property name="args.copycss" value="yes"/>
```

The example below illustrates how to add a CSS to your build file.

```
<?xml version="1.0" encoding="UTF8" ?>
<!-- (c) Copyright IBM Corp. 2004, 2005 All Rights
   Reserved. -->
<project name="ComstarUserGuide_xhtml" default="all"
   basedir="..">
   <path id="dost.class.path">
      <pathelement location="${basedir}${file.separator}
      lib${file.separator}dost.jar"/>
   </path>
   <taskdef name="integrate" classname="org.dita.dost.
      platform.IntegratorTask">
      <classpath refid="dost.class.path"/>
   </taskdef>
   <target name="all" depends="integrate,
      ComstarUserGuide2xhtml"></target>
   <target name="integrate">
      <integrate ditadir="${basedir}"/>
   </target>
   <target name="ComstarUserGuide2xhtml">
```

```
        <ant antfile="${basedir}${file.separator}
           conductor.xml" target="init">
           <property name="args.input" value="myprojects/
              ComstarUserGuide/ComstarUserGuide.ditamap"/>
           <property name="output.dir" value="out/
              myprojects/ComstarUserGuide/css"/>
           <property name="transtype" value="xhtml"/>
           <property name="dita.extname" value=".dita"/>
        <property name="args.css" value="${basedir}$
              {file.separator}myprojects${file.separator}
              Samples${file.separator}ComstarUserGuide$
              {file.separator}phones.css" />
           <property name="args.csspath" value="
              ComstarUserGuide/resources" />
           <property name="args.copycss" value="yes"/>
        </ant>
     </target>
  </project>
```

Adding a header and footer

In this exercise, you learn to use your Ant build file to insert a custom header and footer in your HTML output files. For example, if you want to add a link to your home page at the top of your web pages without including the header in your stylesheet, you can use this Ant process to create a single file containing the HTML markup and include the header automatically when you build your output. You can also add custom HTML navigation to each of your builds or place a copyright statement at the end of your web pages. Adding custom headers and footers improves your content reuse capabilities because you can produce custom header and footer information for different users' needs. Figure 6.7 shows the default output for your HTML output looks.

Figure 6.7 Default HTML output from the open toolkit

Figure 6.8 shows the output when you add a custom header and footer.

Figure 6.8 Output with generated header and footer

1. Save the following example HTML markup in a file named header.html in your ComstarUserGuide folder.

```
<p><font style="color:red; font size: 20pt;">
   Visit <a href="http://www.comtech-serv.com">
   Comtech Services, Inc.</a></font></p>
```

2. Save the following example HTML markup in a file named footer.html in your ComstarUserGuide folder.

```
<p>Copyright 2006 Comtech Services, Inc.</p>
```

3. Create a new build file for your deliverable.

   Your build file should look like the following example:

```
<?xml version="1.0" encoding="UTF8" ?>
<!-- (c) Copyright IBM Corp. 2004, 2005 All Rights
   Reserved. -->
<project name="ComstarUserGuide_xhtml" default="all"
   basedir="..">
   <path id="dost.class.path">
      <pathelement location="${basedir}${file.separator}
         lib$ {file.separator}dost.jar"/>
   </path>

   <taskdef name="integrate" classname="org.dita.dost.
      platform.IntegratorTask">
      <classpath refid="dost.class.path"/>
   </taskdef>
   <target name="all" depends="integrate,
      ComstarUserGuide2xhtml"></target>
   <target name="integrate">
      <integrate ditadir="${basedir}"/>
   </target>
   <target name="ComstarUserGuide2xhtml">
      <ant antfile="${basedir}${file.separator}
        conductor.xml" target="init">
         <property name="args.input" value="myprojects/
            ComstarUserGuide/ComstarUserGuide.ditamap"/>
         <property name="output.dir" value="out/
            myprojects/ComstarUserGuide/web"/>
         <property name="transtype" value="xhtml"/>
         <property name="dita.extname" value=".dita"/>
      </ant>
   </target>
</project>
```

4. Add the args.hdr and args.ftr parameter definitions to your build file.

```
<property name="args.hdr" value="file:/${basedir}$
   {file.separator}myprojects${file.separator}Samples$
   {file.separator}ComstarUserGuide${file.separator}
   header.html" />

<property name="args.ftr" value="file:/${basedir}$
   {file.separator}myprojects${file.separator}Samples$
   {file.separator}ComstarUserGuide${file.separator}
   footer.html" />
```

For the DITA Open Toolkit to correctly process the HTML header and footer files, you must precede the file location with file:/ to indicate to the DITA Open Toolkit that you are linking to another file. The ${basedir} is the location from which you run the ant build command. In this example, the ${basedir} value is C:/DITAOT. **Note:** Make sure you do not have spaces, tabs,or soft returns in your build file.

```
<?xml version="1.0" encoding="UTF8" ?>
<!-- (c) Copyright IBM Corp. 2004, 2005 All Rights
   Reserved. -->
<project name="ComstarUserGuide_xhtml" default="all"
   basedir="..">
   <path id="dost.class.path">
      <pathelement location="${basedir}${file.separator}
      lib${file.separator}dost.jar"/>
   </path>
   <taskdef name="integrate" classname="org.dita.dost.
      platform.IntegratorTask">
      <classpath refid="dost.class.path"/>
   </taskdef>
   <target name="all" depends="integrate,
      ComstarUserGuide2xhtml"></target>
   <target name="integrate">
      <integrate ditadir="${basedir}"/>
   </target>
   <target name="ComstarUserGuide2xhtml">
      <ant antfile="${basedir}${file.separator}
         conductor.xml" target="init">
         <property name="args.input" value="myprojects/
            ComstarUserGuide/ComstarUserGuide.ditamap"/>
         <property name="output.dir" value="out/
            myprojects/ComstarUserGuide/headerandfooter"/>
         <property name="transtype" value="xhtml"/>
         <property name="dita.extname" value=".dita"/>
```

```
            <property name="args.hdr" value="file:/$
               {basedir}${file.separator}myprojects$
               {file.separator}Samples${file.separator}
               ComstarUserGuide${file.separator}header.html" />
            <property name="args.ftr" value="file:/$
               {basedir}${file.separator}myprojects$
               {file.separator}Samples${file.separator}
               ComstarUserGuide${file.separator}footer.html" />
         </ant>
      </target>
   </project>
```

Ant review questions

1. What is the purpose of the Ant build file?
2. What are the four placeholders that must be changed in the Ant build file?
3. What command do you use to run an Ant build file?
4. How would you create a table of contents for your HTML output?
5. How would you create a PDF and an HTML output using a single build file?
6. Can you add a cascading style sheet to your output?

SECTION K

Understanding Conditional Processing

Conditional processing in DITA allows you to filter content that you want or do not want in a particular deliverable. With conditional processing, you create a master topic that contains content variations for different users, products, platforms, versions, or other conditions that you define. When you process the topic, you exclude content that should not be part of a specific deliverable. DITA conditional processing enables customized output from a single source.

In DITA, almost every element has a common set of attributes you can use for conditional processing. These attributes include

- *audience* — the intended audience of the content
- *platform* — the platform on which the product is deployed
- *product* — the product that is the subject of the discussion
- *rev* — the revision or draft number of the current document
- *otherprops* — any other attribute you include

You can use the audience attribute to specify parts of a topic that apply to two different audiences. For example, you may have written a concept that is appropriate for an advanced user, but you want to include the first paragraph in a version for a beginner. By adding an *audience* attribute with the value "beginner" to the first paragraph, you can extract this paragraph during processing to develop a beginner's manual.

You can enter more than one value for the *audience* attribute. You may decide that the second paragraph of your concept is appropriate for a beginner and an administrator. The value you enter to label this paragraph would be "beginner administrator". During processing you could produce a beginner and an administrator version of the topic, in addition to the advanced version.

LESSON 20

Conditional Processing File

For conditional processing to function correctly, you must label your content correctly and create a .ditaval file to activate your conditional processing rules. The properties you include in the .ditaval file dictate the content to include or exclude.

In the .ditaval file, you indicate the attributes and values that you want to process conditionally and the processing rules you want to apply. In the <prop> element, you can set parameters to include, exclude, or flag content. These parameters are defined by the following attributes:

- *att* — the attribute you want to filter on, such as product, platform, audience, or otherprops
- *val* — the value you assign to the attributes that you want to filter on, such as internal/external (audience), windows/linux (platform)
- *action* — the activity you want to perform, such as include, exclude, or flag
- *img* — the image you will use for flagged content
- *alt* — the alternate text to use if the image is not visible for the flagged content

The revision property <revprop> element in the .ditaval file allows you to flag a specific version of your document. Use flagging to highlight content in your deliverable for review. Highlighting can be handled with color changes in electronic output or with symbols in print or PDF output. Using the <revprop> element lets you create a version for editors or reviewers so that they focus on new or changed content they have not yet reviewed.

The revision property <revprop> element uses attributes to control its behavior. They include the following:

- *val* — the version number of your output, such as 7.01. Unlike the <prop> attribute, you need not specify an attribute because the revision attribute is assumed.
- *action* — the activity you want to perform on your content, such as flag or noflag
- *char* — the symbol you want to use to flag your content, such as | or *
- *style* — the color you want to use to highlight revisions. The style should be either a name or an SRGB value. There are sixteen possible values for color.

Black=#000000	White=#FFFFFF	Yellow=#FFFF00	Green=#008000
Silver=#C0C0C0	Navy=#000080	Maroon=#800000	Gray=#808080
Lime=#00FF00	Red=#FF0000	Blue=#0000FF	Olive=#808000
Purple=#800080	Teal=#008080	Fuchsia=#FF00FF	Aqua=#00FFFF

Filtering

Filtering is the most common option for conditional processing. To include or exclude content specific to a deliverable, you must use the "include" or "exclude" value for the *action* attribute in your .ditaval property element. You can filter at the map or at the topic level. The *att* attribute in the property element identifies the name of the attribute you want to process conditionally. The *val* attribute indicates the value you are using to distinguish the pieces of content.

Flagging

The other value you can use in the *action* attribute on the <prop> element is "flag". Flagging allows you to attach a graphic to a specific piece of information during processing. For example, if you have different information that applies to users in Canada versus the US, you might indicate Canadian-specific information using a Canadian flag image. Use the *img* attribute to "flag" content with a special image indicator, and use the *alt* attribute to apply an alternative for the image. Figure 6.9 shows the Quicken help system using a Canadian flag image to identify information specific to Canadian tax laws.

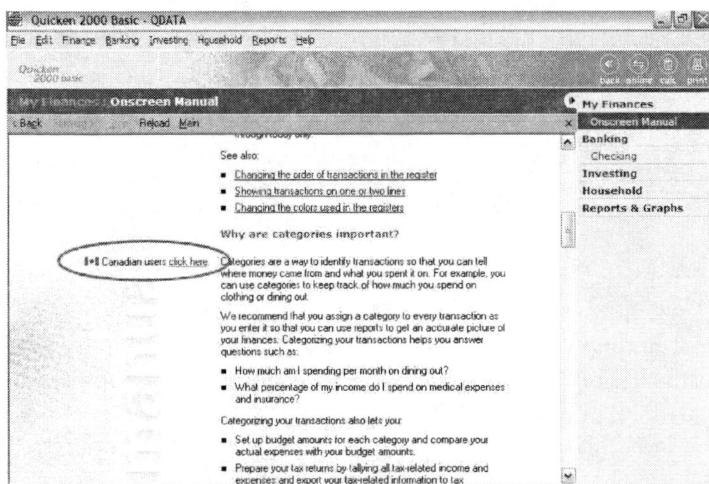

Figure 6.9 Flagging example rendered

Adding conditional processing metadata attributes

This exercise explains how to set up your topics to be filtered correctly during conditional processing.

For this exercise, use the content for the phone deliverable created throughout this guide. For example, consider using a topic you often duplicate to accommodate minor modifications for different users' situations. You must identify a topic for which you would originally have created two very similar files that have small differences in the content.

In this lesson, you learn to add ID attributes to the elements you want to filter.

1. Open the Transferring a call topic you created in Lesson 2: Task Information Type.

   Use the task to create an administrative and a user guide.

```
<?xml version="1.0" encoding="utf-8"?>
<!DOCTYPE task PUBLIC "-//OASIS//DTD DITA Task//EN"
   "../../dtd/task.dtd">
<task id="TransferringACall" xml:lang="en-us">
   <title>Transferring a call</title>
   <shortdesc>When you transfer a call to another person
     in your office, you have two ways of handling the
     transfer.
   </shortdesc>
   <taskbody>
```

```
<context>
   <p> When you transfer the call without speaking
      to the person, it is an unannounced transfer.
      When you speak to the person receiving the
      transferred call, it is an announced transfer.
   </p>
</context>
<steps>
   <step>
      <cmd>Press the transfer button.</cmd>
   </step>
   <step>
      <cmd>Dial the number.</cmd>
      <info>Dial the number manually or using your
         pre-defined speed dial keys. </info>
   </step>
   <step>
      <cmd>Transfer the call.</cmd>
      <choicetable>
         <chhead>
            <choptionhd>Type of Announcement
            </choptionhd>
            <chdeschd>Steps to complete
               announcement </chdeschd>
         </chhead>
         <chrow>
            <choption>Announce a call transfer
            </choption>
            <chdesc>
               <ol>
                  <li>Speak to the person</li>
                  <li>Hang up the phone</li>
               </ol>
            </chdesc>
         </chrow>
         <chrow>
            <choption>Transfer a call unannounced
            </choption>
            <chdesc>
               <ul>
                  <li>Hang up the phone</li>
               </ul>
            </chdesc>
         </chrow>
      </choicetable>
      <info>
```

```
            <note>If you announce a call and the person
               refuses the transfer, do not hang up the
               phone. Press the transfer button again to
               retrieve the call on your phone station.
            </note>
         </info>
      </step>
   </steps>
   <result>The call is transferred.</result>
  </taskbody>
</task>
```

2. Insert information for a different audience.

   In this example, you add two steps and a post requirement for administrators only.

```
<?xml version="1.0" encoding="utf-8"?>
<!DOCTYPE task PUBLIC "-//OASIS//DTD DITA Task//EN"
   "../../dtd/task.dtd">
<task id="TransferringACall" xml:lang="en-us">
   <title>Transferring a call</title>
   <shortdesc>When you transfer a call to another person
      in your office, you have two ways of handling the
      transfer.</shortdesc>
   <taskbody>
      <context>
         <p> When you transfer the call without speaking
            to the person, it is an unannounced transfer.
            When you speak to the person receiving the
            transferred call, it is an announced transfer.
         </p>
      </context>
      <steps>
         <step>
            <cmd>Activate the phone to use the transfer
            feature.</cmd>
            <info>To activate your phone, go to the
               options screen and turn the transfer feature
               from off to on. Information about the options
               screen is in the Options section of this
               manual.</info>
         </step>
         <step>
            <cmd>Test the transfer feature to ensure
               your phone is working correctly.</cmd>
            <info>Use the steps below to test your
               phone</info>
         </step>
```

```
    <step>
        <cmd>Press the transfer button.</cmd>
      </step>
      <step>
        <cmd>Dial the number.</cmd>
        <info>Dial the number manually or using your
          pre-defined speed dial keys. </info>
      </step>
      <step>
        <cmd>Transfer the call.</cmd>
        <choicetable>
          <chhead>
            <choptionhd>Type of Announcement
            </choptionhd>
            <chdeschd>Steps to complete
            announcement </chdeschd>
          </chhead>
          <chrow>
            <choption>Announce a call transfer
            </choption>
            <chdesc>
              <ol>
                <li>Speak to the person</li>
                <li>Hang up the phone</li>
             </ol>
            </chdesc>
          </chrow>
          <chrow><choption>Transfer a call
            unannounced</choption>
            <chdesc>
              <ul>
                <li>Hang up the phone</li>
              </ul>
            </chdesc>
          </chrow>
        </choicetable>
        <info>
          <note>If you announce a call and the
            person refuses the transfer, do not hang
            up the phone. Press the transfer button
            again to retrieve the call on your
            phone station.</note>
        </info>
      </step>
    </steps>
    <result>The call is transferred.</result>
  <postreq>If you encounter any problems testing
      your phone, contact the manufacturer.</postreq>
  </taskbody>
</task>
```

If you use an XML editor, your screen image may render the first two steps. However, in the user guide, step 3 becomes step 1 when you produce your deliverable. After you process the information, the stylesheet numbers the steps correctly for the guide you produce.

3. Add an *audience* attribute to the information specific to the administrator.

   Enter "administrator" for the attribute value.

```
<step audience="administrator">
   <cmd>Activate the phone to use the transfer feature.
   </cmd>
   <info>To activate your phone you must use go to the
      options screen and turn the transfer feature from off
      to on. Information about the options screen is in the
      Options section of this manual.</info>
</step>
<step audience="administrator">
   <cmd>Test the transfer feature to ensure your phone
      is working correctly.</cmd>
   <info>Use the steps below to test your phone.
   </info>
</step>
<postreq audience="administrator">If your
   encounter any problems with testing your phone, please
   contact the manufacturer to report your issues.
</postreq>
```

4. Add audience attributes to distinguish the original content specific for the user guide.

   In the example, some content is specifically for the enduser. For these elements, add "enduser" for the *audience* attribute value. For all other elements, you can either omit the audience attribute, or you can indicate that these elements apply to both audiences. Both options are shown in the example below.

```
<context audience="enduser">
   <p> When you transfer the call without speaking to the
   person, it is an unannounced transfer. When you speak to
   the person receiving the transferred call, it is an
   announced transfer.</p>
</context>
<steps>
   <step audience="administrator enduser">
      <cmd>Transfer the call.</cmd>
```

```
      <choicetable>
         <chhead>
            <choptionhd>Type of Announcement
            </choptionhd>
            <chdeschd>Steps to complete announcement
            </chdeschd>
         </chhead>
         <chrow>
            <choption>Announce a call transfer
            </choption>
            <chdesc>
               <ol>
                  <li>Speak to the person</li>
                  <li>Hang up the phone</li>
               </ol>
            </chdesc>
         </chrow>
         <chrow>
            <choption>Transfer a call unannounced
            </choption>
            <chdesc>
               <ul>
                  <li>Hang up the phone</li>
               </ul>
            </chdesc>
         </chrow>
      </choicetable>
      <info>
         <note audience="enduser
            enduser_important">If you announce a
            call and the person refuses the transfer,
            do not hang up the phone. Press the
            transfer button again to retrieve the call
            on your phone station.</note>
      </info>
   </step>
</steps>
```

Conditional processing example

The following example illustrates the topic with the combined administrator and enduser content identified with conditional processing metadata.

```
<?xml version="1.0" encoding="utf-8"?>
<!DOCTYPE task PUBLIC "-//OASIS//DTD DITA Task//EN"
   "../../dtd/task.dtd">
<task id="TransferringACall" xml:lang="en-us">
   <title>Transferring a call</title>
   <shortdesc>When you transfer a call to another person
      in your office, you have two ways of handling the
      transfer.</shortdesc>
```

```
<taskbody>
   <context audience="enduser">
      <p> When you transfer the call without speaking
         to the person, it is an unannounced transfer.
         When you speak to the person receiving the
         transferred call, it is an announced transfer.
      </p>
   </context>
   <steps>
      <step audience="administrator">
         <cmd>Activate the phone to use the transfer
            feature.</cmd>
         <info>To activate your phone you must use go
            to the options screen and turn the transfer
            feature from off to on. Information about the
            options screen is in the Options section of
            this manual.</info>
      </step>
      <step audience="administrator">
         <cmd>Test the transfer feature to ensure
            your phone is working correctly.</cmd>
         <info>Use the steps below to test your phone
         </info>
      </step>
      <step>
         <cmd>Press the transfer button.</cmd>
      </step>
      <step>
         <cmd>Dial the number.</cmd>
         <info>Dial the number manually or using your
            pre-defined speed dial keys. </info>
      </step>
      <step audience="administrator enduser">
         <cmd>Transfer the call.</cmd>
         <choicetable>
            <chhead>
               <choptionhd>Type of Announcement
               </choptionhd>
               <chdeschd>Steps to complete
                  announcement</chdeschd>
            </chhead>
            <chrow>
               <choption>Announce a call transfer
               </choption>
               <chdesc>
                  <ol>
                     <li>Speak to the person</li>
                     <li>Hang up the phone</li>
                  </ol>
               </chdesc>
```

```
                </chrow>
                <chrow>
                    <choption>Transfer a call unannounced
                    </choption>
                    <chdesc>
                        <ul>
                            <li>Hang up the phone</li>
                        </ul>
                    </chdesc>
                </chrow>
            </choicetable>
            <info>
                <note audience="enduser enduser_
                    important">If you announce a call and
                    the person refuses the transfer, do not
                    hang up the phone. Press the transfer
                    button again to retrieve the call on your
                    phone station.</note>
            </info>
        </step>
    </steps>
    <result>The call is transferred.</result>
    <postreq audience="administrator">If your
        encounter any problems with testing your phone,
        please contact the manufacturer to report your
        issues</postreq>
  </taskbody>
</task>
```

Creating the .ditaval file

To successfully produce output using conditional processing, you must create a .ditaval file to indicate which properties you want to filter or flag. The DITA Open Toolkit comes packaged with the .ditaval file DTD for your reference. It is located at **samples > filterflag > DITAval.dtd.**

1. Open a new file in your text editor.
2. Enter the xml declaration as the first line of your file.

   ```
   <?xml version="1.0" encoding="utf-8"?>
   ```

3. Add <val> element start and end tags for the .ditaval file.

   ```
   <?xml version="1.0" encoding="utf-8"?><val>
   </val>
   ```

4. Add two empty <prop> elements between the <val> element start and end tags.

You use the property element to add the metadata needed to conditionally process your topic. You can add as many <prop> elements as needed.

```
<val>
   <prop />
   <prop />
</val>
```

5. Add the following attributes and associated values to your <prop> elements.

   The attribute values shown below represent the values used in the previous exercise in this lesson: Adding Conditional Processing Metadata Attributes . In that exercise, you used the attribute *audience* to distinguish between the information for the enduser and the administrator. For this sample .ditaval file, assume you are creating the User Guide. Exclude everything labelled administrator and include everything labelled enduser. The first property element includes attributes from the first column and the second property element includes attributes from the second column.

att="audience" *val*="administrator" *action*="exclude"	*att*="audience" *val*="enduser" *action*="include"

```
<val>
   <prop att="audience" val="administrator"
      action="exclude" />
   <prop att="audience" val="enduser" action="include" />
</val>
```

6. Add a third <prop> element.

   Use this <prop> element to flag steps you indicated were for endusers. For example, you may have an image of an exclamation point to indicate to your user that a certain step is critical.

```
<val>
   <prop att="audience" val="administrator"
       action="exclude" />
   <prop att="audience" val="enduser" action="include" /
   <prop />
</val>
```

7. Add the following attributes and associated values to the third <prop> element.

att="audience"

val="enduser_important"

action="flag"

img="important.gif"

alt="Critical step"

8. Save your .ditaval file in the ComstarUserGuide folder.

This example excludes the administrator audience and places an image (important.gif) in the note for the end user audience.

phone.ditaval

The example below shows a .ditaval file. The .ditaval file is usually a short file, but it becomes more complex as your conditions increase in complexity.

```
<?xml version="1.0" encoding="utf-8"?>
<val>
   <prop att="audience" val="administrator"
      action="exclude" />
   <prop att="audience" val="enduser" action="include" />
   <prop att="audience" val="enduser_important"
      action="flag" img="important.gif"
      alt="Critical step" />
</val>
```

Processing the .ditaval file

To process the .ditaval file, you must include a property in your Ant build file to point to your .ditaval file's location.

1. Add another <property> element for the DITA.input.valfile parameter after your last <property> element in the build file you created in the Creating build files section.

   The processor uses the dita.input.valfile in the build file to process your conditional content. The dita.input.valfile value identifies the location of your .ditaval file. You should include the .ditaval file in the same folder as your DITA map. If you place your .ditaval file in a central location to conditionally process multiple deliverables, you need to reference the .ditaval file using a relative path from the base DITA Open Toolkit directory.

   In your Ant build file, you must replace the forward slashes in your path names with ${file.separator} for conditional processing to work. You must also start your path names at the DITA Open Toolkit base directory using ${basedir}.

```
<property name="dita.input.valfile"
  value="${basedir}$
    {file.separator}myprojects
     {file.separator}
    ComstarUserGuide{file.separator}
        phones.ditaval"/>
```

The example below illustrates a .ditaval file.

```
<?xml version="1.0" encoding="UTF8" ?>
<!-- (c) Copyright IBM Corp. 2004, 2005 All Rights
   Reserved. -->
<project name="ComstarUserGuide_xhtml" default="all"
   basedir="..">
   <path id="dost.class.path">
      <pathelement location="${basedir}${file.separator}
         lib${file.separator}dost.jar"/>
   </path>
   <taskdef name="integrate" classname="org.dita.dost.
      platform.IntegratorTask">
      <classpath refid="dost.class.path"/>
   </taskdef>
   <target name="all" depends="integrate,
      ComstarUserGuide2xhtml"></target>
   <target name="integrate">
      <integrate ditadir="${basedir}"/>
   </target>
   <target name="ComstarUserGuide2xhtml">
      <ant antfile="${basedir}${file.separator}
         conductor.xml" target="init">
         <property name="args.input" value="${basedir}$
            {file.separator}myprojects${file.separator}
            ComstarUserGuide${file.separator}
            ComstarUserGuide.ditamap"/>
         <property name="output.dir" value="${basedir}$
            {file.separator}out${file.separator}myprojects
            {file.separator}ComstsrUserGuide$
            {file.separator}web"/>
         <property name="transtype" value="xhtml"/>
         <property name="dita.extname" value=".dita"/>
         <property name="dita.input.valfile" value="${basedir}$
            {file.separator}myprojects{file.separator}
            ComstarUserGuide{file.separator}
            phones.ditaval"/>
      </ant>
   </target>
</project>
```

Conditional processing review questions

1. What is the purpose of a .ditaval file?
2. What values can you filter using conditional processing?
3. What is the benefit of using conditional processing?
4. How do you reference the .ditaval file?
5. How would you create different deliverables for endusers and administrators?

Appendix A

Appendix A provides a set of example DITA files and the corresponding DITA code needed to produce the output. The purpose of Appendix A is to demonstrate the DITA methodology, including what a topic should look like, and a proposed DITA markup for the content. The collection of examples is a small user guide for a phone system. The DITA code for the example map is located at the end of Appendix A.

Comstar overview

The Comstar User and Attendant's Guide is designed to help you use your telephone's features to your best advantage.

Terms you'll need to know

The following terms will help you understand some of the instructions in this guide.

Attendant
: A receptionist or other person responsible for answering incoming calls.

Dialpad
: The numbered keys on your telephone, including the # and *.

Function buttons
: The buttons or keys on your telephone that allow you to press a single button to make conference calls, program your telephone, use the speakerphone, and others.

Handset
: The telephone receiver that you use to listen and speak.

Intercom calls
: The calls you make to other telephones inside your organization.

Line buttons
: The buttons you use to select the outside line you want to use to make a call.

Line lamps
: The small lights next to the line buttons on your telephone.

Speakerphone
: A built-in feature of your telephone that lets you speak and hear a conversation without using the handset. The following telephones have a built-in speakerphone: 16-button, 30-button, and 42-button.

Station
: An individual telephone set.

Station buttons
: The buttons you use to select other extensions in the system.

Switchhook
: On the single-line telephone, the button in the handset cradle.

64-button DSS/BLF

The 64-button accesory that contains 60 telephone line buttons and lamps and four function buttons. DSS/BLF stands for Direct Station select/Busy Lamp Field.

Comstar overview code

The code below illustrates the example shown.

```
<?xml version="1.0" encoding="utf-8"?>
<!DOCTYPE concept PUBLIC "-//IBM//DTD DITA Concept//EN"
   "../../../dtd/concept.dtd">
<concept id="comstaroverview" xml:lang="en-us">
   <title>Comstar overview</title>
   <shortdesc>The Comstar User and Attendant's Guide is
      designed to help you use your telephone's features to
      your best advantage.</shortdesc>
   <conbody>
      <section>
         <title>Terms you'll need to know</title>
         <p>The following terms will help you understand
            some of the instructions in this guide.</p>
         <dl>
            <dlentry>
               <dt>Attendant</dt>
               <dd>A receptionist or other person
                  responsible for answering incoming calls.
               </dd>
            </dlentry>
            <dlentry>
               <dt>Dialpad</dt>
               <dd>The numbered keys on your telephone,
                  including the # and *.</dd>
            </dlentry>
            <dlentry>
               <dt>Function buttons</dt>
               <dd>The buttons or keys on your telephone
                  that allow you to press a single button to
                  make conference calls, program your
                  telephone, use the speakerphone and
                  others.</dd>
            </dlentry>
            <dlentry>
               <dt>Handset</dt>
               <dd>The telephone receiver that you use to
                  listen and speak.</dd>
            </dlentry>
            <dlentry>
               <dt>Intercom calls</dt>
```

```
                <dd>The calls you make to other telephones
                   inside your organization.</dd>
             </dlentry>
             <dlentry>
                <dt>Line buttons</dt>
                <dd>The buttons you use to select the
                   outside line you want to use to make
                   a call.</dd>
             </dlentry>
             <dlentry>
                <dt>Line lamps</dt>
                <dd>The small lights next to the line
                   buttons on your telephone.</dd>
             </dlentry>
             <dlentry>
                <dt>Speakerphone</dt>
                <dd>A built-in feature of your telephone
                   that lets you speak and hear a
                   conversation without using the handset.
                   The following telephones have a built-in
                   speakerphone: 16-button, 30-button, and
                   42-button.</dd>
             </dlentry>
             <dlentry>
                <dt>Station</dt>
                <dd>An individual telephone set.</dd>
             </dlentry>
             <dlentry>
                <dt>Station buttons</dt>
                <dd>The buttons you use to select other
                   extensions in the system.</dd>
             </dlentry>
             <dlentry>
                <dt>Switchhook</dt>
                <dd>On the single-line telephone, the
                   button in the handset cradle.</dd>
             </dlentry>
             <dlentry>
                <dt>64-button DSS/BLF</dt>
                <dd>The 64-button accesory that contains
                   60 telephone line buttons and lamps and
                   four function buttons. DSS/BLF stands for
                   Direct Station select/Busy Lamp Field.
                </dd>
             </dlentry>
          </dl>
       </section>
    </conbody>
</concept>
```

Quick Guide to Basic Telephone Use

The Quick Guide provides a brief description of the buttons on your phone.

Action	Indicator	Description
Talk	TALK	Press the talk key to receive a dial tone.
Speaker phone	SPEAKERPHONE	Press the speaker phone button to place a call on speaker phone.
Forward	FORWARD	Press the forward button to forward all incoming calls to another phone number or voice mail.
Transfer	TRANSFER	Press the transfer button to transfer a call to another person.
Hold	HOLD	Press the hold button to place a call on hold.
Mute	MUTE	Press the mute button to mute your end of the call.

Quick guide code

The following code illustrates the example shown.

```
<?xml version="1.0" encoding="utf-8"?>
<!DOCTYPE reference PUBLIC "-//OASIS//DTD DITA
   Reference//EN" "reference.dtd">
<reference id="QuickGuide" xml:lang="en-us">
   <title>Quick Guide to Basic Telephone Use</title>
   <shortdesc>The Quick Guide provides a brief
      description of the buttons on your phone.
   </shortdesc>
   <prolog>
      <author>John Smith</author>
   </prolog>
   <refbody>
      <properties>
         <prophead>
            <proptypehd>Action</proptypehd>
            <propvaluehd>Indicator</propvaluehd>
            <propdeschd>Description</propdeschd>
         </prophead>
         <property>
            <proptype>Talk</proptype>
            <propvalue>
               <image href="talk.jpg"/>
            </propvalue>
            <propdesc>Press the talk key to receive a
               dial tone.</propdesc>
         </property>
         <property>
            <proptype>Speaker phone</proptype>
            <propvalue>
               <image href="speakerphone.jpg"/>
            </propvalue>
            <propdesc>Press the speaker phone button to
               place a call on speaker phone.</propdesc>
         </property>
         <property>
            <proptype>Forward</proptype>
            <propvalue>
               <image href="forward.jpg"/>
            </propvalue>
            <propdesc>Press the forward button to
               forward all incoming calls to another phone
               number or voice mail.</propdesc>
         </property>
```

```
        <property>
           <proptype>Transfer</proptype>
           <propvalue>
              <image href="transfer.jpg"/>
           </propvalue>
           <propdesc>Press the transfer button to
              transfer a call to another person.
           </propdesc>
        </property>
        <property>
           <proptype>Hold</proptype>
           <propvalue>
              <image href="hold.jpg"/>
           </propvalue>
           <propdesc>Press the hold button to place a
              call on hold.</propdesc>
        </property>
        <property>
           <proptype>Mute</proptype>
           <propvalue>
              <image href="mute.jpg"/>
           </propvalue>
           <propdesc>Press the mute button to mute
              your end of the call.
           </propdesc>
        </property>
     </properties>
  </refbody>
     <related-links>
         <link href="TransferringACall.dita"
            scope="local"/>
     </related-links>
</reference>
```

About hold

The hold feature allows you to keep a phone call on the line while you step away from your desk. The person on the call will still be connected but will hear silence or music depending upon how your system was configured.

About hold code

The code below illustrates the example shown.

```
<?xml version="1.0" encoding="utf-8"?>
<!DOCTYPE concept PUBLIC "-//OASIS//DTD DITA Concept//EN"
   "../../../dtd/concept.dtd">
<concept id="abouthold" xml:lang="en-us">
   <title>About hold</title>
   <conbody>
      <p>The hold feature allows you to keep a phone call
         on the line while you step away from your desk. The
         person on the call will still be connected but will
         hear silence or music depending upon how your
         system was configured.</p>
   </conbody>
</concept>
```

Holding a call

1. Press Hold/Callback to place a call on hold.
2. Press the Hold/Callback to retrieve a call on hold.

Holding a call code

The code below illustrates the example shown.

```
<?xml version="1.0" encoding="utf-8"?>
<!DOCTYPE task PUBLIC "-//OASIS//DTD DITA Task//EN"
   "../../../dtd/task.dtd">
<task id="holding" xml:lang="en-us">
   <title>Holding a call</title>
   <taskbody>
      <steps>
         <step>
            <cmd>Press Hold/Callback to place a call on
               hold.</cmd>
         </step>
         <step>
            <cmd>Press the Hold/Callback to retrieve a
               call on hold.</cmd>
         </step>
      </steps>
   </taskbody>
</task>
```

About transfer

When you transfer a call to another person in your office, you have two ways to handle the transfer. When you transfer a call without speaking to the person, it is an unannounced transfer. When you speak to the person receiving the transferred call, it is an announced transfer.

About transfer code

The code below illustrates the example shown.

```
<?xml version="1.0" encoding="utf-8"?>
<!DOCTYPE concept PUBLIC "-//OASIS//DTD DITA Concept//EN"
   "../../../dtd/concept.dtd">
<concept id="abouttransfer" xml:lang="en-us">
   <title>About transfer</title>
   <conbody>
      <p>When you transfer a call to another person in
         your office, you have two ways to handling the
         transfer. When you transfer a calll without
         speaking to the person, it is an unannouced
         transfer. When you speak to the person receiving
         the transferred call, it is an announced transfer.
      </p>
   </conbody>
</concept>
```

Transferring a call

When you transfer a call to another person in your office, you have two ways of handling the transfer.

When you transfer the call without speaking to the person, it is an unannounced transfer. When you speak to the person receiving the transferred call, it is an announced transfer.

1. Press the transfer button.
2. Dial the number.

   Dial the number manually, use your pre-defined speed dial keys or go to your company directory.
3. Transfer the call.

Type of Announcement	Steps to complete
Announce a call transfer	1. Speak to the person. 2. Hang up the phone.
Transfer a call unannounced	Hang up the phone.

Note: If you announce a call and the person refuses the transfer, do not hang up the phone. Press the transfer button again to retrieve the call on your phone station.

The call is transferred.

Transferring a call code

The code below illustrates the example shown.

```
<?xml version="1.0" encoding="utf-8"?>
<!DOCTYPE task PUBLIC "-//OASIS//DTD DITA Task//EN"
   "task.dtd">
<task id="TransferringACall" xml:lang="en-us">
   <title>Transferring a call</title>
   <shortdesc>When you transfer a call to another person
      in your office, you have two ways of handling the
      transfer.</shortdesc>
   <prolog>
      <copyright>
         <copyryear year="2006"></copyryear>
         <copyrholder>Comtech Services</copyrholder>
      </copyright>
      <permissions view="all"/>
```

```
    <metadata>
       <keywords>
          <keyword>phone</keyword>
          <keyword>transfer</keyword>
          <keyword>transferring a call</keyword>
       </keywords>
    </metadata>
 </prolog>
 <taskbody>
    <context>
       <p>When you transfer the call without speaking
          to the person, it is an unannounced transfer.
          When you speak to the person receiving the
          transferred call, it is an announced transfer.
       </p>
    </context>
    <steps>
       <step>
          <cmd>Press the transfer button.</cmd>
       </step>
       <step>
          <cmd>Dial the number.<</cmd>
          <info>Dial the number manually, use your
             pre-defined speed dial keys or go to your
             company directory.</info>
       </step>
       <step>
          <cmd>Transfer the call.</cmd>
          <choicetable>
             <chhead>
                <choptionhd>Type of Announcement
                </choptionhd>
                <chdeschd>Steps to complete</chdeschd>
             </chhead>
             <chrow>
                <choption>Announce a call transfer
                </choption>
                <chdesc>
                   <ol>
                      <li>Speak to the person.</li>
                      <li>Hang up the phone.</li>
                   </ol>
                </chdesc>
             </chrow>
             <chrow>
                <choption>Transfer a call unannounced
                </choption>
```

```
                <chdesc>
                    <ul>
                        <li>Hang up the phone.</li>
                    </ul>
                </chdesc>
            </chrow>
        </choicetable>
        <info>
            <note>If you announce a call and the
                person refuses the transfer, do not hang
                up the phone. Press the transfer button
                again to retrieve the call on your phone
                station.</note>
        </info>
    </step>
  </steps>
  <result>The call is transferred.</result>
</taskbody>
  <related-links>
    <link href="AboutTransfer.dita" format="html"
        scope="local"/>
    <link href="../GeneralTopic/Glossary.dita"
        format="html" scope="peer"></link>
    <link href="http://www.comtech-serv.com/Comstar"
        format="html" scope="external">
    <linktext>Comstar Phones</linktext>
        <desc>Order your Comstar phone today.
        </desc>
    </link>
  </related-links>
</task>
```

About forward

You can ask the system to forward all your calls to another extension or to an outside telephone number.

When you forward your calls, inside and outside calls are forwarded to another extension. While your phone is in "call forwarding," you will hear a single ring to remind you that you are using this feature.

You also have the ability to forward your calls in a chain with up to four forwardings. With chaining, call A will forward to phone B, phone B to phone C, and so on. The fourth phone will always ring even if it is also on call forwarding.

And, if you have programmed a distinctive ring for your phone, the extension that receives your forwarded calls will ring your calls with the same distinctive sound.

About forward code

The code below illustrates the example shown.

```
<?xml version="1.0" encoding="utf-8"?>
<!DOCTYPE concept PUBLIC "-//OASIS//DTD DITA Concept//EN"
   "../../../dtd/concept.dtd">
<concept id="aboutforward" xml:lang="en-us">
   <title>About forward</title>
   <shortdesc>You can ask the system to forward all your
      calls to another extension or to an outside telephone
      number.</shortdesc>
   <conbody>
      <p>When you forward your calls, an inside and
         outside calls are forwarded to another extension.
         While your phone is in "call forwarding," you will
         hear a single ring to remind you that you are using
         this feature.</p>
      <p>You also have the ability to forward your calls
         in a chain with up to four forwardings. With
         chaining, call A will forward to phone B, phone B
         to phone C, and so on. The fourth phone will always
         ring even if it is also on call forwarding.</p>
      <p>And, if you have programmed a distinctive ring
         for your phone, the extension that receives your
         forwarded calls will ring your calls with the same
         distinctive sound.</p>
   </conbody>
</concept>
```

Forwarding a call

1. Press Program.
2. Press Forward.
3. Press an idle line button.
4. Dial the outside number.
5. Press Program.

Forwarding a call code

The code below illustrates the example shown.

```
<?xml version="1.0" encoding="utf-8"?>
<!DOCTYPE task PUBLIC "-//OASIS//DTD DITA Task//EN"
   "../../../dtd/task.dtd">
<task id="forwarding" xml:lang="en-us">
   <title>Forwarding a call</title>
   <taskbody>
      <steps>
         <step>
            <cmd>Press Program.</cmd>
         </step>
         <step>
            <cmd>Press Forward.</cmd>
         </step>
         <step>
            <cmd>Press an idle line button.</cmd>
         </step>
         <step>
            <cmd>Dial the outside number.</cmd>
         </step>
         <step>
            <cmd>Press Program.</cmd>
         </step>
      </steps>
   </taskbody>
</task>
```

About conference calls

Use a conference call to speak with more than two people in two different locations at the same time.

Use one of the following types of conference calls to speak with multiple people.

Three-way conference call
: Three-way conference calling connects two other people to a call.

Multi-line conference call
: Multi-line conference calling connects you to more than two but fewer than eight other people on a call.

Dial-in conference call
: Dial-in conference calling uses a single conference call number to connect multiple people.

About conference call code

The code below illustrates the example shown.

```
<?xml version="1.0" encoding="utf-8"?>
<!DOCTYPE task PUBLIC "-//OASIS//DTD DITA Concept//EN"
   "concept.dtd">
<concept id="AboutConferenceCalls" xml:lang="en-us">
   <title>About conference calls</title>
   <shortdesc>Use a conference call to speak with more
      than two people in two different locations at the same
      time.</shortdesc>
   <prolog>
      <author>John Smith
      </author>
   </prolog>
   <conbody>
      <p>Use one of the following types of conference
         calls to speak with multiple
         people.</p>
      <dl>
         <dlentry>
            <dt>Three-way conference call</dt>
            <dd>Three-way conference calling connects
               two other people to a call.</dd>
         </dlentry>
```

```
        <dlentry>
        <dt>Multi-line conference call</dt>
           <dd>Multi-line conference calling connects
              you to more than two but fewer than eight
              other people on a call.</dd>
        </dlentry>
        <dlentry>
           <dt>Dial-in conference call</dt>
           <dd>Dial-in conference calling uses a single
              conference call number to connect multiple
              people.</dd>
        </dlentry>
     </dl>
  </conbody>
     <related-links>
        <link href="SettingUpConfCall.dita"
           scope="local"/>
     </related-links>
</concept>
```

Placing a call

1. Lift the handset or press speaker.
2. Dial the number.

Placing a call code

The code below illustrates the example shown.

```
<?xml version="1.0" encoding="utf-8"?>
<!DOCTYPE task PUBLIC "-//OASIS//DTD DITA Task//EN"
   "../../../dtd/task.dtd">
<task id="placingcall" xml:lang="en-us">
   <title>Placing a call</title>
   <taskbody>
      <steps>
         <step>
            <cmd>Lift the handset or press speaker.</cmd>
         </step>
         <step>
            <cmd>Dial the number.</cmd>
         </step>
      </steps>
   </taskbody>
</task>
```

Leaving a conference call temporarily

1. Press Hold/Callback.
2. Hang up the phone.

   The other parties can continue to talk together until you return.

Leaving a conference call temporarily code

The code below illustrates the example shown.

```
<?xml version="1.0" encoding="utf-8"?>
<!DOCTYPE task PUBLIC "-//OASIS//DTD DITA Task//EN"
   "../../../dtd/task.dtd">
<task id="leavingconferencecall" xml:lang="en-us">
   <title>Leaving a conference call temporarily
   </title>
   <taskbody>
      <steps>
         <step>
            <cmd>Press Hold/Callback.</cmd>
         </step>
         <step>
            <cmd>Hang up the phone.</cmd>
            <info>The other parties can continue to talk
               together until you return.</info>
         </step>
      </steps>
   </taskbody>
</task>
```

Reentering a conference call

1. Lift the handset or press Speaker.
2. Press the appropriate line or station button of the parties you wish to consult with.
3. Press Conference.

   This will connect you with the parties on the conference call.

Reentering a conference call code

The code below illustrates the example shown.

```
<?xml version="1.0" encoding="utf-8"?>
<!DOCTYPE task PUBLIC "-//OASIS//DTD DITA Task//EN"
   "../../../dtd/task.dtd">
<task id="reenteringconference" xml:lang="en-us">
   <title>Reentering a conference call</title>
   <taskbody>
      <steps>
         <step>
            <cmd>Lift the handset or press Speaker.
            </cmd>
         </step>
         <step>
            <cmd>Press the appropriate line or station
               button of the parties you wish to consult
               with.</cmd>
         </step>
         <step>
            <cmd>Press Conference.</cmd>
            <info>This will connect you with the parties
               on the conference call.</info>
         </step>
      </steps>
   </taskbody>
</task>
```

Consulting privately on the conference call

1. Press the appropriate line or station button of the person you wish to consult with.

   You will be privately connected with that person. The third party will be placed on Hold.

2. Press Conference to connect with one person.

   The system will choose the person. The other person will be placed on Hold.

Consulting privately on the conference call code

The code below illustrates the example shown.

```
<?xml version="1.0" encoding="utf-8"?>
<!DOCTYPE task PUBLIC "-//OASIS//DTD DITA Task//EN"
   "../../../dtd/task.dtd">
<task id="consulting" xml:lang="en-us">
   <title>Consulting privately on the conference call
   </title>
   <taskbody>
      <steps>
         <step>
            <cmd>Press the appropriate line or station
               button of the person you wish to consult
               with.</cmd>
            <info>You will be privately connected with
               that person. The third party will be placed
               on Hold.</info>
         </step>
         <step>
            <cmd>Press Conference to connect with one
               person.</cmd>
            <info>The system will choose the person. The
               other person will be placed on Hold.
            </info>
         </step>
      </steps>
   </taskbody>
</task>
```

Reentering a call with all people

1. Lift handset or press Speaker.
2. Press Conference or Hold/Callback.

Reentering a call with all people code

The code below illustrates the example shown.

```
<?xml version="1.0" encoding="utf-8"?>
<!DOCTYPE task PUBLIC "-//OASIS//DTD DITA Task//EN"
   "../../../dtd/task.dtd">
<task id="reenteringcall" xml:lang="en-us">
   <title>Reentering a call with all people</title>
   <taskbody>
      <steps>
         <step>
            <cmd>Lift handset or press Speaker.</cmd>
         </step>
         <step>
            <cmd>Press Conference or Hold/Callback.
            </cmd>
         </step>
      </steps>
   </taskbody>
</task>
```

About using the telephone's features

Your Comstar telephone has many features that allow you to handle calls in a variety of powerful ways.

In this chapter, you will learn how to use the features of your phone. If you have any questions about these features, contact your system administrator.

The features discussed in this chapter are

- automatic callback
- automatic preselect
- automatic speakerphone answer
- background music
- call forwarding
- call waiting

About using the telephone's features code

The code below illustrates the example shown.

```
<?xml version="1.0" encoding="utf-8"?>
<!DOCTYPE concept PUBLIC "-//OASIS//DTD DITA Concept//EN"
   "../../../dtd/concept.dtd">
<concept id="AboutPhoneFeatures">
   <title>About using the telephone's features</title>
   <shortdesc>Your Comstar telephone has many features
      that allow you to handle calls in a variety of
      powerful ways. </shortdesc>
   <conbody>
      <p>In this chapter, you will learn how to use the
         features of your phone. If you have any questions
         about these features, contact your system
         administrator.</p>
      <p>The features discussed in this chapter are
      </p>
      <ul>
         <li>automatic callback</li>
         <li>automatic preselect</li>
         <li>automatic speakerphone answer</li>
         <li>background music</li>
         <li>call forwarding</li>
         <li>call waiting</li>
      </ul>
   </conbody>
</concept>
```

Warnings

FCC Warning	This equipment generates, uses, and can radiate radio frequency energy and if not installed and used in accordance with the instruction manual, may cause interference to radio communications. It has been tested and found to comply with the limits for a Class A computing device pursuant to Subpart J of Part 15 of FCC rules, which are designed to provide reasonable protection against such interference when operated in a commercial environment. Operation of this equipment in a residential area may cause interference, in which case the user, at his own expense, will be required to take whatever measures may be required to correct the interference.
Liquids	Do not expose your phone to any liquid of any kind. Exposure may result in an electric shock to yourself and loss of your equipment.

Warnings code

The code below illustrates the example shown.

```
<?xml version="1.0" encoding="utf-8"?>
<!DOCTYPE reference PUBLIC "-//IBM//DTD DITA Reference//EN"
   "reference.dtd">
<reference id="Warning" xml:lang="en-us">
   <title>Warnings</title>
   <refbody>
      <simpletable>
         <strow>
            <stentry>FCC Warning</stentry>
            <stentry>This equipment generates, uses, and
               can radiate radio frequency energy and if not
               installed and used in accordance with the
               instruction manual, may cause interference
               to radio communications. It has been tested
               and found to comply with the limits for a
               Class A computing device pursuant to
               Subpart J of Part 15 of FCC rules, which are
               designed to provide reasonable protection
               against such interference when operated in a
               commercial environment. Operation of this
               equipment in a residential area may cause
               interference, in which case the user, at his
               own expense, will be required to take
               whatever measures may be required to correct
               the interference.</stentry>
            </strow>
            <strow>
               <stentry>Liquids</stentry>
               <stentry>Do not expose your phone to any
                  liquid of any kind. Exposure may result in
                  an electric shock to yourself and loss of
                  your equipment. </stentry>
            </strow>
      </simpletable>
   </refbody>
</reference>
```

Glossary

account code
: A one to five digit number you can use to identify calls made to your customers for accounting purposes.

after-hours call
: A call made when your office is closed.

button
: The "keys" next to the lamps on the telephone. You press the buttons to call other telephones or to make an outside call.

call forwarding
: The ability to forward a call to another user in your company or to an outside line.

call transfer
: The feature that lets you send a call to another telephone.

call waiting
: The feature that lets a call wait at your telephone if you are busy on another call and reminds you the call is waiting.

conference call
: A call between up to 10 people.

do not disturb
: The feature that allows you to keep all calls from ringing at your telephone.

handset
: The telephone receiver that you use to listen and speak.

intercom calls
: The calls you make to other telephones within the system.

line-to-line call
: A call forwarded or transferred between two different outside lines.

privacy/flash button
: Prevents automatic answering of intercom calls. If PRIVACY/FLASH is preselected (pressed before lifting the handset or pressing Speaker), it will force the other telephone to answer without the speakerphone.

program button
: The button that you use to begin programming your telephone.

speakerphone
: A built-in feature of your telephone that lets you speak and hear a conversation without using the handset.

speed dial button
: The button, in conjunction with another button, that lets you speed dial an outside number or automatically redial the last number dialed.

speed transfer
: A feature that allows you to transfer a call without waiting for a reply from the person you are transferring to. Also called unscreened automatic speed transfer.

station
: An individual telephone set.

station buttons
: The buttons you use to select other extensions in the system.

system manager
: The person authorized to make changes to the telephone system and to keep records of the modifications.

telephone extension number
: A number from 200 to 263 that identifies each telephone in your system.

tone
: A series of distinctive sounds used by the system to indicate the type of events occurring with your telephone.

transfer hold
: Allows a user on a call to press an SS button to place a party on hold and initiate a transfer.

64-button DSS/BLF
: The 64-button accessory that contains 60 telephone and line buttons and lamps and 4 function buttons. It is used to see the status of all lines and stations and to quickly access them.

Glossary code

The code below illustrates the example shown.

```
<?xml version="1.0" encoding="utf-8"?>
<!DOCTYPE reference PUBLIC "-//IBM//DTD DITA Reference//EN"
   "reference.dtd">
<reference id="Glossary" xml:lang="en-us">
   <title>Glossary</title>
   <refbody>
      <section>
         <dl>
            <dlentry>
               <dt>account code</dt>
```

```
   <dd>A one to five digit number you can use
      to identify calls made to your customers
      for accounting purposes.</dd>
</dlentry>
<dlentry>
   <dt>after-hours call</dt>
   <dd>A call made when your office is
      closed.</dd>
</dlentry>
<dlentry>
   <dt>button</dt>
   <dd>The "keys" next to the lamps on the
      telephone. You press the buttons to call
      other telephones or to make an outside
      call.</dd>
</dlentry>
<dlentry>
   <dt>call forwarding</dt>
   <dd>The ability to forward a call to
      another user in your company or to an
      outside line.</dd>
</dlentry>
<dlentry>
   <dt>call transfer</dt>
   <dd>The feature that lets you send a call
      to another telephone.</dd>
</dlentry>
<dlentry>
   <dt>call waiting</dt>
   <dd>Lets a call wait at your telephone
      if you are busy on another call and
      reminds you the call is waiting.</dd>
</dlentry>
<dlentry>
   <dt>conference call</dt>
   <dd>A call between up to 10 people.
   </dd>
</dlentry>
<dlentry>
   <dt>do not disturb</dt>
   <dd>The feature that allows you to keep
      all calls from ringing at your telephone.
   </dd>
</dlentry>
<dlentry>
   <dt>handset</dt>
   <dd>The telephone receiver that you use to
      listen and speak.</dd>
</dlentry>
<dlentry>
```

```
   <dt>intercom calls</dt>
   <dd>The calls you make to other telephones
      within the system.</dd>
</dlentry>
<dlentry>
   <dt>line-to-line call</dt>
   <dd>A call forwarded or transferred
      between two different outside lines.
   </dd>
</dlentry>
<dlentry>
   <dt>privacy/flash button</dt>
   <dd>Prevents automatic answering of
      intercom calls. If PRIVACY/FLASH is
      preselected (pressed before lifting the
      handset or pressing Speaker), it will
      force the other telephone to answer
      without the speakerphone.</dd>
</dlentry>
<dlentry>
   <dt>program button</dt>
   <dd>The button that you use to begin
      programming your telephone.</dd>
</dlentry>
<dlentry>
   <dt>speakerphone</dt>
   <dd>A built-in feature of your telephone
      that lets you speak and hear a
      conversation without using the handset.
   </dd>
</dlentry>
<dlentry>
   <dt>speed dial button</dt>
   <dd>The button, in conjunction with
      another button, that lets you speed dial
      an outside number or automatically redial
      the last number dialed.</dd>
</dlentry>
<dlentry>
   <dt>speed transfer</dt>
   <dd>A feature that allows you to transfer
      a call without waiting for a reply
      from the person you are transferring to.
      Also called unscreened automatic
      speed transfer.</dd>
</dlentry>
<dlentry>
   <dt>station</dt>
   <dd>An individual telephone set.</dd>
</dlentry>
```

```
            <dlentry>
               <dt>station buttons</dt>
               <dd>The buttons you use to select other
                  extensions in the system.</dd>
            </dlentry>
            <dlentry>
               <dt>system manager</dt>
               <dd>The person authorized to make changes
                  to the telephone system and to keep
                  records of the modifications.</dd>
            </dlentry>
            <dlentry>
               <dt>telephone extension number</dt>
               <dd>A number from 200 to 263 that
                  identifies each telephone in your system.
               </dd>
            </dlentry>
            <dlentry>
               <dt>tone</dt>
               <dd>A series of distinctive sounds used
                  by the system to indicate the type of
                  events occurring with your telephone.
               </dd>
            </dlentry>
            <dlentry>
               <dt>transfer hold</dt>
               <dd>Allows a user on a call to press an SS
                  button to place a party on hold and
                  initiate a transfer.</dd>
            </dlentry>
            <dlentry>
               <dt>64-button DSS/BLF</dt>
               <dd>The 64-button accessory that contains
                  60 telephone and line buttons and lamps
                  and 4 functions buttons. It is used to see
                  the status of all lines and stations and
                  to quickly access them.</dd>
            </dlentry>
         </dl>
      </section>
   </refbody>
</reference>
```

Comstar map code

```
<?xml version="1.0" encoding="utf-8"?>
<!DOCTYPE map PUBLIC "-//OASIS//DTD DITA Map//EN"
   "../../../dtd/map.dtd">
<map title="Comstar User Guide" id="Comstaruserguide">
   <topicref href="ComstarOverview.dita" format="dita"
      scope="local"  id="comstaruserguide">
      <topicref href="QuickGuide.dita"
         navtitle="Quick guide" format="dita" scope="local">
           <topicmeta>
            <author>Jennifer Linton</author>
            <author>Kylene Bruski</author>
            <publisher>Comtech Services, Inc.
            </publisher>
            <copyright>
               <copyryear year="2005" />
               <copyrholder>Comtech Services, Inc.
               </copyrholder>
            </copyright>
            <audience audience="beginner" />
            <audience audience="intermediate"/>
         </topicmeta>
      </topicref>
      <topicref href="AboutHold.dita" navtitle="Hold"
         format="dita" scope="local" >
         <topicmeta>
            <author>Kylene Bruski</author>
            <publisher>Comtech Services, Inc.
            </publisher>
            <copyright>
               <copyryear year="2005"/>
               <copyrholder>Comtech Services, Inc.
               </copyrholder>
            </copyright>
            <audience audience="beginner" />
         </topicmeta>
         <topicref href="HoldingACall.dita"
            navtitle="Putting a call on hold" format="dita"
            scope="local" />
      </topicref>
      <topicref href="AboutTransfer.dita"
         navtitle="Transfer" format="dita" scope="local" >
         <topicref href="TransferringACall.dita"
            navtitle="Transferring a call" format="dita"
            scope="local" />
      </topicref>
      <topicref href="AboutForward.dita"
         navtitle="About forward" format="dita">
         <topicref href="ForwardingACall.dita"
            navtitle="Forwarding a call" format="dita"
```

```
            scope="local" />
      </topicref>
      <topicref href="AboutConferenceCalls.dita"
         navtitle="About conference calls" format="dita"
         scope="local" >
         <topicref href="PlacingACall.dita"
            navtitle="Placing a conference call"
            format="dita" scope="local" />
         <topicref href="
            LeavingAConferenceCallTemporarily.dita"
            navtitle="Leaving a conference call temporarily"
            format="dita" scope="local" />
         <topicref href="ReEnteringAConferenceCall.dita"
            navtitle="Reentering a conference call"
            format="dita" scope="local" />
         <topicref href="
            ConsultingPrivatelyOnTheConferenceCall.dita"
            format="dita" scope="local" />
         <topicref href="
            ReEnteringACallWithAllPeople.dita"
            navtitle="ReEntering a call with all people"
            format="dita" scope="local"/>
      </topicref>
      <topicref href="AboutPhoneFeatures.dita"
         scope="local" format="dita" />
      <topicref href="Warnings.dita" scope="local"
         format="dita" />
      <topicref href="
         http://www.comtech-serv.com/Comstar/" format="html"
         navtitle="Comtech Services: Comstar Phone
         Information" locktitle="yes" scope="external">
         <topicmeta>
            <linktext>Order Comstar Phones</linktext>
            <shortdesc>Online ordering for your choice
               of any Comstar phones.
            </shortdesc>
         </topicmeta>
      </topicref>
      <topicref href="../../ComstarPricing.pdf"
         format="pdf" scope="external">
         <topicmeta>
            <linktext>Comstar Pricing List</linktext>
            <shortdesc>Comstar phones provide a variety
               of different plans you can purchase to use
               with your phone.</shortdesc>
         </topicmeta>
      </topicref>
```

```
    <topicref href="../GeneralTopic/Glossary.dita"
          format="dita"  scope="peer" navtitle="Glossary"/>
    </topicref>
</map>
```

Appendix B

Appendix B provides a table of elements mentioned in this book. Because the book does not account for all the elements in the *DITA Language Specification*, this table includes the main elements needed to get started with DITA. The table illustrates the element name, the formal name, and the type of element it is. If you need an element not mentioned in Appendix B, reference the *DITA Language Specification* for the full list.

DITA element glossary

Below you will find a list of elements described in this book. This list does not include all elements available in DITA. For a complete list of elements, see the *DITA Language Specification.*

element	element name	Type of element
<apiname>	API name	text
<audience>	audience	metadata
<author>	author	metadata
<b>	bold	text
<body>	body	container
<brand>	brand	metadata
<chdesc>	choice description	text
<chdeschd>	choice description head	text
<chhead>	choice head	container
<choice>	choice	text
<choices>	choices	container
<choicetable>	choice table	container
<choption>	choice option	text
<choptionhd>	choice option head	text
<chrow>	choice row	container
<cmd>	command	text
<cmdname>	command name	text
<codeblock>	code block	text
<colspec>	column specification	container
<conbody>	concept body	container
<concept>	concept	container

element	element name	Type of element
<context>	context	text
<copyrholder>	copyright holder	metadata
<copyright>	copyright	metadata
<copyryear>	copyright year	metadata
<created>	created date	metadata
<critdates>	critical dates	metadata
<dd>	definition description	text
<ddhd>	definition head	text
<dl>	definition list	container
<dlentry>	definition list entry	container
<dlhead>	definition list head	container
<dt>	definition term	text
<dthd>	term head	text
<entry>	entry	text
<example>	example	text
<fig>	figure	container
<filepath>	file path	text
<i>	italic	text
<image>	image	container
<info>	information	text
<keyword>	keyword	metadata and text
<keywords>	keywords	metadata
<li>	list item	text
<link>	link	text
<linkinfo>	link information	text
<linklist>	link list	container

element	element name	Type of element
<linkpool>	link pool	container
<linktext>	link text	text
<menucascade>	menu cascade	container
<metadata>	metadata	metadata
<msgph>	message phrase	text
<navtitle>	navigation title	text
<note>	note	text
<ol>	ordered list	container
<p>	paragraph	text
<parml>	parameter list	container
<pd>	parameter description	text
<permissions>	permissions	metadata
<ph>	phrase	text
<platform>	platform	metadata
<plentry>	parameters list entry	container
<postreq>	post requirement	text
<prereq>	prerequisite	text
<prodinfo>	product information	metadata
<prodname>	product name	metadata
<prolog>	prolog	container
<prop>	conditional processing property	container in ditaval file
<propdesc>	property description	text
<propdeschd>	property description head	text
<properties>	properties	container

element	element name	Type of element
<property>	property	container in ant build file
<property>	property (DITA element)	container
<prophead>	property head	container
<proptype>	property type	text
<proptypehd>	property type head	text
<propvalue>	property value	text
<propvaluehd>	property value head	text
<pt>	parameter term	text
<refbody>	reference body	container
<reference>	reference	container
<related-links>	related links	container
<relcell>	relationship table cell	map text
<relcolspec>	relationship column specification	map container
<relheader>	relationship head	map container
<relrow>	relationship table row	map container
<reltable>	relationship table	map container
<result>	result	text
<revised>	revised date	metadata
<row>	row	container
<searchtitle>	search title	text
<section>	section	container
<shortdesc>	short description	text
<simpletable>	simple table	container
<sl>	simple list	container

element	element name	Type of element
<sli>	simple list item	text
<stentry>	simple table cell (entry)	text
<step>	step	container
<stepresult>	step result	text
<steps>	steps	container
<steps-unordered>	steps unordered	container
<stepxmp>	step example	text
<sthead>	simple table head	container
<strow>	simple table row	container
<sub>	subscript	text
<substep>	sub-step	container
<substeps>	sub-steps	container
<sup>	superscript	text
<systemoutput>	system output	text
<table>	table	container
<task>	task	container
<taskbody>	task body	container
<tbody>	table body	container
<term>	term	text
<tgroup>	table group	container
<thead>	table head	container
<title>	title	text
<titlealts>	title alternatives	container
<topicgroup>	topic group	map container
<topichead>	topic heading	map container
<topicmeta>	topic metadata	map metadata container

element	element name	Type of element
<topicref>	topic reference	map container
<tt>	teletype	text
<uicontrol>	user interface control	text
<ul>	unordered list	container
<userinput>	user input	text
<varname>	variable name	text
<xref>	cross reference link	container

Index

A

action attribute 256, 257
alt attribute 256, 257
ant 226
    installing 228
ant build file
    adding a frameset 240
    adding cascading stylesheet 247
    adding HTML headers and footers 250
    copying files 240
    creating 237
    defined 237
    invoking multiple builds 244
    modifying 240
    modifying template 238
    processing 239
    properties 242, 249, 253
    review questions 254
ANT_HOME environment variables 232
Apache FOP 226
    installing 230
api name <apiname> 82
att attribute 256, 257
attributes 255
    adding 258
audience <audience> 102
    adding 118
audience attribute 255
author <author> 102
    adding to map 117

B

block elements 63
    adding 61
        paragraph 61
        unordered list 62
    introduction 61
    rendered example 63
    review questions 71
    XML code example 62
body <body> 30
bold <b> 86
brand <brand> 102
build files 236
    defined 224
bulleted list <ul> 62, 65
    See unordered list

C

Cascading Style Sheets (CSS) 223, 247
char attribute 256
choice <choice> 45
choice description <chdesc> 46
choice description head <chdeschd> 46
choice head <chhead> 46
choice option <choption> 46
choice option head <choptionhd> 46
choice row <chrow> 46
choice table <choicetable> 46
    adding to steps 38
choices <choices> 45
class attribute 199
CLASSPATH environment variables 232

code block <codeblock> 80
collaborative work environment 107
collection-type attribute
  assigning 159
  controlling map linking 153
  family 155
    assigning 159
  in relationship table 172, 176
  introduction 155
  review questions 163
  sequence 157
    assigning 161
  XML code example 161
column specification <colspec> 68
command <cmd> 43
command name <cmdname> 83
command prompt 239
concept <concept> 29, 31
  XML code example 31
concept body <conbody> 30
  adding 26
concept information type
  adding
    conbody 26
    definition description 26
    definition list 26
    definition list entry 26
    definition term 26
    paragraph 26
    prolog 25
    related links 27
    root element 24
    short description 25
    title 25
  base structure 23
  creating 24
  defined 20
  introduction 23
  review questions 33
  XML code example 27
conditional processing
  adding attributes 258
  attributes 255
  ditaval file 256
  filtering 257
  flagging 257
  introduction 255
  preparing for 258
  review questions 269
  XML code example 263
conref attribute 188
  adding to a map 193
  adding to a topic 189
  content reuse 183
  review questions 196
  XML code example 192, 195
content inventory 15
content reuse 185
  conref attribute 183
  introduction 183
  reusing components 187
  reusing maps 186
  small content units 186
  topic reuse 186
context <context> 43
  adding 36
copy <copy> 242
copyright <copyright> 102
  adding to map 118
copyright holder <copyrholder> 102
copyright year <copyryear> 102
created date <created> 102
critical dates <critdates> 102
cross reference link <xref> 79
  adding 75
customized deliverables 107, 108, 111

D

Darwin Information Typing Architecture 7
  See also DITA
definition description <dd> 67
  adding 26
definition head <ddhd> 66
definition list <dl> 66
  adding 26
  XML code example 67
definition list entry <dlentry> 67
  adding 26
definition list head <dlhead> 66
definition term <dt> 67
  adding 26
departmental domain specialization 203

description <desc> 92
DITA
- authoring tools 226
- benefits of 9
- business advantages of 10
- content reuse 185
- core information types 19
- generalizing 200
- introduction 7
- maps 107
- Open Toolkit 225, 226
- overview of topic elements 59
- processing 236
- relationship table 171
- specialization 197
- topic-based authoring 13

DITA map
- adding the root element 113
- collaboration 107
- content reuse 185
- creating hierarchy 120
- customized deliverables 108
- elements 122
  - review questions 125
- folder location 111
- format attribute 128
- including PDFs 128
- introduction 107, 111
- linking attribute 164
- map linking 152
- metadata 111, 112, 126
- processing 223
- processing attributes 146
- product development 108
- referencing non-DITA file types 128
- reusing content 186
- scope attribute 133
- solutions-oriented deliverables 108
- starting 113
- structure 112
- type attribute 141

DITA topic elements
- introduction 59

ditaval file 256, 267
- creating 265
- XML code example 267

domain elements
- defined 80
- introduction 72

domain specialization 202

DTD
- declaration assignment 24, 35, 50, 113
- file introduction 203
- modifying 214
- topic 197

duplicate file copies, avoiding 134

duplication of effort, avoiding 107

E

element name
- modifying element names 208
- specializing 219

entry <entry> 68

environment variables 231
- ANT_HOME 232
- CLASSPATH 232
- JAVA_HOME 232
- JHHOME 232
- Path 232

example <example> 31, 47, 64
- adding to a task 39

external value
- scope attribute 134

F

family linking 153

family value
- collection-type attribute 155

figure <fig> 64

file path <filepath> 84

file types
- referencing in a DITA map 128

filtering 257, 266

flagging 257, 266

folder structure
- example 134
- topics and maps 111

format attribute
- adding to related links 90
- assigning 128
- dita value 130
- html value 130

- introduction 128
- review questions 132
- XML code example 130

G

glossary, creating a specialization 221
- implementing a specialized topic 219

H

hierarchical relationships in a map 112
hierarchy
- organizing topics 111

href attribute
- assigning to topic reference 114, 176
- in cross reference element 75
- in peer references 133
- in related links 91
- introduction 126

HTML
- elements 61
- output 223

HTML help 226
- installing 231

hyperlink 170
hyperlinks 88
- linking to non-DITA topics 88

I

ID attribute
- assigning 24, 35, 50
- assigning to map 113
- in a conref 188
- in cross reference element 75
- used with conref 194

image attribute 256
img attribute 257
industry domain specialization 202
information <info> 43
- adding to steps 37

information types
- base structure 19
- concept 20, 23
- domain specialization 203
- introduction 19
- reference 22, 49
- task 20, 34

inheritance 199
- DITA map 127
- specialization 199

inline elements 72
italic <i> 86

J

Java Development Kit (JDK) 226
- installing 229

Java help 226
- installing 229

JAVA_HOME environment variables 232
JHHOME environment variables 232

K

keyword <keyword>
- adding 74
- in phrase elements 78
- in prolog metadata 103

keywords <keywords> 99, 103

L

link <link> 93
- adding 90

link information <linkinfo> 94
link list <linklist> 93
link pool <linkpool> 94
link text <linktext> 94
- adding 91

linking attribute 152
- assigning 165
- in relationship table 172, 177
- introduction 164
- none 165
- normal 165
  - assigning 167
- review questions 169
- sourceonly 164
  - assigning 166
- targetonly 164
  - assigning 168
- XML code example 168

list item <li> 65, 66
local value
- scope attribute 133

locktitle attribute

assigning to topic reference 115
using with scope attribute 137

M

map
See DITA map
map linking 188
introduction 152
menu cascade <menucascade> 85
message phrase <msgph> 82
metadata
adding to topics 96
HTML 97
in a map 111, 112, 126
prolog 97
metadata <metadata> 103
adding 99
minimalist agenda 170
mod file
introduction 203
modifying 206
mod file introduction
See specialization

N

name attribute 245
navigation title <navtitle> 30
navtitle attribute
assigning to topic reference 115
using with scope attribute 137
none, linking attribute 165
normal, linking attribute 165
note <note> 44
numbered list 66

O

Open Toolkit 225
applications 226
contents 227
installation requirements 225
installation testing 233
installing 228
introduction 226
review questions 235
ordered list <ol> 66
otherprops attribute 255

P

paragraph <p> 31, 63
adding 26, 61
parameter description <pd> 81
parameter list <parml> 81
parameter list entry <plentry> 81
parameter term <pt> 81
parent/child relationships in maps 126
Path environment variable 232
PDF, including in a DITA map 128
peer value
scope attribute 133
permissions <permissions> 97, 103
adding 99
personalized deliverables 108
phrase <ph> 78
phrase elements 78
adding 73
cross reference link 75
href 75
ID attribute 75
keyword 74
type attribute 75
user interface control 75
introduction 72
review questions 87
XML code example 76
platform <platform> 103
platform attribute 255
post requirement <postreq> 48
adding to a task 39
prerequisite <prereq> 42
print attribute 149
in processing 146
processing
adding HTML headers and footers 250
ant build files 239
cascading stylesheet 247
command prompt 239
ditaval file 267
introduction 223, 236
multiple media 244
processing attributes
assigning 147
introduction 146

print 146
print attribute 149
review questions 151
toc attribute 146, 149
XML code example 146, 149
product attribute 255
product information <prodinfo> 103
product name <prodname> 103
programming elements 80
prolog <prolog> 30
adding 25, 36, 51
prolog metadata 102
adding 97
keywords 99
metadata 99
permissions 99
introduction 96, 97
review questions 105
XML code example 100
prop <prop> 256
adding 265
attributes 256
assigning 266
filtering 266
flagging 266
properties <properties> 56
adding 51
XML code example 57
properties elements 52
property <property> 57
property description <propdesc> 57
property description head <propdeschd> 57
property head <prophead> 51, 56
property type <proptype> 57
property type head <proptypehd> 56
property value <propvalue> 57
property value head <propvaluehd> 56
publisher <publisher> 117

R

reference <reference> 29
reference body <refbody> 30
adding 51
reference elements 56
reference information type
adding
prolog 51
properties table 51
properties table elements 52
property head 51
refbody 51
related links 53
root element 50
short description 50
title 50
basic structure 49
creating 49
defined 22
introduction 49
review questions 58
XML code example 54
related links
implementing in maps 155, 171
related links <related-links> 30, 93
adding 27, 39, 53, 88
description 92
format attribute 90
href attribute 91
link 90
link text 91
scope attribute 91
introduction 88
review questions 95
XML code example 92
related-link groups, creating 141
relationship column specification <relcolspec> 181
adding 174
relationship head <relheader> 181
adding 174
relationship table
collection-type attribute 172
complex example 172
creating 173
elements 181
introduction 170, 171
linking attribute 172
review questions 182
simple example 171
XML code example 178
relationship table <reltable> 181
adding 173
relationship table cell <relcell> 182

adding 175
relationship table row <relrow> 181
adding 174
result <result> 47
adding to a task 39
reusing
admonishments 186
content 185
content units 188
topics 188
topics and content units 183
revised date <revised> 103
revision (rev) attribute 255
revision property <revprop> 256
attributes 256
root elements
adding 24, 35, 50, 113
concept 29
reference 29
task 29
row <row> 68

S

Saxon XSLT processor 226
installing 230
scope attribute
adding to related links 91
assigning 135
external 136
external value 134
introduction 133
local 136
local value 133
peer 136
peer value 133
review questions 140
XML code example 138
search title <searchtitle> 30
section <section> 31, 64
sequence value
collection-type attribute 157
sequential linking 153
short description <shortdesc> 30
adding 25, 35, 50
simple list <sl> 65
simple list item <sli> 65
simple table <simpletable> 70
simple table cell (entry) <stentry> 70
simple table head <sthead> 70
simple table row <strow> 70
software elements 82
solutions-oriented deliverables 107, 108, 111
sourceforge.com 225
sourceonly, linking attribute 164
specialization
adding ATTLIST definitions 211
adding DTD entity declaration 217
adding element entity declarations 210
class attribute 199
core DITA information types 197
domain 202
DTD file
modifying 214
XML code example 217
generalizing 200
glossary 205
glossary <glossary>
adding 220
glossary elements
adding 221
defining 208
ID attribute
assigning 220
implementing a specialized topic 219
inheritance 199
introduction 197, 199
mod file
modifying 206
XML code example 212
modifying element names 208
modifying topic structure 208
review questions 222
short description element 220
structural 200
title element 220
specializing
benefits of 200
step <step> 43
step example <stepxmp> 44
step result <stepresult> 44
steps <steps> 43
adding 37

steps unordered <steps-unordered> 43
streamlining processes with content reuse 183
structural specialization 200
    example 201
structure elements 29
    XML code example 31
structured writing
    benefits of 14
    performing a content inventory 15
structuring DITA maps 112
style attribute
    color value 256
stylesheets, developing 223
subscript <sub> 86
sub-step <substep> 44
sub-steps <substeps> 44
superscript <sup> 86
system output <systemoutput> 84

T

table <table> 67
    rendered example 70
    XML code example 68
table body <tbody> 68
table group <tgroup> 68
table head <thead> 68
table of contents, managing 146
targetonly, linking attribute 164
task <task> 29
task body <taskbody> 30
    adding 36
task elements 42
task information type
    adding
        choice table 38
        context 36
        post requirement 39
        prolog 36
        related links 39
        root element 35
        short description 35
        step information 37
        steps 37
        task body 36
        task example 39
        task result 39
        title 35
    base structure 34
    creating 34
    defined 20
    introduction 34
    review questions 48
    specialization 198
    XML code example 40
teletype <tt> 86
term <term> 79
term head <dthd> 66
title <title> 29
    adding 25, 35, 50
title alternatives <titlealts> 29
title attribute, assigning to a map 113
toc attribute
    assigning 149
    in processing 146
    using with scope attribute 137
topic DTD 197
topic elements
    introduction 59
    structure 59
topic group <topicgroup> 123
    adding 176
topic heading <topichead> 123
topic hierarchy
    organizing in maps 111
topic metadata <topicmeta> 124
    adding 116
    introduction 96
    using with scope attribute 137
    XML code example 119
topic reference
    managing in a TOC 146
topic reference <topicref> 122
    adding 114
    adding to relationship table 175
    hierarchy 120
        XML code example 121
    nesting 120
    parent and child relationships 121
    XML code example 116
topic-based authoring
    adding specialized information types 16
    content reuse 185, 186

core information types 19
creating a concept 24
creating a reference 49
introduction 13
mixed topic types 16
planning topics 108
removing topics easily 109
reusing topics and content units 188
simplifying 184
well-structured topic 16
type attribute
adding to relationship table 174
assigning 142
concept 144
example of related links 142
in cross reference 75
introduction 141
reference 144
review questions 145
task 144
XML code example 144
typographic elements
defined 86
introduction 72

U

unordered list <ul> 65
adding 62
URL, referencing 134
user input <userinput> 84
user interface control <uicontrol> 85
adding 75
user interface elements 85

V

val <val> 265
val attribute 256, 257
variable name <varname> 83
view attribute 99

X

XHTML output 223
XML code example
block elements 62
collection-type attribute 161
concept 31
concept information type 27
conditional processing 263
conref attribute 192, 195
definition list 67
ditaval file 267
DTD file specialization 217
format attribute 130
linking attribute 168
mod file specialization 212
phrase elements 76
processing attributes 146, 149
prolog metadata 100
reference information type 54
related links 92
relationship table 178
scope attribute 138
structure elements 31
table 68
task information type 40
topic metadata 119
topic reference 116, 121
type attribute 144
XML declaration
assigning 24, 35, 50, 113
assigning to ditaval file 265